ADVENTURES

PART 1

LEPRECHAUNS IN LATIN AMERICA

Norman Magowan

IndePenPress

First published in Great Britain by IndePenPress

All paper used in the printing of this book has been made from wood grown in managed, sustainable forests.

ISBN13: 978-1-78003-023-4

Printed and bound in the UK
Indepenpress Publishing Limited
25 Eastern Place
Brighton
BN2 1GJ

A catalogue record of this book is available from the British Library

Cover design by Jacqueline Abromeit

Dedicated to my father, George

Contents

Foreword

"The world is a book, and those who do not travel read only one page."

Quote attributed to Saint Augustine in the 4th Century AD, found on a welcome card at Pauls Inn Motel, Victoria, BC, Canada 2006 AD. Still true today…

1. Santiago / Valparaiso
2. Pucon / Villarica
3. San Carlos de Bariloche
4. Rio Mayo
5. Comodoro Rivadavia
6. Rio Gallegos
7. Moreno Glacier & Torres Del Paine
8. Ushuaia
9. Chos Malal
10. Mendoza
11. San Juan / Vallecito
12. Cordoba
13. Puerto Iguazú
14. Salta

15. San Pedro De Atacama
16. Iquique
17. La Paz
18. Lake Titicaca
19. Cusco / Machu Picchu
20. Abancay
21. Paracas
22. Lima
23. Trujillo
24. Cuenca
25. Quito
26. Galapagos Islands
27. Apuela

SOUTH AMERICA

Prelude: The Bridge

We arrived at the bridge to find it blocked, just like they said, with welded steel work strong enough to stop a tank never mind a motorcycle.Standing idly on a dirt road off to one side we surveyed the scene, considered the chaos. The two bikes leaned lazily on their side stands, tink, tink, tinking, the peculiar little sounds of hot metal cooling in the slight breeze off the river. All around, people were busily engaged in either sustaining or circumventing the obstruction.

We watched as commuters and backpackers scrambled both ways over the barrier, aided and abetted by an army of local porters. Once across, they hopped onto minibuses and taxis to complete their journeys either north around the lake into Peru, or south, back to Bolivia down the road we had just travelled. Little old women sporting ubiquitous bowler hats took advantage of the bottleneck and set up thriving enterprises selling cold water, snacks and soft drinks under the cloudless blue sky.

Our way forward was well and truly blocked. Twenty-five days ago, the locals had closed the bridge over some grievance with the local mayor. '*No passeran!*' and the 'Gringo Trail' was choked to a trickle of pedestrian traffic. The 'Trail' runs from La Paz in Bolivia, through Copacabana on Lake Titicaca, over the border into Peru, where we now stood at Ilave on the Lake, before running on to Puno and Cusco, our intended destination. Retreat meant 2500 miles back into Chile and along the Pacific coast that would take weeks; we had to figure out a way across.

From our perch on the dirt road we scanned the river, a fast, wide, boulder-strewn run of water, thankfully not deep enough to obstruct the passage of heavy vehicles. The town lay on the far side. Two rusting open-topped lorries waited on the riverbank below ready to ferry across the next paying freight. A heavy farm tractor stood in the middle, ready to pull out anyone who got stuck. Two smiley locals approached, eager to make some money. They would take us across on one of the trucks for ten bucks a bike. We didn't even haggle on the price, but first had to figure a way off the road down the steep mud embankment onto the riverbank fifteen feet below.

A deaf and dumb guy, trying to be helpful, pointed to a dirt track that ran around and underneath the bridge. I took a walk with him to check it out but found the way well and truly blocked by a huge blue artic', stuck and sinking in the glutinous red mud. An army of locals, every one a foreman, tried to extract it using picks and shovels to clear a way forward while others placed rocks from the riverbed under its mired wheels. At some unseen signal, they all stood back, the driver revved hard, the truck lurched forward... and then settled back on its suspension, wheels spinning uselessly. Rusty gloop took to the air, fan tailing the truck, showering everyone in sight.

Back at the bikes I was explaining to Maggie that 'No Passeran' really looked like no way across. We were pondering whether or not our loaded motorcycles could somehow mule-train it down to the riverbank when the day was shattered by the loud roar of an angry mob as a cast of thousands, straight from a David Lean epic, suddenly deluged out of Ilave and headed for the bridge. From our panoramic view we watched awestruck as ant sized infantry ran from doorways, down streets and alleys, converging on the bridge. A very dangerous situation was developing and things now turned real scary, really quickly.

All of the hawkers, loiterers and travellers at the blockade ran for their lives in every direction, as if fleeing some impending air raid announced by the siren wail of the Frankenstein lynch mob marching on the bridge. Vans and taxis, minibuses and mopeds kicked up a pell-mell of noise, dust and smoke as engines roared into life and made their getaway. Have you ever seen your granny run? Grannies, as a general rule, do not run; they sit in comfy chairs knitting cardigans and sucking mint sweeties while watching soaps on daytime TV. But today we saw 'grannies' aplenty in full sprint, portly little old ladies with their wares gathered in their aprons, legging it for all they were worth away from the danger. We leapt on our bikes and joined the rout, finally stopping a short way off with a stand of gaping bystanders to see what would happen next.

The crowd had crossed the bridge and reached the barricade. It was difficult to tell at this distance what was going on. At times there seemed to be two factions all shouting at each other; at others it seemed as if all the people were united in one unruly menacing mob, all sounding off at once. I looked at Maggie. She looked terrified and rightly so. Our dash away from the bridge meant that our only way out of this mess, back to Bolivia, was now blocked by a snarling angry rabble. We had to no other option but to cross the river.

The bridge was impassable. We might wait and see if the crowd dissipated and then try to get down that mud bank to the lorries... Cross the river; then what? What event had unfolded in town to set off such excitement? This was not what we'd envisaged when planning our Pan American Adventure to ride from Chile to Alaska.

Just a tad too much 'Adventure' today when we would prefer the locals to be a little more 'Pan-American.' Still, it was just another problem for us to solve on our route to Alaska and by now we were travel-hardened veterans ready for anything, or so we thought...

Chapter 1: Adventures in Yellow

Ambling around Trafalgar Square that last Sunday morning, a huge ugly mural caught our eye. Plastered across a plywood hoarding despoiling the front of the National Gallery, the mural was themed around one painting: a typical Van Gogh of a poorly drawn chair, sat on a red tile floor, angled against the pale blue background of an interior wall. The chair was painted in vivid yellows, enhanced by thick child-like outlines in blue, brown and black that emphasised its shape and presence. A pipe and what looked like a crumpled hanky lay abandoned on its wicker seat. Strange subject for a painting, why paint a chair?

As I studied it, the lines of the painting drew me into the canvas, begging further questions. The chair looked recently vacated although the position of the articles on the seat suggested a temporary abandonment and that the sitter would return soon to finish the pipe. Who had been sitting there and where had they gone? What urgent errand demanded their attention? The chair was an ordinary, sturdy, everyday pinewood chair, the kind found in rustic kitchens just about everywhere. A good 'sit up proper and eat up your dinner' chair, or maybe the sort of chair to set yourself down in to tell an expectant audience a good story or two…

The display was titled 'An Adventure in Yellow' and the subject was the artist's passion for the colour, explaining how it ran as a theme throughout his short, tragic life. Van Gogh was treated for a wide range of mental disorders, including schizophrenia, neurosis, and epilepsy, and his doctor administered doses of digitalis as an 'anti-manic' potion. Digitalis is a drug distilled from poisonous foxglove flowers and is known to cause xanthopsia, an optical defect in which the yellow-blue vision range is distorted and bright lights appear glary and haloed. The world appears as if viewed through a yellow filter and xanthopsia has been offered as one possible explanation for the tragic genius's peculiar style.

The hoarding described how yellow is the colour traditionally used to represent the sun, happiness and also, apparently, madness. Van Gogh loved the colour, especially during his time in the South of France where he applied it most famously in his portrayals of sunflowers and cornfields. It was also the colour of his death; he killed himself 'in yellow', putting a shotgun to his head in a field of wheat.

Standing there on that grey November morning other happy associations with yellow sprang to mind. Daffodils and buttercups, bananas and lemons, smiley faces and submarines. Or for those whose glass is half empty, cowardice and running away, fever and disease, sulphur and toxic odours. On this day, 'Adventure in Yellow' held for us a more immediate and personal association. Somewhere at sea, a battered rusty cargo hulk was braving mid-Atlantic swells with two yellow motorcycles crated up on deck. Both bikes had departed on a two-month voyage to Chile via the Panama Canal for the start of our Pan-American Adventure. We had been planning the trip for over a year: to ride from Chile to Alaska on a journey we estimated would cover 22 000 miles through some of the hottest, coldest, wettest and driest conditions on Earth. Then it struck me: 'Adventures in Yellow' – what a wonderful title for our enterprise!

Later, on the train out of London, I dozed in the late watery afternoon sun, allowing my mind to drift back to earlier associations with 'Yellow', the colour of childhood happiness and summer holidays. Born not far from the big yellow cranes of the Harland & Wolff shipyard in East Belfast, I had a great childhood, brought up with two younger sisters by very loving parents. Every July the whole family took a taxi to Belfast docks for the steamship to the Isle of Man and our annual two-week vacation. They were superb holidays: a B&B in Douglas, never-ending sunny days on the beach, rides on the horse trams, losing your pocket money in the slot-machines up at White City and bus runs to all points on the island. I loved these holidays and have very strong and happy memories from them.

As a kid I had little interest in two wheels and could just about stay upright on a bicycle. My first motorcycle, a Honda C50, was bought simply as an expedient means of transport (given that my folks had no car), yet that little bike really changed my life. I now had freedom to roam where I pleased and began visiting places only twenty or thirty miles from home for the first time in my life. I met and fell in love with Maggie from Holywood who I encountered at a Saturday night disco in the heyday of 'Night Fever'. She had notions of travel, a longing to see far off places, and I had a Honda 50.

Reading Ted Simon's book *'Jupiter's Travels'*, describing his 1973 round-the-world- trip on a 500cc Triumph, gave us the mad notion of riding from Belfast to the South of France on a bike: our first two wheel trip outside the Emerald Isle. At the age of eighteen, we clubbed together to buy a little green 200cc Kawasaki and loaded it with camping gear procured at minimum cost and weight stowed in throw-over saddle-bags. A top box with a rack on top for the tent completed our luggage. We stocked up on Pot Noodles and Cup-a-Soup in case the foreign muck wasn't up to much and there was a huge golf umbrella (à la Ted Simon) strapped to the front fork in case it did rain in France. We were young and green, the headlamp was painted yellow and the days were filled with golden sunshine!

In many ways that first trip could be viewed as a disaster. Our first night camping had us shivering horribly in lightweight sleeping bags in a cheap nylon tent, soaked by condensation that made everything soggy wet. Doubled up on a small over-loaded bike we were prone to punctures – on one occasion having three in one day – and we realised that the back tyre that looked fine back home in Belfast would never last the trip. Disaster? *Au contraire*, it was an awakening. Communication was effected by the most appalling schoolboy French and when that failed, improvised with comedy sign language. Generally, when we had problems, people turned out to be mostly decent. All we had to do was ask and they would help. The 'foreign muck' proved to be the most amazing cuisine and the rubbish we'd brought from home was soon in the bin.

The most incredible aspect of the trip was the sheer joy and delight to be had from experiencing new places, especially on a motorcycle. You are really out there totally immersed in your environment, constantly bombarded with sights, smells and sounds. Riding across the plains of Northern France, down through the Massif Central, Avignon, purple sunsets on the Cote d'Azur; getting kicked out of the Casino in Monte Carlo for inappropriate dress and on the way home arriving skint in Paris where we could only afford for one of us to ascend the Eiffel Tower (we pledged to postpone the event until we could do it together one day).

After this first foray there was no stopping us. In 1982 we married and over the following years acquired bigger and better bikes, embarking on numerous trips all over Europe. As the train arrived in Stevenage station I alighted with a contented smile at the warm recollection of those happy days.

Not all associations with yellow offer such happy and comforting recollections. 'Yellow' is the colour of illness and disease and in succeeding years this sad shade would stain our lives. In 1987, at an age when we still possessed belief in youthful immortality, a very close friend was diagnosed with Multiple Sclerosis. The news came at a time when we were planning a six-week trip across North Africa and our reaction was to turn the trip into a fundraiser. We spent weekends out with our bike at motorcycle events and in shopping malls across Northern Ireland collecting for the charity Action MS. The fundraising was a lot of fun and intensely rewarding. We met other people with MS and gained a wider appreciation of the condition and stood in awe at how they coped with it.

Easter 1987 we set off on a blue Kawasaki GT550 for a six-week, 6000 mile trip, riding down through England, Spain, crossing into Morocco, Algeria, Tunisia, then back across the Med to France and home. In Spain we met lots of folk from the UK, down for two-week sun and sand packages, who were horrified when they found out where we were headed. Many had been on day trips to Tangiers and returned with lurid tales of drug dealing, beggary, thievery, poverty and robbery in every possible combination. We began to wonder at the sanity of our adventurous leanings. Our own guidebook warned that our first destination, the Rif Mountains, was a notorious hashish-producing region complete with all the crime and thuggery to match. A particular warning singled out marauding 'Big Black Mercedes' cars crewed by violent thugs: get stopped by one of those and lose everything. We were by now somewhat tense at the prospect of our first excursion outside Europe.

In Morocco we rode through dusty farmland with friendly field workers waving us on our way as we headed for the Rif Mountains and Chechaouan, our first stop in North Africa. Leaving the coastal plains, the road ascended through pine forested hill country more reminiscent of the Scottish Highlands than the Atlas Mountains, ice blue lakes completing this illusion. It was comforting to ride in semi-familiar scenery with fewer weird people around and we stopped at various places to take photos of ever more stunning mountain vistas. At one of these halts we had just finished snapping when we heard the screech of tyres on gravel as a car pulled up behind us. It was a big black saloon... that sported a three spoke gun-sight badge… of the Mercedes marque. The windows rolled down to reveal four guys inside – all young, fit and very confident. We looked at each other. Guidebook Druggies! This is it: Day One in North Africa – The End.

"*Avez-vous un problem?*"

"What? … *Pardon… que?*"

"*Avez-vous un problem avec le moto?*"

"Oh…Ah... I see!…No, No. *Je prends les photos.*"

Damn! I'd just held up my camera to illustrate why we'd stopped. Now they knew we had valuables; how stupid can you get? It was at this point I noticed that all of the guys were smiling at us, big friendly smiles too. They thought we had broken down and had simply stopped to help. They asked if it was our first time in Morocco. We said yes and we were stunned and amazed at how beautiful their country was. This pleased them no end. They recommended a few places to stay and eat on the road ahead and then took off, the rear window full of big beaming smiles as they waved madly and wished us *bon voyage*.

Over the next few days we grew to love this treasure of a country, as the rich tapestry of the flying carpet that is Morocco unfolded before us. We rode south to the Cascades D'Ouzoud, a magnificent waterfall paradise hidden high in the Atlas Mountains, where we camped overlooking the falls. We spent a whole day swimming in glorious cool pools around the bottom of 100 metre tall water chutes and took a hike with a local kid in the afternoon to look for monkeys in the trees downstream. In the evening the women of the house brought out platters of local food – couscous and rice dishes with lamb or chicken – to a small table laid by our tent, our mealtimes accompanied by heady sunset views over the falls.

We ambled through Marrakech, getting pleasantly lost in its miles of rambling Souks; bartering for souvenirs amidst colourful markets shambled together; a tented city filled with saffron silks and ochre cottons; tinsmiths working brass and copper; the witches' market with its cures and potions and of course the carpet shops with their musty smell of new wool, carpets rolled and ready to fly through any Arabian Night. Every now and then an alley would spill into a small square where we'd stop to have a mint tea or join the throng to watch snake charmers at work.

And so it continued for the rest of the trip. Up early to see a Saharan sunrise atop the massive sand dunes near Erfoud and on to the border at Figuig and into Algeria. Ramadan, the Moslem period of fasting, began and lasted for the rest of the trip. Our problems in finding somewhere to eat in Tipaza were resolved by the local Police who brought us into the station and fed and watered us, honouring the Moslem tradition of helping travellers on the road. Finally Tunisia, where we rode down to the semi-desert island of Djerba, not far from the Libyan border, before turning north to Tunis and the ferry to Marseilles. We arrived back to Belfast and home with heavy hearts, wishing that we could simply continue on. One day we would.

In 1989 we moved to England, when I took employment with a company that built satellites. We continued our motorcycling adventures completing a four-week, 5000-mile coast-to-coast ride across the USA on our 1200cc Honda Gold Wing. We flew out to Vancouver and rode down through Yellowstone Park, on south to the Grand Canyon and then east across New Mexico, Texas, Oklahoma and up into Tennessee. In Virginia we picked up the Blue Ridge Parkway and rode north to Gettysburg, Niagara and finally Toronto and the flight home. It was another memorable trip but North America lacked the raw edge and sheer excitement of travel in North Africa.

As the 20th century drew to a close, I had the opportunity to join a spacecraft test and launch campaign and life just could not be any better. The satellites were built in Stevenage, England and transported to a special facility in Munich for environmental testing to ensure that each spacecraft would withstand the horrendous noise, vibration and shocks encountered during the launch into space atop an Ariane IV rocket. We had to further demonstrate that it was capable of surviving the harsh thermal environments it would encounter once operational.

With testing complete, each satellite was then taken to the European Spaceport at Kourou, French Guyana, for the launch campaign itself. Kourou was our introduction to South America and exposure to life in the jungle. We visited Devil's Island, the old French penal colony (made famous by the book *Papillon* and the movie with Steve McQueen) and once more there was that edge to life only to be found when venturing off the beaten track into truly remote places. We were on a high; quite simply, life could not possibly be better.

Chapter 2: The Storm Before The Calm

In 1999 dark clouds appeared on the horizon. Back in Belfast my father, normally healthy and full of beans, was suddenly ill with an ulcer and needed to go into hospital for a 'wee operation', to have it sorted. In Northern Ireland we make much use of this word 'wee'. It usually signifies a diminutive, for example a wee house or a wee car being a small house or car, but is sometimes used to trivialise things such as when the dentist says 'this'll only hurt a wee bit,' you know that a lot of pain is headed your way. Ditto the statement from my father, 'I need a wee operation'. It was only after surgery we found out that the 'wee operation' was to cut out a cancerous tumour on the duodenum, my father deliberately holding back the truth from the family. The surgery seemed to take a lot out of him and although he was soon up and about, he was never quite the same thereafter.

In work too, my dream job in space turned to a nightmare on the ground when I was promoted against my own wishes, and made Quality Manager over a satellite ground station we were supplying to a foreign government. The contract was over budget, behind schedule and everyone was putting in crazy hours trying to play catch up. The long hours away from home, combined with uncertainty over my father's condition, saw my own health begin to deteriorate.

At first I suffered bouts of light-headedness followed by pains in the left side of my chest. My arms felt like they were trembling but when I looked they would be fine. I developed an undue concern for my health and well being. A good physiotherapist traced the chest pains to a back muscle going into spasm, sending shooting pains around under my arm and up into the chest. It was some relief to know that I wasn't about to die from a heart attack. These fears seem ridiculous now but at the time they were very real and I was slowly losing my way.

The situation in work deteriorated further. I was forcing myself to go in every day, working long hours trying to 'win' the odd battle but knowing that every day I was losing the war. I hung on for six months until one day I went in and just tidied up my desk. The following day I took one look at the clean desk and left, not to return for five months. I now know that I was suffering from stress and was in denial at my condition, refusing to take the necessary steps to redress it. It was unfeasible to think that I couldn't cope but the truth was I was operating in such an environment of uncertainty and instability, trying to control events over which I could not possibly have any influence both in the family and at work, that I was bound to lose.

In April 2001 my father's cancer was back and consuming his body with a vengeance. The family GP gave us the bad news: he had only a matter of weeks left. He was only in his mid sixties and had been a decent, honest, hard-working man all his life. Now, when he should be enjoying his retirement years, his life was to be horribly taken away. He died in July and it was a sledgehammer blow. To date, I had only ever experienced the loss of grandparents, which as a child I had easily accepted; in my eyes they were 'old' people and you die when you get old. But my father was different and both Maggie and I really started to question for the first time where we were going with our own lives.

In the months after my father's death, I had some excellent counselling at our local NHS hospital. My stress symptoms were explained to me in clear and simple terms. The body has a natural response mechanism to stress whereby it produces short kicks of adrenaline, enabling a 'fight or flight' response as the situation demands, a totally normal occurrence that you employ every day. On crossing a road, you see a fast car approaching. You may decide to immediately run across the road (fight) or wait until later to find a safer place to cross, thus avoiding the threat (flight). Either way you get a little zap of adrenaline readying your advance or retreat. In an environment of perpetual stress, this mechanism goes haywire and the body produces these adrenaline shots continually, even when there is no threat. Your body enters a state of anxiety, charged with adrenaline, causing classic side effects of muscle spasms, chest pains, light-headedness and trembling limbs as your body is enervated by its own chemistry. These side effects cause more anxiety, producing more adrenaline, in short a never-ending cycle of despair.

I was subjected to a technique called EMDR (Eye Movement Desensitisation and Reprogramming) a significant weapon that enabled me to break the adrenaline cycle without using drugs. Gradually, over a period of weeks I employed the method to smash anxiety and regain focus and control over my life. I realised there were basic changes needed and that only I could effect them. My father was gone, but I owed it to him to go on. Maggie was a stalwart support throughout, alternately offering sympathy, assistance and the odd kick up the backside when it was needed to wake me to reality. My employer was also very supportive, allowing me to transfer back into the space side of the business where I was able to slowly ease myself back into performing a useful role.

Events took a further downward spiral the following year. Maggie's older brother, David, went to his GP suffering from chest pains and breathing difficulties. A trip to the hospital and an X-ray found the dreaded black spot on his lung. It was lung cancer. Forty six years old, another smoker who thought it would never happen to him. It did. It was a devastating blow. Barely a year after my father died we were back to square one again, facing another battle with cancer. He lasted six weeks, dying from a massive heart attack while in hospital for further investigations. The tumour had grown, spreading to his pulmonary artery, slowly blocking it off and causing the heart attack. What happened to my father was sad; David's death was tragic, but it served as a wake up call.

We had just endured the worst two years of our lives and could no longer see ourselves staying in the same jobs, waiting for retirement in twenty years' time or worse. James Dean once said, "Dream as if you'll live forever; live as if you'll die today." Our dreams involved travel and motorcycling and we now realised that if we didn't act on them soon, then maybe that's all they'd ever be: dreams. We read every book and magazine article on motorcycle travel we could get our hands on; spent evenings trawling the internet looking at travel web sites, everything from resource sites for motorcycle travellers like '*Horizons Unlimited*' down to individual travelogues such as the excellent '*Rocinantes Travels*', an online tale of a Norwegian couple who rode through the Americas from New York to Tierra Del Fuego.

In January 2005, two major events decided our future course in life. First, we visited the Daily Telegraph Adventure Sport & Travel Show in London where we were utterly enthralled at a talk by Chris Scott, author of the book '*Adventure Motorcycling*', about his travels in the Sahara. Then work announced that things were not going so well. The company's latest business plans to turn lead into gold were once again failing miserably and there would be redundancies at the end of the year… any volunteers? A quick calculation based on fifteen years' service showed I could walk away with sufficient funds for the two of us for at least one year on the road.

It was a big deal to walk away from what was, all things considered, a very comfortable lifestyle. Looking back on our lives to date, we realised we had travelled a path through a series of key points, each of which required a major decision to be made. We reasoned that we had done fairly well to date based on the decisions made so far so why shouldn't this latest decision be another good one? In our hearts and minds we knew it was the right move to make. At last we were back in control of our own destiny. The storm had run its course and calmer waters beckoned. All we had to do now was to decide where to go…

Chapter 3: New World, New Beginnings

As we pored over atlases and maps one route consistently caught our attention: the Pan-American Highway, a ride through South, Central and North America, an incredible journey encompassing just about every condition and climate on earth, from frozen wastelands to steamy jungles. We would need a new bike for the trip. Our journey would take us over some appalling roads, so the bike would have to have some off-road capability. Here we suffered a major handicap, both being 'Leprechauns' from the old country. (I wasn't always this short. In my earlier years I stood proud at six foot six inches tall and was a major in the Irish Guards – but I was thrown out for drinking and womanising with the Colonel's wife. Reduced to the ranks, I now stand at my current five foot five and a bit...)

In all seriousness, I was the smallest kid in my class at school and Maggie was the smallest baby in the hospital where she was born. Today we are short-asses with a 28½″ inside leg at full stretch. With these off-roading motorcycles, we depart from the realms of Marks & Spencer where the short inside leg is readily catered for off-the-shelf. Prepare to enter the world of Tonka Toy Motorcycles: roughtie-toughtie bikes, all chunky and knobbly, built to withstand the vilest abuses Planet Earth can throw at them. The bikes are relatively light in weight and have good ground clearance thanks to their long suspension travel. The downside of this is a high seat height that can make them feel top heavy. It is possible to alter the suspension and cut away the seat foam to lower any bike but this compromises comfort and performance.

Offerings from KTM, Honda, Triumph, Kawasaki, Yamaha and Suzuki were all too high in the saddle. That left BMW. Their adventure-touring flagship, the GS1150, was a monster of a bike but its smaller sibling, the single cylinder F650GS, was a pleasant surprise. Built in Berlin with a big beaky front mudguard, the little 650 looks like a Teutonic Toucan. Maggie arranged a test ride on a sunny winter afternoon and when I arrived home from work that evening, her big beaming smile said it all. She loved the bike; it was light, very easy to ride on the road with no nasty habits and impeccable handling. The seat was just a little high but we reckoned once the bike was loaded with panniers and touring gear the suspension would settle just enough to grant us a perfect footing.

Our bike was bright Mandarin Yellow, six months old and barely run in with just over 2000 miles on the clock. Cruising at 60mph the bike returned over 70mpg, amazing fuel economy for a bike of this size. We quickly realised that for both of us to make the trip on this bike would mean real compromises on what we could carry; everything would have to be pared down to a bare minimum.

Already we were thinking of setting up a website to communicate our whereabouts with folks at home and this, with the need to process digital photographs, meant that a laptop was essential, creating a mound of kit that would take up a whole pannier. Then we had to carry bike spares, clothing for both on and off the motorcycle, wet gear for riding in the rain, camping gear, cooking gear, wash kit, medical kit, maps and guidebooks. There would be a raft of documentation too: vehicle registration documents, passports, insurance documents and vaccination certificates, not to mention travellers' cheques and the fact that we would have to carry wads of local currencies and a supply of US Dollars.

The obvious solution was to take two bikes. Although it meant doubling our road costs, it meant we could comfortably carry more or less as much kit as deemed necessary and would have a safety advantage in that if one bike failed in any way we would always have the second to go get assistance. A few weeks later we stumbled across a bargain pre-registered bike with only three miles on the clock at a dealer in Northampton.

And so our 'Pan-American Adventure' began to take shape with funding sorted, bikes sussed and a general idea of where we wanted to go all outlined. The past few years we had been through the mill on the receiving end of cancer; now was the time to strike back and so we dedicated our journey as a fundraiser for Cancer Research UK, the largest independent cancer charity in the world. A summer campaign followed that proved to be a whole adventure on its own, attending major motorcycle rallies and events across England, setting out our stall and putting our well-practised blarney to good use. We started in Peterborough at the annual British Motorcycle Federation (BMF) Rally, a show that draws some 80 000 motorcyclists to the largest outdoor event of its type in Europe.

Early on at the BMF, I was chatting to a guy, explaining to him how the loss of my father inspired our trip, when he started to well up a little. He looked me in the eye and asked did it get any better? Any easier? He had just lost his own father to cancer and was having a hard time coping with it. He caught me off guard, as up to now we had been so absorbed in our campaign, refining our collection patter on how to best persuade folk to part with money that we had somehow stupidly failed to anticipate an encounter like this. Our fundraising would hit home how widespread the disease is and just how many are affected. One in seven people will have cancer in their lifetime. Of the one in seven, one in four will die from the disease. Of the 80 000 people at the BMF, that meant 11 500 would have cancer and of these, almost 3000 would die: sobering statistics.

The guy wanted an answer from me to a difficult question, one I wasn't sure that I'd fully answered for myself. But then it hit me that, yes, it does get better and it will get easier. Life must always go on, no matter what, and it is for the living. When someone dies, they leave a hole in the fabric of your existence; the closer the person, the bigger the hole. In time you can fill that void with other people, other things, but look closely and you will always see and feel the shape of the hole.

And so I replied, "What would your father want you to do? Sit around moping, perpetually grieving over things that now can never be? I think not. You have to absorb your loss but learn from it. Do something that would make your Old Man proud. We are here but for a limited time and there are no second chances. Do what makes you happy and if you need to make changes in your life to attain this, then just get out there and do it. Do it now." I can't claim to have fully answered his question and I knew I couldn't end all the grief, but maybe our encounter would make a start.

Later I met a couple with their little boy around seven, maybe eight years old. They had a bike, had toured a little in their day and like us had lost close family members to cancer. They listened attentively as I explained our story; how we had decided on our life change, details about our bikes, our trip, where we intended to go and why, how we reckoned the idea of the trip was worth money for the charity and how all of the money we collected would fund research into cancer that would maybe spare another family a loss like ours.

"Sure, sure, we'll give something," they said and both made separate donations. Throughout these proceedings we were all guilty of ignoring the little boy. This was adult talk, important grave matters for discussion by grown-ups. He just stood there, lost somewhere down round our feet, waiting patiently. I thanked his mum and dad for their time, their donations, and they wished us well. They gathered the little man up and were ready to leave when he said, "Wait Mummy, wait." He wriggled out of his mum's clutch and dug his hand into his pocket and brought out a twenty pence piece. "This is for the sick people," and he popped his pocket money into the collecting bucket. His mum and dad's eyes welled up. I was fair choking back the tears myself at this most heart-warming gesture, one that filled me with hope for the future of all mankind.

In parallel with the fundraising activities, life became increasingly governed by lists: an essential kit list, spares lists, a list of things we wanted but probably couldn't afford, lists of things to read, lists of things to do with the house before renting it out, there was even at one time a 'list of lists'... Then, one sunny November morning, we set off for Dartford to the offices of Kuehne & Nagel, who proved to be a professionally competent shipping company. With the fundraising complete, all of the lists ticked off and the bikes cocooned and crated for their two-month sea voyage to Valparaiso in Chile, we were finally ready to go.

Chapter 4: Latin America, Bienvenidos...

We shouldn't be here in cold, wet, wintry Paris. We should be in sunny Chile, haggling with customs officials and getting our bikes un-crated to blast off into the wilds of South America. But thanks to Air France we've missed the connection between our London-Paris flight and the Paris-Santiago flight so we have a 24-hour wait for the next plane. On the up side we have been fed and watered at the expense of the airline and plonked in a posh hotel, giving us a little time to reflect on our forthcoming Pan-American Adventure.

The first part of our journey would take us through Latin America and the more we planned the trip, the more we realised just how little we really knew or understood about the region. From our European distance and perspective, South America was a relatively unknown quantity, a backwater. Recollections from schoolboy geography lessons told of a lost continent squeezed between the South Atlantic and Pacific Oceans, consisting for the most part of the vast Amazon jungle populated with brightly coloured poisonous frogs and poison dart-blowing Indians with the odd monster anaconda thrown in.

On the map, the Amazon region hangs like a tattered green flag from the rippling spine of the snow-capped and forbidding Andes mountain range, exchanging the biggest snake in the world for the biggest bird: the condor. Here on the Altiplano under the condor sky, chubby, bowler-hatted, rosy-cheeked women run after herds of idiot llamas and their cousins the vicuñas and guanacos. Below the Amazon region, the land tapers off into pampas grassland and the

Patagonian wilderness, the range of the splendid leather-chapped *gaucho*, who spends all day chasing cows alongside long-lost Welsh immigrants who still chase sheep over the same grasslands. The whole landmass is finally punctuated at its southern extremity by Tierra del Fuego, end of the world and last stop before Antarctica.

Turning around, riding north between the Andes and the Pacific Ocean, will take us through the Atacama Desert, one of the most arid climates on earth. The road ascends into jungly highlands containing the lost cities of the Incas through Peru to Ecuador and the northern hemisphere. Ecuador is a convenient jump-off point to explore the Galapagos Islands with their famous tortoises, flora and fauna that so inspired Charles Darwin.

Central America promises jaguar-ridden muggy jungle rides through a plethora of banana republics where stereotypical Zapata moustachioed *banditos* still sport criss-crossed bullet belts and machetes but have exchanged their traditional white pyjamas and straw hats for tiger-stripe camouflage denim and Ché berets. If we survive Central America, we will end up in Mexico, whose cuisine has indelibly coloured that of all Latin America. Outside of Chilli Con Carne and other such hot and spicy Tex-Mex standards we really know very little about the food where we're going, although in my case, being an omnivorous pedal-bin is sure to be an advantage.

All along the Pacific Rim, volcanoes line our route, some two hundred active monsters in South America alone. Central America, in addition to volcanoes, is subject to the vicious hurricane season, spawning torrential rain and tornadoes that could destroy bridges and wash away roads. If we survive the volcanic eruptions, hurricanes and all the encounters with jaguars, anacondas, foul spitting llamas and squillions of poisonous snakes, not to mention those tree frogs, then mosquitoes are sure to bring us down with malaria or dengue fever. To be honest, none of the above really scares or deters us. Our biggest source of danger, as with almost everywhere in the world, is liable to come from our fellow human beings.

There were people in the Americas long before the arrival of the Europeans in the 16th century. The indigenous peoples were of Asiatic origin, migrating over a now broken land bridge from Asia to Alaska and then drifting south through Central America and into the southern continent. In the north they lived as hunter-gatherers on the plains and in the mountains, while further south they became more settled, establishing a number of city based civilisations, such as the Mayans who dwelt in the area from Panama up to central Mexico. In fact the Mayans had been and gone by the time the Spanish arrived, leaving behind fabulous abandoned cities, their empire mysteriously fading away some 700 years before Columbus. Their more northerly neighbours, the Aztecs, superseded the Mayans, while on into South America proper lay the Inca Empire. Both of these civilisations were about to be shattered by the Europeans' 'discovery' of the Americas. .

The Europeans had, by the time of Columbus, suspected that there was 'something interesting' over the western horizon as they gazed out onto the Atlantic. By the late 1400s it was a known fact that the Earth was round and a number of clever-clogs had actually calculated its hypothetical circumference. It was therefore just a question of someone setting out to prove the theories and enquire as to whether it was just ocean all the way round to China and India or if there might be something else along the way. Columbus' discovery of the Caribbean islands in 1492 followed a few years later by the mainland (at Panama - he never set foot in North America) opened the doors for invasion and colonisation of the Americas. Within a hundred years the Spanish had spread throughout South and Central America up into Louisiana and Florida, the Portuguese were in Brazil and the British and French were expanding north and westward through Canada and North America.

It must have been an amazing time for the old world to be suddenly presented with these whole new continents; in effect a huge library full of blank pages just waiting for men to write large their own stories. Across Europe, where traditionally the eldest son inherited the familial wealth, there was suddenly untold opportunity for the lesser offspring to sail west and claim reputation and reward for themselves. Freethinking men too escaped the strict ways and confinement of crowns and churches to set up colonies where new social experiments and religious ideas could be set forth and practised.

Of course, the European monarchies and governments eventually held sway over their areas of influence but a spark had been ignited and people were already questioning the established ways. Things came to a head in Britain's North American colonies, which were providing the motherland with a steady income of revenue from crops like tobacco, sugar and cotton. The problem was that the colonists wanted fairer representation; they paid taxes to the British crown but felt they were getting very little in return for their money. To begin with they wanted only local government, happy to defer to the crown for matters of foreign affairs and to pay some taxes to the mother country but the Crown would not yield on principle to a bunch of colonials and so by 1777 it all escalated into war.

The American War of Independence not only ended with the formation of the United States of America; it had major worldwide consequences. Colonials everywhere looked to the success of the North Americans and began to question what they were getting from their own far-off mother countries: Old World monarchies who received plenty of tribute from the labours of their colonists, yet gave very little back in return. The French dabbled in the War of Independence, providing considerable quantities of ships and troops to uphold the colonial cause, their king taking great delight at the discomfort and unravelling of the British colony; it would all led to his own demise.

Troops returning to France after the war were charged with revolutionary fervour; the seeds sown for *liberté, egalité* and *fraternité.* They had witnessed the North American colonials challenge the established order and win. Within twenty years, France was plunged into revolution and the king literally lost his head. The whole of Europe was in turmoil as other monarchies feared similar fates, so they ganged up to fight the French, led now by Napoleon Bonaparte. The Napoleonic Wars, fought in the early 1800s, lasted around twenty years, in which Napoleon successfully fought off the combined empires of Britain, Austria, Prussia, Spain and Russia. His failure to defeat the British at sea and on land (in Spain and Portugal) would be his ultimate undoing and so ended the immediate threat of further revolution in Europe, with the monarchy restored in France.

For Spain, the Napoleonic Wars were an unmitigated disaster. Siding first with the French, they lost their fleet at Trafalgar. Then Napoleon, fed up with the pontifications of further Spanish involvement in his wars, came to Madrid and deposed the Spanish King, replacing him with his brother Joseph. Spain rose against the French invaders, siding with the British under Wellington, who eventually drove the French out by 1814. The restored Spanish monarchy was but a slight shadow compared to the mighty Empire that had set out to find and colonise the Americas.

Spain no longer had the wherewithal to maintain her colonies. In Latin America a series of wars of independence took place through the 1820s. Simon Bolivar became liberator of Venezuela, Columbia, Ecuador and Peru. Further south, General San Martin overran Argentina and Uruguay and in Chile the unlikely sounding General Bernardo O'Higgins (bastard son of an Irish priest in Spanish service) became the nation's forefather. Likewise in Central America, a stream of declarations of independence saw the formation of the countries there today.

The remainder of the 19th century saw a series of internal wars as the new countries squabbled over territorial division and the establishment of borders. In the 20th century, they became synonymous with revolution and dictatorships. Today bold posters of Ché Guevara stare out in student bed-sits the world over. Names like Pinochet and Galtieri, men who ran dark paramilitary regimes linked with mass 'disappearances' and wholesale corruption, still strike a chord of fear. No wonder these places made excellent hideouts for run-away Nazis after World War II.

Then there was the US paranoia in the post-war years that every banana republic would grow another Castro, destabilising the country with socialist ideas, turning everyone into communists overnight and wrecking the country; so the CIA would go in first and destabilise it themselves, doing a much better job of destroying the place than any petty revolutionary could ever dream of. Their legacy: decades of unstable and corrupt puppet democracies; reams of revolutionary bandits roaming the country, way-laying any unfortunates who stray into their path, especially unwary *gringos*. A few of the countries became host to drug lords and traffickers, keen to safeguard their interests from prying officials and spawning further legions of militia as the drug war hotted up in the latter part of the 20th century.

Fortunately most of the countries along our chosen route had weathered this storm and were now enjoying some return to stability and normality, but the image of wholesale disorder, bribery and corruption throughout Latin America is a hard one to shake. We would be wary of encounters with local police and army on the road and with customs officials at border crossings on the lookout for an easy dollar.

Such was our knowledge and preconceptions of our destination on the eve of our departure. Why on earth were we going? At the end of the day, taking everything into consideration, the geography simply outweighed the history, luring us to ride into and experience first hand these vast and lurid landscapes so unlike anywhere we had ever travelled before. Putting it quite simply, we wanted adventure.

We would be throwing off the yokes of day-to-day life to become modern day Indiana Joneses sporting Arai crash helmets in place of a battered Fedora as we set out to thrash our way through the lands of the Incas and the Aztecs on our trusty Teutonic Toucans. People too: it has been our experience that local people are mostly kind and good in spite of what history tells us and how it colours our perceptions. An old cliché tells us that there are no strangers in life, only friends you have yet to meet. It's one we both hold dear and we would find it fully vindicated as we embarked on the course of our Pan-American Adventure.

Chapter 5: Chilean Arrival; The Adventure Begins

Our first night on South American Soil was spent in the hotel 'General Holly' in La Providencia, the bustling business district of Santiago, capital of Chile. The room was painted bright yellow and a print of one of Van Gogh's illustrious sunflowers hung over the bed, a good omen for the start of our trip indeed. The hotel was just around the corner from the Kuehne & Nagel Office.

Riding the elevator up to their office on the fourth floor we both felt a mild sense of panic, worried that for some reason the bikes might not have arrived. Stuck in a customs shed somewhere like the Panama Canal, costing us thousands of dollars to grease the wheels of corrupt officialdom to release them. Maybe they had arrived but their crate had been dropped from a crane at the harbour and the bikes were smashed to pieces. The worry snakes churning in the pits of our stomach went into overdrive, writhing and wriggling with heightened anxiety. It didn't help when the young girl on reception looked blankly at us.

We spluttered a quick smiley introduction in our best Spanglish but it was clear we were not expected, even though we had previously emailed the office with the details of our arrival. The receptionist disappeared, returning a few moments later with Catalina Enriquez, the shipping agent I had corresponded with, and we were finally relieved at this contact with a familiar name. Catalina was a stunningly beautiful woman and had my vote right away for the next Miss World. We followed her into her office where the receptionist brought us coffees. Luscious dark curls nestled round the nape of her neck, tumbling down onto her shoulders and big brown eyes, reading our anxiety and discomfort, flashed us reassuring "it'll be alright" looks. She continuously plucked stray strands of errant hair from her face as she called the customs agent in Valparaiso. Within minutes she had confirmed that the bikes had safely arrived and arranged for us go over to collect them tomorrow.

Day Two – Valparaiso; In researching the trip, we'd read horror stories of other motorcyclists stuck in Latin American Ports waiting weeks for bikes to clear customs, with rolling duties, fees and stamps to be paid amounting to hundreds and hundreds of dollars. We had chosen Chile as our point of arrival deliberately on the grounds that it seemed to suffer the least corruption in all of South America, but now we would find out first-hand if the stories were true.

And so we found ourselves in the heart of the harbour area in search of the customs agent's office. The neighbourhood was a decidedly run-down, 'seen-better-days' warren of shabby back streets with grubby whitewashed walls the colour of a coal-miner's collar. José, our agent, explained it would cost $125 per bike for all the customs stamps and necessary release paperwork at the *Aduanas*. In cash... Here we go. He called in Ingrid, a swarthy Chileno-Swiss beauty, and explained she would accompany and guide us through the various customs protocols.

Leaving with Ingrid we wandered the short distance to the first of the *Aduanas* offices, a modern looking glass and concrete building down by the harbour. Forms were completed in triplicate and boxes stamped. Ingrid clearly enjoyed her work. Armed with a quick smile and an easy manner, she bantered her way through the various offices and we gradually accumulated all the right bits of paper. At lunchtime she sent us off to grab a bite to eat, telling us to meet her back at the office. There we found that she had worked her lunch break on our behalf.

We paid José and trotted off with Ingrid to complete the final paperwork at the *Aduanas* headquarters, an imposing old colonial style red-roofed building with cool, dark fusty corridors and a myriad of offices all hidden behind closed doors with dusky smoked glass windows that looked like they would more likely host an array of dodgy 1950s detective agencies. Again Ingrid knew the right doors to open and by mid afternoon she announced '*todos estan completo*'.

Next stop, the bonded stores where our wooden crates were waiting collection. We acquired a small army of freight handlers, all of them eager to help us break down the two big ply-wrapped Christmas presents, prising them apart with jemmy bars and claw hammers. Released from their wooden cocoons, we went to work on the pupate motorcycles, putting everything back together, reconnecting batteries, filling fuel tanks that had been drained prior to packing and sorting the various boxes and bags that contained everything we would need for the next year on the road. We were elated when both bikes fired-up first time after two months at sea. During all this time, Ingrid refused to go home. We pleaded with her that she had more than done her job getting all the release paperwork sorted but she still insisted on staying until the two bikes were running and ready to go. It was after 9pm when we dropped her back at the office.

Today began with us both nervous about what would happen at the *Aduanas* and worried whether we would have our bikes released at the end of it. Instead we had found something we'd been sadly missing over the past few years at home: good service. Everyone did their job; sure there were customs procedures, with forms to fill aplenty, but everything was correct and above board. The people we dealt with were polite, friendly and keen to help at every stage along the way. There is an old idiom in the Quality Management business that says you should seek to 'delight your customer'. We were delighted in spades today. We paid José the agreed fee and that was all there was to it apart from a few voluntary gratuities, gladly paid with thanks.

We rode the bikes to a hotel in Viña Del Mar, a very upmarket seaside resort, adding a touch of glamour to the start of our trip with its splendid Casino along the sea front surrounded by tall wavy palm trees. Scores of laid back, wealthy Chilenos strolled the promenade in the evening sun or rode up and down the boulevard in cabriolets and convertibles. the whole scene was set to a percussive soundtrack provided by the Pacific Ocean crashing against the long sandy beach. We found a perch on the sea wall and sat and watched the sun sink to the west, far across a boiling sea, the first of many glorious Pacific sunsets.

For all that Viña was a lovely place to be, especially for a North European in January, we were both feeling a little wound-up in nervous anticipation at the start of our trip. After all our planning and preparation this was it; we were now fully committed to our new life. When we rose tomorrow the bikes would be starting up, this time for real, heading out on mile one of a long road on a journey that would not end until we reached Alaska. How would the bikes behave? Were they overloaded? There seemed to be an awful lot of stuff, yet had we forgotten anything?

A take-away pizza and a bottle of Chilean Red in our room served as the inaugural meal of the trip. We hit the sack early, soothed by the light intoxication of the red wine, yet still uneasy. With the sash window raised and slat-wood shutters open, the cool evening breeze eventually sent us off to the land of nod. Suddenly we were awakened. It was pitch black. A glass of water on the bedside table was chink-chinking violently against the empty wine bottle beside it, the surface of the water a splash of circular ripples. Elsewhere we could hear toothbrushes rattling in their tumbler in the bathroom. A pen fell off the table onto the floor and a loose door rattled in its frame. Then it stopped and the night-time peace resumed. This slight tremor that reckoned low on the Richter scale was a common occurrence in these parts; it was our first experience of an earthquake.

We awoke bleary-eyed and unsettled. We wheeled the bikes out onto the street, where they immediately drew attention from passers-by, mostly curious well-wishers, whose myriad smiles and thumbs-ups helped ease the tension as we readied for the road. Within five minutes we even had the address of a place to stay in Buenos Aires from a passing friendly Argentine.

A southeast back road took us out of Viña and onto the Ruta 5, the Pan-American Highway, the spinal road of the Americas that runs along the Pacific from Chile to Alaska, with only a short interruption at the impassable Darien Gap. Our first impression was of a good hard top dual carriageway that swooped along the length of this 2 500-mile long stick of a country. There was even an Armco barrier separating the two-way traffic and a hard shoulder too, giving the road some semblance of a proper interstate highway. The 100kph speed limit seemed a little slow but we soon found why.

In the West, motorways or interstates are high-speed expressways for getting directly from A to B and are closed to all pedestrian activity and traffic. Not so the Pan-American. We had started our journey on a weekend and at first traffic was light, the odd car or truck being the only other vehicles on the road. Thinking 'we could clip along here nicely on this lovely road', we were alarmed a little by the sight of a pedestrian walking along the hard shoulder. A little further on, some livestock capered alongside the road, chickens and goats unrestrained and liable to stray onto our path. Then a cyclist; OK, he was on the hard shoulder out of harms way. A second cyclist was definitely in harms way however, travelling the wrong way, coming towards us in the fast overtake lane! Later we would see bus stops full up with bored waiting passengers, their kids playing out on the road.

Finally there were the interminable tollbooths. On the bike we had to remove gloves, dig out and collate unknown coinage buried deep in pockets, hoping it was enough to cover the due toll, (a few pennies) to ride the next section of road. One of these every thirty or forty miles and our average speed began to suffer, as we spent more time paying tolls than riding the bikes.

Leaving the Pan-American we chased the Rio Bio Bio under cobalt skies. In the afternoon, the wind rose, making for a blustery dusty ride. We ran into a little town called Chol Chol and promptly got lost, ending up on our first dirt road of the trip. We rode on, rear wheels spitting little plumes of dust as we ate up the miles in the late afternoon. Then we hit road works. The men had finished for the day but what lay ahead was a nightmare. Chunks of rocks and coarse gravel had been piled up into a causeway as footings for a new hard top road. Tire tracks from big trucks and road construction equipment had gouged wide tracks into the surface, making for some horrible riding, for while it was reasonably compact in the tire tracks there were rocks and loose gravel everywhere else.

I go first, cursing under my breath as I ride onto the causeway. Stones clang bang off my bash plate like glancing armour-piercing shot, and the bike is bucking and heaving, demanding a hundred percent concentration as I struggle to stay in control. Over the helmet intercom I hear the rants and raves, huffs and puffs, of Maggie as she follows me. I shut it out; the road ahead demands my full attention. The secret is to keep speed up so that the bike flies over the ruts and obstacles rather than battering into each and every one of them. Don't look too closely at the road in front of your wheel, lift the eye and look well ahead at where you want to go and keep on the throttle for power and momentum.

I know the theory well but this is my first time putting it into practice, on a heavily laden bike to boot. I get a gunmetal mouthwash of adrenaline and my heart and pulse go crazy. Even writing this now I can still taste that fear. I lift my vision but all I can see is this endless dusty, sharp gravelly road stretching on to infinity. I am distracted by increasingly ultra violent clangs as huge rocks smack the underside of the bike and I make the cardinal error of looking down. A glance aside reveals a precipitous drop into thick gravel off the causeway so I try to stay well away from there. The tire tracks too criss-cross off into the distance like missile tracks in a dogfight and I have to make snap decisions as to which one offers the best way ahead. From time to time three or four of the buggers come together and then fan apart again. Riding quicker to try and smooth out the bumps and grinds means making these decisions faster and faster with the result that I now find myself drifted well over to the left of the road.

I look up, horrified, to see a green and white police car coming the other way at a rapid rate of knots, trailing a blaze of dust in its wake. I am out of control on the wrong side of the road about to crash into a speeding police car! There is a huge berm of gravel piled up to my right, denying safe passage across the road; nevertheless

I have a go. Next thing the bike is fishtailing like a landed lamprey. The handlebars are oscillating from side to side as the front end digs in and the back, still under power, tries to come round and overtake. I cling on for a few seconds but am inevitably spat off, releasing the handlebars to perform a magnificent somersault through the air.

I sit on my arse in the gravel for a moment, making a quick assessment of my state of life and limb. The limbs are all there and seem to be working fine and there is no loss of bodily fluids so I am relieved to conclude that I am alive and not hurt. I wish I could say the same for my bike. It is wrecked. One of the panniers has been ripped off along with the number plate and the Scottoiler chain lubricator mounted behind it. The front end is twisted and the plastic bodywork on the fairing and tank are gouged deep from the impact with the gravel.

I'm joined by Maggie and the two police officers and all three of them are grabbing at me to check that I'm alright. Dazed but not confused. The cops help us get the bikes to the side of the road and then, sure that I'm not hurt, they depart. The biggest damage here is to my pride. I never fall off my bike, as a rule, and now I'm looking at my lovely little BMW and it's been crashed and wrecked so early in the trip.

'What now?' Panic washes over me in waves. We are in the middle of nowhere on a horrible road with no idea of how much more of this there is to follow. My bike is in pieces, but first things first. It is late afternoon but there are still a good four or five hours of daylight left, so we should be able to get ourselves out of here. Then we meet two young French lasses: surreal to meet these two students sauntering down the road. They tell us the road continues like this for twelve or fifteen kilometres and gets better towards the end. Good news; at least it isn't far. There is a gutter at the side of the road, which is flatter and wide enough for a bike and much easier going than up on the causeway, so we have an easier path to follow. Now for the bike.

I am able to re-secure the pannier to the bike, the number plate and Scottoiler assembly can be bungee corded on too and there is no damage to the rear light. On closer inspection the damage to the front end is all cosmetic and superficial and can be ignored and 'hey presto' the bike isn't such a wreck after all and is good to go. We teeter along the gutter path, taking our time and soon the gravel pilings lessen. My bike rides fine, confirming nothing is seriously out of alignment and soon we are back on brand new tarmac.

Our final destination for this dramatic day was the little town of Pucon. A twisty mountain road led us through dense pine forest, which suddenly opened up to reveal, towering over the road, the majestic snow capped cone of Volcan Villarica, the first ever volcano we had encountered in our lives. We stopped the bikes, got off for a big hug and drank in the sight before us. At just under 3000 metres (9338 feet to be precise) it was a monster stood there in all its splendid symmetrical glory, the setting sun burnishing the mountain face with beaten hues of gold, blue, purple and orange. At the top a plume of smoke spiralled lazily into the evening sky, where we caught the odd twinkle of an early star.

We reached Pucon just as it was getting dark and set up tent in the serenely tranquil Camping Parque la Poza. We sauntered into town for a late dinner and pondered on what a day it had been. We were feeling every emotion that evening, sat outside a bar sipping Escudo beers: highs and lows, excitement and terror, all in one big mixed bag. Our first encounter with bad roads had ended so quickly in disaster; how many more miles of similar substrate lay ahead? Maybe next time we wouldn't be so lucky?

Neither of us had any prior experience riding off-road, our thousands of touring miles to date all accomplished on well-paved roads. We tried a one-day off-road skills course in Essex prior to the trip but all that did was to show us both how scary it could be riding on wet dirt. We stupidly concluded we wouldn't really encounter anything that bad on our trip and were now finding this to be a very false assumption. I realised now that we were relying heavily on the bikes themselves to see us through any off-road difficulties.

A grand day of motorcycling had started on tremendous roads that degenerated to a sea of gravel with the crash, the wrecked bike and worse still, the damaged pride and confidence. But then, at the end of it all, was the spectacular vista of Villarica and a safe haven in Pucon to repair for a few days. If this could all happen in a single day on the road, what would the rest of the trip be like? Our thoughts turned to "what would we be doing at home if we weren't here?" *Nine to five on a Tuesday in early January. Going to work and coming home in the dark. A bit of dinner, making conversation over a day that proceeded like the one before and the one to follow. Watching a bit of TV and then off for an early night to get up for work in the morning...* No comparison is there?

A few days later and I'm sat on my arse in gravel once again, puffing and wheezing, only this time it's deliberate and doesn't involve being flung off a motorcycle down a rocky road. The past few days at Pucon were spent resting and straightening out the bike. The damage really was all superficial and easily repairable and the bike now bears proud scars of her encounter with the road. We repacked some of our kit, now better organised for whatever comes next. It is so easy to unwind in this touristy little mountain town, a place where you can rent mountain bikes, go kayaking and generally gorge on outdoor pursuits to your heart's content.

We signed up for a hiking trip to the summit of Villarica; the opportunity to get up there and have a gander inside its big stinky crater was too hard to resist. Maybe see what hell looks like! At the tour office we were issued with a waterproof jacket, some trousers with plastic knees and ass, an ice axe and some crampons. Then a sleepy minibus ride up to the ski lift that would take us halfway up the mountain. A short stomp up and over a boulder field and we were into the snow line. Then a five and a half-hour hike to the top, following a zigzag route up and across the snow fields. At the end of it I was knackered.

If you are reading this book under some sort of assumption that because I'm doing this rugged motorcycle-adventuring caper, I must be rough, tough and well fit, well I'm sorry to disappoint. Maggie is the athletic half of our partnership. Lithe, lively and light she is and could easily have sprinted to the top in half the time it took me. She gladly eats birdseed and rabbit food and gets a buzz from jogging round any local park. For myself, I'm a wee tubby with a little paunch of cuddles that expands and contracts from time to time, depending on how much alcohol abuse my current lifestyle demands. Oh, and I'm fond of the odd cake and choccie bar in front of the TV, which I suppose doesn't help.

I have very small feet (UK size 5 or 38 Euro) and when I was 25 smashed my legs up in a motorcycle accident; I still have a metal plate in my left leg today, so walking tends to hurt after a while. Having said all that, I do love the outdoors but my approach to hiking is more along the lines of "If I can put one foot in front of the other I will get there eventually in my own time" rather than feeling some need to go and get super fit before I tackle these things. As it happened, there were a few other 'tubs' in our hiking group and a few of them didn't make it to the top, so I was delighted to complete the final ascent out of the snow onto the rocky crown.

We sat down around the crater rim, munching snacks and drinking water, feeling inadequate and ill-equipped to deal with so much startling scenery. The views from the top were magnificent in every direction. Stretched ahead to the north and south lay a chain of Andean volcanoes, their snow-clad cones sticking out like proud sentinels above the cloud base. To the east, Villarica dropped off towards the Pacific while to the west lay the Andes proper: a freeze-frame close-up of an ice-frozen sea in distress, a tableau of mad meringue. The ground around us was strewn with clinker-like rubble that fell off into the crater itself, a gawping hell-mouth several hundred metres across all strata'd round its rim with sulphurous red, green and yellow deposits. A farty smelling fug lingered at the bottom of the crater and every now and again the wind would waft its noxious odour in our direction to sting our nostrils.

Although we couldn't see any live lava in the crater, Villarica is very much an active volcano. In 1971 eruptions melted snow and ice on the upper reaches of the mountain, causing major disruption to the surrounding area when mud slides wrecked roads and bridges with some loss of life. The guides called us to re-group for the descent. A ten-minute scramble down from the rocky summit led us back onto the snow. Here we were introduced to the art of 'glissading', the polite term for sliding down a volcano on your ass. That plastic panel on the posterior of those snazzy trousers now came into its own as a personal in-built sled; tuck the ice axe under your arm for use as a brake and off you go. Our five and a half-hour ascent became a rapid one and a half-hour descent as we hurtled down the mountain yelling at the top of our lungs.

From Pucon we rode south towards Osorno. Volcanoes were now a regular sight, like telegraph poles and lampposts, yet they never failed to wow. At Osorno we stopped at a roadside café to debate our onward course. We could continue on south, following the Pan-American to Puerto Montt, the island of Chiloe and on to the Carretera Austral, a dirt road that would eventually take us into Argentina and the Moreno Glacier. Alternatively we could head east across the Andes into Argentina where we would pick up the Ruta 40, another dirt road that would also lead to the glacier.

Chile had been a lot of fun and a great introduction to South America. The people were very charming, very polite and mild-mannered. The food was stunning too; my paunch was definitely expanding on a diet of *empanadas* (the Latino equivalent of a Cornish pasty) and Chileno beers. As for Argentina, we had already avoided shipping our bikes to Buenos Aires due to too many tales of corruption and hassle there and the country had not really featured much in our original plans. We reckoned on a two-week foray through Patagonia just to get to Tierra del Fuego and to see the Moreno Glacier before returning to Chile. It nearly came down to the toss of a coin. In the end the stunning views previously glimpsed from the top of Villarica swayed us and we set off into the mountains. Little did we know it was a road that would lead us to catastrophe, to beautiful and lasting friendships and to some of the best days of our lives.

Chapter 6: On into Argentina

The road over the Andes took us through country that was quickly exhausting our range of superlatives for describing astounding scenery. The deserted road climbed and snaked into the mountains. Springtime flowers lined the verges in a rash of yellows, blues, purples and whites. In places they carpeted whole fields providing a multi-hued alpine foreground to a backdrop of awesome volcanoes. A few days previously, we had stumbled onto our first ever volcano at Villarica. Now there were five of the monsters spread across our horizon, including the snow-clad bulk of the enormous Volcan Osorno and the pointy 'witch's hat' of Puntiagado. All too soon we reached the Chilean *Aduanas* and the first of many border crossings of the trip.

The basic procedure for every border was that we had to get ourselves stamped out of the country we were leaving and then cancel our *'permisos'*: temporary import permits for the bikes that guaranteed we would not sell the vehicles without paying any import duties before leaving. There was usually a final police check that everything was completed before we were permitted to ride to the entry customs for the land ahead, get ourselves stamped in and arrange new *'permisos'* for the bikes.

At the Chilean customs, I went inside to sort the paperwork, where I joined a small queue of locals who seemed a little agitated at my presence. They shuffled nervously until one man stepped forward to point out the cause of their agitation: I was in the wrong queue. They were only pedestrians; I could use an adjacent empty window that dealt with vehicles and be processed quickly. When I did this they all relaxed and smiled. What lovely people! Ten minutes later it was all done. We rode to the police checkpoint, showed that we were all stamped up and off we went to Argentina.

The entry port lay ten miles further on and we rode through a mountainous no-man's land on a winding dirt road that chased rivers and gullies even higher up into the Andes. Finally the road reverted to tarmac and we reached the *Aduanas*. We parked the bikes a short distance from the customs post and the plan was for Maggie to stay there while I did the paperwork. One of the *Aduanas* came out shouting at us, indicating we should move the bikes up to the post. That way, we could park them in the cool shade out of the scorching afternoon sun. Inside, the customs procedures were easily completed by friendly staff, who bade us a warm welcome to Argentina and wished us a safe journey on, all completed in another ten minutes. If it all goes like this…

We rode on through mountain forests that pine-scented the early evening air, past lakes the colour of lapis lazuli. Another pleasant whiff now joined the evening bouquet as we rode along roads lined with hundreds of thousands of lupins, taking us down and around Lake Nahuel Huapi and into the lakeshore city of San Carlos de Bariloche, gateway to Patagonia and our stop for the day. Riding into Bariloche, we noticed many of the buildings were made of stone and wood and had the appearance of so many little cuckoo clocks. The surrounding mountains gave the place an Alpine feel and it was no surprise when we learned that Germans and Bavarians had settled in this area, making it their home-from-home.

Wandering the streets, we found restaurants and cafes selling schnitzel, äpfel-strudel and kirsch-torte. We found a little Celtic themed wooden joint called the 'Breoghan' for our first dinner in Argentina, where an extremely attentive Brazilian waiter showed us to our seats and proceeded to go over the menu with us. José-Eduardo took us through their selection of meat and fish mains and then gave us a run through some of the local wines available, making sure we understood all the courses and explaining anything we didn't understand. In the end we settled for *'Trucha con Hongos'*, locally caught lake trout served with sautéed wild mushrooms, washed down with a bottle of Torrente, a local Patagonian white.

We chatted about our trip so far and when we said we had ridden today from Chile he interrupted and asked if we'd had Pisco Sours. We had heard of this beverage, a major area of dispute between Chile and Peru, who both claim it as their national drink. It is made from white grape brandy with egg white, limejuice, crushed ice and icing sugar and so we had our first tipple of the Chilean/Peruvian national drink in Argentina. It was to be the first of very, very many Pisco Sours, a drink that is addictively delicious: smooth, sweet and tangy all at the same time and very easy to imbibe, especially after a dusty day in the saddle in hot sunny climes.

The trout was, at that time, one of the best pieces of fish we've ever eaten. The hongos, served in a creamy buttery sauce, were a perfect complement and the Torrente wine a delightful introduction to Patagonian wines, some of the finest table wines we've drunk anywhere and all of this for less than £10. We finished with a complementary home made herbal liqueur and a photo snapped with José-Eduardo.

We spent several days in Bariloche, our last city stop before heading south into the wilds of Patagonia. We could have stayed much longer, as this place is a jewel; its setting on Lago Nahuel Huapi, surrounded in every direction by snow-capped Andean peaks is like no other place on earth. We had lazy saunters along the lakeshore and took a cable car ride up to Cerro Otto for even more magnificent views of the mountains. On our final evening, we visited *'El Refugio de Montana'*, an Argentine *Parrilla*. It was a small family run place and the immediate thing that struck us was a natural happiness amongst the staff as they went about their work.

Our waiter was the eldest son who took us to a big wooden meat counter where we were invited to select our dinner from a tableau of choice cuts of meat. We settled on *'Bife de Chorizo'* (sirloin), which was then taken for cooking by the father on the *parrilla*, a huge metal-grated barbeque over an open wood fire that looked like a torture rack taken from some deep dungeon and put to better use. We had our first sampling of *Chimichurri*, a locally made starter consisting of olive oil, vinegar, garlic, coriander and fresh shredded oregano, served as a dip with some fresh bread. The steak arrived with a basket of chips, a simple tomato and lettuce salad and a bottle of Pinot-Merlot (Patagonian of course). It was quite simply the best piece of meat to ever pass our lips. Tender, moist, juicy, succulent, it could almost be eaten without a knife so easily did it rend apart.

Sat in this rustic little restaurant on a quiet Wednesday evening, quaffing the dregs of our Pinot-Merlot, I contemplated what we had found so far on our trip. First of all, Chile and Argentina were nothing like what either of us had expected. 'Latin America' conjures up the image of swarthy-skinned, dark-haired folk but almost everyone we'd encountered so far looked decidedly European. The German influence in Bariloche was so great that if you transplanted someone here blindfolded, with no idea of where they were in the world, they would swear they were indeed in Bavaria. But another aspect that was far more striking is how much happier and more content everyone in our new life seemed to be compared with the folk we'd left back home. We had stumbled on a real sense of '*Joie de Vivre*' and, while it's a beautiful thing to behold, it is somewhat unsettling and it started me thinking that maybe we've lost our way in the West, where everyone is out for a fast buck; to make money, own property, have a big car, get the kids to the best school, hold down a successful career, work their fingers to the bone. Ultimately this translates to a very poor quality of life, even if it may look good on paper.

Take the restaurants referenced above, for example. They were just ordinary 'off the street' joints that we chose on appearance and cost. We were travelling on a budget with the simple rule that the longer that budget lasted, the longer we stayed on the road. Yet the service we received is like nothing we <u>ever</u> had before anywhere in Europe or North America. The waiters and chefs are simply delighted that you have chosen to patronise their establishment and they go out of their way to make you feel welcome and to enjoy their experience. We never felt pressured to leave just to clear a table or because it was late and the staff wanted to get home. And we certainly never ever felt that staff were being nice to us just so we'd leave a big tip, as is often the case with the insincere pap that passes for service in the USA. People have time for others here, like the folk in the Chilean *Aduanas* directing me to the right queue. It will be interesting to see how this develops as our journey continues.

We filled up with petrol in a small gas station on the road out of Bariloche.

"What did he say?" Maggie asked.

"Haven't got a clue but I think he thinks we're Mexicans."

This conversation followed an exchange with the young chap on the pump while he'd fuelled the two motorcycles. We were getting used to the inquisitive Latinos and had stock answers ready now for the obligatory '*de donde vienen?*' and '*de donde van's?*'

that bombarded us at every stop as they inquired where we were coming from or going to. But this guy had gone on, hurtling into a machine gun staccato of unintelligible chatter from which I, with my infantile Spanish, understood only a single word: '*Mexicanos*'. I looked at myself in the wing mirror, deciding there was no way my grey grizzled facial hair would mark me as a Zorro or a Zapata.

We rode off with a mystery unresolved, continuing south, following winding roads out of the mountains and on to first glimpses of those Patagonian plains. Cold grey granite peaks gave way to lower elevations and softer grass-covered hill country, all earths and browns, the matted colour of Spitfire camouflage. Flocks of little dust-coloured twitter birds scattered in front of our wheels with a brilliant white flash of tail and a fleck of rusty red under-feather on their wings.

Today we learned a new word of dread on the roads of South America: '*Desvio*'. It was printed on an orange lozenge and heralded the fact that the road up ahead had been excavated and a 'diversion' was in place to get round the roadworks. Usually they scraped a wide dirt track up the side of the road under repair. If we were lucky, this would be a short stretch of reasonable dirt surface, sufficiently well impacted by passing traffic that we could hurtle over, but more often it would be several kilometres of shitty track strewn with mud, gravel or small rocks that demanded our full attention and taking it easy with the bikes. We rode a few of these today and they all served to remind us both of how dreadful we were at riding off road. Even scarier was the fact that we both felt we were getting worse, not better.

The sensation we were travelling in lands more European than Latin American was further reinforced at today's halt at a small town called Trevelin, deeper into Patagonia. The welcome sign at the edge of town was seated in a full bloom bed of red roses and purple lavenders. Riding through, many of the small local businesses sported red rampant dragons on a green and white background a telltale sign that we had arrived in one of Argentina's Welsh settlements. Back in 1865 some 150 Welshmen, taking up an invite from the Argentine government to settle the wilds of Patagonia, arrived and established a small community here. The area has retained strong ties to its traditional roots to this day.

We retired for afternoon tea in 'Nain Maggie's Tea Room'. Maggie, of the tea house, was born in 1878, migrated to Argentina in 1891 and then lived here, running the tea room, until she died in 1981 at the ripe old age of 103. *'Te de Galles'* was served: a Welsh Afternoon Tea consisting of home made buttered bread with cheese, home made strawberry and cherry jams and an assortment of scones and heavenly pastries all served on a quaint patterned china tea-set. In fact, we consumed so much 'tea' that we had to skip dinner that evening. We sat awestruck throughout, listening to our waitress (a freckly-faced local lass sporting voluminous curls of bright ginger hair) chatting first in the restaurant in Spanish and then shouting out orders to the kitchen in Welsh.

The road straightened out and departed away from the Andes, the chain of mountains diminishing further and further off to our west. We were heading into wilder, more desolate, landscape, flat grassland that stretched off in every direction forever. Riding became a tedious countdown of miles to the next fuel stop with the odd halt to get off for a photograph of nothing much or a leg-stretch. At one of these stops, a photo-shoot of a rather impressive stand of giant thistles, three motorcycles came rumbling down the road, sped by with a rippling wave, then U-turned and rode back to see if we were OK. All three sported Mexican license plates.

Ahh! The young man in the gas station in Bariloche the other day: he had been telling us they had seen three bikes just like ours and they were from Mexico! With the peso dropped, we finally met Joaquin de Uriarte, José Ramon and Muceo: the Three Amigos. Introductions complete, we rode on together to a little town called Rio Mayo and the start of Ruta 40. The turn off the main road to Rio Mayo was labelled on our maps as a possible town or settlement but when we got there we found only a deserted road junction. We had two maps covering this area, one bought in Argentina and one in Chile. On the Argentine map the junction was labelled as '*El Puerto del Virgien*' but the Chilean map called it '*El Puerto del Diablo*'; it remained to be seen whether this gateway would lead to virgins or devils up ahead...

Rio Mayo was one of the most desolate god-forsaken places we've ever been. We had an increasingly unsettling feeling as we rode into town that just maybe we had bitten off more than we could chew here. The town itself feels like it sits in a hole in the ground. The approach is across wind-swept grasslands until suddenly the road drops into a broad river valley. The paved road ends at a bridge over a river, with Rio Mayo on the other side, a most pronounced one-horse town, its streets paved with sharp thick gravel. The road continues on through town and climbs out the other side back onto the elevated grassland, where it continues south for hundreds of kilometres, all of it on gravel. The view from town in any direction ends at muddy coloured canyon walls, hence the sensation that you are living in a hole.

Joaquin sussed the best hotel from some locals on a street corner; the Hotel Residencia '*El Viejo Covadonga*' where for around £7 a night you can have bed, breakfast and evening meal; no menu, just whatever is in the pot that day. The bikes had lodging too in the old

50

function room at the back of the hotel; we rode through the lobby one by one to get there. Over dinner and a few beers, we heard the Mexicans' story from Joaquin who spoke excellent English. He was quite a character, with a fair drop of Irish blood in him from a MacRory grandmother (we suspected he inherited a 'gift of the gab' gene from her as well). They were heading, like us, for Ushuaia, 'the southernmost city on earth' before riding north and back home.

The discussion turned to road conditions and I confessed my spill and our inexperience on riding dirt roads. Maggie too was finding the going harder and harder and her initial confidence had been badly eroded after a few hairy episodes on the Desvios. Tomorrow we would be heading out on the Ruta 40, a 'Ripio' road named from the sharp gravel it is made from. It was clear we were both uneasy and nervous. The Three Amigos, on the other hand, were raised on diets of Baja dirt and looked forward to the morrow's challenge. Joaquin, sensing our unease, suggested that we set off early in the morning; if mishap befell us, we would have some comfort knowing that help was on its way. We turned in for an early night, unsettled by the after dinner conversation and neither of us slept well.

In the morning, all the nervousness of our first day was back as we loaded the bikes. I looked at Maggie as she donned her helmet. Her normally soft, smiling blue eyes were wide open, pupils fully dilated, and her face seemed to have been diminished by the grave concern and misgivings currently racing through her mind. I knew if I checked myself in my wing mirror I would see the same face. *"Consider it as a road to a beautiful place, not a path to the gallows,"* I thought as I wobbled off up the gravelly main street of Rio Mayo and out of town, failing to convince myself.

The road climbed back up a short slippery switchback section onto the grassland where it disappeared to a vanishing point way beyond the horizon. We reached a fork with no signpost to show the correct way. A plume of dust like the Roadrunner in the cartoons arrived on the right hand track, the car stopping briefly in a cloud of sand to confirm our route with a wave of a friendly hand. We were off.

The road was elevated up on a causeway with a nasty looking ditch on either side but at least it ran straight and to begin with we were able to ride in reasonably compacted tyre tracks. But it seemed, just as we were settling down a little, we would hit a softer patch and that front wheel would start digging in with the bike fishtailing just like it did when I crashed in Chile. We were starting to figure out what to do and keeping up speed seemed to help. I looked down at the trip meter and we'd covered ten miles already, clipping along at 30 to 40mph. I stopped for Maggie to catch up and we both smiled, glad to be riding and getting on top of that terror. She gave me a thumbs-up and off we went again.

The next ten miles was more of the same: settled periods with the bike flying along, riding over the bumps and grinds, taking it all in its stride and then those terror moments when that wheel dug in and the bike would start shaking all over. But we were winning! Just past the twenty-mile mark, we swapped places, with Maggie taking the lead for a while. I allowed my mind to wander just a little. *Let's see, so far, so good. Twenty miles and we're both upright. Maybe this off road stuff is really falling into place and we'll be experts in no time.* I was rudely and literally shaken from my thoughts by a tank-slapping motorcycle.

All of a sudden we hit a big patch of soft stones and that front end was digging in as the bike entered stage one crash mode. I looked across to Maggie in time to see her enter stage two when that back end, still under power, comes round to overtake the front wheel, now bogged well and truly down in the soft stony substrate. Everything ran in slo-mo as her bike went down spectacularly, like a shot buffalo. It flipped over, turning upside down and burying its handlebars in the gravel. With Maggie nowhere in sight, the bike shot across my path blazing a trail of smoke, grit and exploding luggage, flying off the causeway and on down into the ditch where it all terminated in a mini-atomic mushroom dust cloud.

To this day I do not know how I stopped. I sat back in the seat, transferring weight to the rear wheel, held on tight and recovered from the fishtail. I leapt off the bike, jettisoning my helmet to find my wife. Her bike lay dead and motionless, upside down in the ditch, engine stalled and front wheel idling in the wind and dust. A few feet away Maggie sat on her ass, cradling her right elbow. She'd been thrown over the handlebars as the bike inverted, tumbling along and off the road to come to a rest by the dead bike. She was white with shock.

"I'm not going home! I'm not going home! We've come all this way and I'm not going home!" she shouted. I sat down beside her to check her out and to reassure her that she was not going home; but looking around I wasn't so sure. There was no blood, so that was a good start and she was conscious, if a little shaken. We comforted each other and let silence reign as the gravity of what had just happened hit us.

Moments later, the silence was broken by the thunder of motorcycles as the Three Amigos arrived. Joaquin gave Maggie another check over and concluded she had whacked her elbow but probably not broken anything. Maggie wasn't convinced. We righted the bike. There was a lot of bodywork damage but I knew from my own crash that it was all superficial. One of the pannier rails was knocked in and the pannier seemed to have absorbed most of the impact. A broken mirror, a distorted nose fairing and some bent handlebars completed the initial damage assessment. There was no way we could continue. At the very least the bike would need to go back to town to be straightened out and Maggie needed that elbow checked.

Between us we recovered the crashed bike from the ditch and returned in relays to Rio Mayo, Maggie as pillion with Joaquin. The hotel owner, a saintly lady by the name of Teresa Basiloff, fussed over us and walked Maggie to the nearby local hospital while I unpacked and moved our luggage back into our recently vacated room. We bade farewell to the Three Amigos and remain forever grateful for their prompt and efficient rescue. Little did we know that our paths were destined to cross again further up the road.

I wandered round to the frontier-town shack of a hospital to check on their latest patient. Approaching the low, grubby-looking, single-storey building I met Teresa, who reassured me that Maggie was OK now, just waiting for a doctor and an X-ray. Inside, the little hospital was clean, if a little ancient in some of its appointments, but staffed by friendly and comforting nurses who explained that, as it was Saturday, they had to radio for the doctor to come in. A small, bearded, soft-spoken young man duly appeared and introduced himself as Dr. Maximillian, at once putting us at ease with his professional demeanour and bearing. An X-ray was taken and he pointed out a small hairline fracture in the elbow socket. He organised a painkiller injection, set the arm in plaster and told us that Maggie would not be riding her bike for a while.

"How long?" we asked.

"Proximo tres semanas" (roughly three weeks). "It depends how the bone heals.." Three weeks in Rio Mayo? Three weeks

until the plaster comes off, then another X-ray, then maybe another plaster? A black hole was opening beneath us and we were about to be swallowed whole into a universe of uncertainty filled with unappetising ifs, buts and maybes. God knows where we would be spat out.

"Do we have to stay here in Rio Mayo for three weeks?" I asked.

Doctor Maximillian laughed and smiled. "No, no, no. You can leave Rio Mayo but maybe not on a bike. Go see some of the country and then get the elbow checked anywhere you like. Just find another hospital and they can remove the plaster and recheck it."

Well maybe we could work something on that. Now for the bad news...

"*Cuanto costa?*" I enquired "*Por el hopital y el traitement. Tenemos insurance de medico – esta bueno?*"

"*Nada,*" replied the doctor. "*Esta libro. No hay una cuenta.*"

Sorry…nothing? It's free? There is no bill? We couldn't believe it. We tried to press some money on him, for the hospital, but he refused. I had noticed a children's ward on the way in and insisted he take the money as a charity donation for the kids and eventually, after some persistence in our worst gobbledegook Spanish, this did the trick.

We stepped outside into the bright Saturday sunshine and sat on the hospital steps considering the unkind hand the morning had dealt us. On the face of it, our journey was in shreds. In a matter of an hour or two we had managed to trash our other bike and now Maggie had a broken elbow. We had barely covered our first thousand miles, with tens of thousands more to go and so far we had suffered two potentially devastating spills. What kind of roads lay up ahead? Chile and Argentina were supposed to be the better countries to visit in South America; what would it be like when we got into the wilds of Bolivia and Peru? Could Maggie even ride again? If there were unforeseen complications with this elbow could it all be over; back to Santiago, put it all in a box and return home, whipped and beaten with our tails between our legs?

On the other hand this morning's adventures had led us into new and unfathomed depths of human kindness. The Three Amigos rescuing us on the road, Teresa at the hotel and the kindnesses and treatments administered at the hospital just blew us away. When we realised they would not take any money for the treatment, we were both close to tears as the penny dropped at just what kind of people we were dealing with here. This knowledge that we were surrounded by kind and goodly people, seemed to counterbalance the bad things that had happened so far.

Back at the hotel, we changed out of our riding kit and sat with Teresa in her bar discussing our misfortunes over a compensatory beer. She kept reassuring us that everything would be all right. We could stay at her hotel as long as we liked, there were people in town that could help straighten the damaged bike and we could work on it in the hotel. Maggie would recover, we'd see. After a while I went out to bring the bikes back indoors. I rode my bike through the foyer, into the function room and parked it beside a long dining table. I went back into the sun and pushed Maggie's mangled machine into the cool dark inside. Closing the doors behind me, my mind was clouded with anxiety and doubts as to when those bikes would ever see sunlight again.

Chapter 7: Homage to Patagonia

They say, "Never judge a book by its cover." The book in question here is Rio Mayo. The place looks like it's fallen into a hole in the ground, with its gravel streets full of dirt and dust that migrates onto and into just about every nook, cranny and orifice imaginable. All the kit in our room was soon covered with a thin film of it. It congealed up our noses, forming crab-apple boogers that had to be picked out frequently to avoid blockage and suffocation. Our new home where we'd been incarcerated through misfortune and injury. But I urge you... "Never judge a book by its cover."

Argentina is the eighth largest country on earth but has never had a population to match. The country contains large tracts of wild and inhospitable land and back in the latter part of the 19th century she was desperate to populate her more remote regions. At a first glance Patagonia looks ideal, with vast tracts of grassland and what looks like a decent network of rivers filled by Andean melt water. But the area lies in the rain shadow of the Andes Mountains to the west and these catch all the moisture coming in off the Pacific, where it precipitates on their western slopes, leaving Patagonia very dry.

Surveyors in the late 1800s decided the area around the Sarmiento Valley would be good for sheep farming. A tributary of the Sarmiento River was named the 'Mayo' after Gregorio Mayo, a lieutenant in one of the early expeditions through this area, and the little settlement of 'Rio Mayo' was formed on its banks. Sheep farming did indeed take hold. According to our *Lonely Planet* guidebook, the high street clothing chain Benetton owns over a million acres of sheep farm here today. Rio Mayo claims itself to be the sheep shearing capital of the country, yet remains a sleepy backwater of under 3000 souls.

The day after the accident was spent in the function room, where we stripped down Maggie's bike and carefully laid out all the damaged parts on a long dining table. We also stripped my bike to the extent necessary to recover 'before' versions of the deformed parts and now had to find somewhere to restore the twisted metal. We marched into the bar, lofting our haul of scrap iron proudly in the air and showed it to Teresa. She smiled at us and said, *"El Mecanico...por reparar,"* whereby we were given directions to *El Mecanico*'s place several streets down and round the corner.

We walked along the pavement half expecting to be overtaken by errant tumbleweed in the little dust storm that was bowling along the road. Turn right here...Ah *'El Mecanico'*! The doors of a half finished block-built garage yawned onto the street, spewing an assortment of rusty cars, pickup trucks and engine blocks, all in terminal stages of life, across the pavement and onto the road. We wandered into the open yard, filled with welding gear and a litter of more dead Fords and Toyotas plus the odd sleeping dog here and there, looking for signs of human life. A shack of a house leaned onto the side of the garage and we poked around the entrance, timidly shouting a few furtive *'holas'?"* and *'buenos dias?'* We heard sounds of life warming up from within and presently *El Mecanico* himself graced us with his remarkable presence.

El Mecanico was a big old boy in both height and girth, obviously an enthusiastic customer at the local *empanada* and beer shop. He was one of those people who looked like they are made from unconnected bits of others. To begin with, he reminded me of an Argentine Oliver Hardy with his round face, fatty tummy and moustache but this illusion was shattered by a shocking mop of very dark hair that exploded from his head like a flock of ducks dipping for bread. His moustache was even more bewildering: a Gallic cropper in burnt ginger and totally at odds with his other body hair. It sat on his upper lip like a pregnant caterpillar or a bad make-up job in one of those cheaply-made period dramas. Maybe it was a wig. Can you get moustache wigs? He wore a turquoise V-necked sweater over a grubby stripy pyjama top that poked out at the collar and a pair of grey jogging bottoms that were pulled up and over his waist in a most unflattering manner with the sweater tucked inside. The whole ensemble suggested that he worked and slept in the same clothes and was liberally sprinkled with stains from the garage, the dining room and... well, let's just forego any further examination at this point.

Through mangled Spanglish and a play acting sign-language extravaganza we managed to convey our disaster to him: we had two bikes, one of them had crashed and we needed these parts (holding up Maggie's damaged bits) to look like these ones (holding up my pristine originals). He communicated back with a series of grunts, shrugs and snuffles, which roughly translated as 'bring them over here and I'll have a go with this big hammer'. A smile and a thumbs-up from us indicated that we wished to proceed with this recommended repair.

He disappeared into the house and returned with a small blue kettle of water in one hand and a little dark brown wooden gourd in the other. What essential part of the repair process was this? The gourd was full of an infusion of some green tea-like substance and had a silver metal straw, with a decorative gold bulge on it, sticking out the top. He uttered the monosyllable *"Maté"*, smiling and holding up the kettle and the gourd so we could see both. He then proceeded to fill the gourd with hot water from the kettle and took a sip from the straw before handing it over to me. I was expected to have some. I was pleasantly surprised at the taste, a little bitter but not unpleasant. Taken with sugar it was actually very refreshing. I passed it back; he topped it up and passed it to Maggie, who was likewise impressed.

Drinking *Maté* is a very big thing in Argentina. It is a dried leaf from a native holly-like tree. It is consumed from a decorative gourd (*calabash*) by means of a metal straw (*bombilla*), which has a flattened end with holes in it and acts as a strainer to filter out the leaves when drinking. It can be taken as it comes or with a little sugar. It is a social event too, and the gourd is passed round whoever is present to take a sip on the *bombilla*. The calabash are fairly small and require regular top ups with hot water. Strangely, the infusion doesn't seem too bitter, like tea would if left brewing and a calabash can last for quite some time on numerous refills. Everywhere we went, cafes, restaurants, gas stations, they all had hot water dispensers as most people travel with a flask to top up their *Maté* along the way.

The twisted bike parts went into the vice and with a bang, a blam, and a few blatters, they were soon knocked into shape. Back at the hotel, we started the rebuild. Teresa came in as we were trying to bond the cracked tank-fairing panel with a mixture of superglues and epoxy adhesives we'd found at the local corner shop. The part had too much flex in it and we couldn't get the break to set properly; once we flexed it to pop it back on the bike it simply broke again. Teresa beckoned us into the kitchen and produced a pair of pliers, a nail and some nylon parcel cord. Then she switched on the gas cooker and heated up the nail, holding it with the pliers.

We melted a series of holes along both sides of the broken plastic and at the end sewed it up with the parcel cord with a jollop of epoxy on the back. Perfect! We rebuilt the bike and 'voila' we were fully operational (at least mechanically) once again. The bike had a Frankenstein battle scar now running across her bodywork, a trophy from our defeat in the dirt.

Rio Mayo, in spite of its small size, is a major nodal point for travellers in this part of the country and a lot of overlanding motorcyclists stop here before hitting the Ruta 40. The day following the accident a BMW 1150GS bearing US plates arrived and we were joined for dinner that evening by a Californian, Peter Deck, with a quick smile and a tale or two to tell. . He was a lawyer working for the UN refugee agency and had served in nearly every major hotspot around the world: Bosnia, Somalia, Liberia and so on. Between postings he went off to see the rest of the world on his motorcycle and his current venture was a tour of South America. We took an instant liking to Peter. He felt sorry for us but there was nothing he could really do to help. The bike was repaired so we were just waiting to see what would happen with Maggie's elbow. We agreed to keep in touch and indeed, additional misfortune would bring us together again further on up the road.

We watched Peter take off next morning and returned to our room. All things considered we had to make progress on our journey south. It was high summer and the best time to see the southern extremes of the Americas. Waiting three weeks for the elbow to mend would take us well into February and we would be racing to play catch-up for the rest of the trip. Besides, who knew what the doctors would say in three weeks: what if the broken elbow had complications? The nearest major city, Comodoro Rivadavia, lay a few hundred miles away on the Atlantic Coast. We decided to go there by bus and attempt to complete the southern leg of our trip by any other means. We would then return to Rio Mayo and, provided Maggie's elbow was sufficiently healed, collect the bikes to continue our travels north.

The bus to Comodoro left at 5am so we had to get up at 3am, carry all our baggage to the station and spend a whole day sweltering on a rough ride to the coast. Teresa was brilliant. She took our excess baggage for safekeeping and when we made a final check on the bikes we found she had draped blankets over them to keep the dust off. There was just the question now of that early morning bus ride…

Two o'clock in the afternoon, Maggie and I had just downed some lunch and were sat at the table reading and enjoying some quiet time when the doors of the Covadonga burst open and a very loud young man shattered the afternoon solitude. He was looking for the *gringos* with the crashed *moto* who wanted to go to Comodoro. Small town; word gets around I suppose. 'Lito' was a bank courier with the handsome look of a George Best about him and drove a little red Volkswagen van from Rio Mayo to Comodoro every day, there and back again. He offered to take us with him.

He communicated all of this information by shouting, for you see Lito was the Argentine equivalent of an Englishman abroad, working on the grounds that, if you're not understood first time, you need to move in closer and repeat yourself louder so maybe they will understand. To begin with we were a little wary, suspicious that he was simply trying to scam some money from us, so we declined and explained that we were OK with the bus. At the end of an exhausting twenty-minute shouting session the penny finally dropped that all he wanted was a paltry $5 each for the ride, pick-up tomorrow at 2pm, so we bade farewell to the prospect of the early morning bumpy bus ride and that was that.

For all his loudness, Lito was a gem. Not only did he take us to Comodoro. On arrival in the city, he showed us the bus station, stopping to pick up timetables for the routes to the south. He then drove us around four or five hotels, negotiated a rate for us in the best of these and gave us his number for a pick-up back to Rio Mayo whenever we returned from our foray to the south.

Comodoro was a fair sized city, if a little soulless, grown in recent years thanks to a boom in the petro-chemical industry. The road into town took us through vast fields of 'nodding donkey' oil heads, each one supping up black gold from the ground. Comodoro has tried to 'make itself interesting' but a 'Museum of Petroleum' will hardly attract massive crowds. All of this was further inspiration, if it were needed, to leave.

We hired a car. It was not appointed with any of those luxuries we now take for granted at home: central locking, power steering, electric windows and so on. Every panel and door was scratched and dented so there was no need for a tedious close-up inspection to mark down every chip and blemish on her paintwork, as required when hiring at Heathrow. The tires were well worn; at home they would be barely legal but we were starting to get the picture that in South America these things weren't really all that important. She was what a second-hand car salesman at home might term a 'nice little runner' and she would do 'nicely' for our southern excursion. Our plan was to drive to the bottom of South America with a diversion west towards the Pacific to visit the Moreno Glacier and Torres Del Paine National Park.

On our first day we drove south for 800km to Rio Gallegos, the last place of any size before crossing to Tierra del Fuego. On the map this part of Patagonia appears flat and empty yet it was quite a stunning drive. The ever-present wind blew unimpeded across vast rolling plains splotched with vivid colour so that we felt we were driving across a giant discarded artist's mixing palette. Bright white salt flats, turquoise and Prussian blue lagoons; mustardy yellow sulphurous earths slashed with veins of rouged dirt; and now and again the road would veer towards the vastness of the South Atlantic with spectacular views of empty beaches on this desolate coast. We saw our first llamas of the trip and panicked herds of crazy rheas, the ostrich like bird of South America and 'oohed' at flocks of shocking pink flamingos sift feeding little lagoons for crustacean dinners.

The temperature dropped and the blustery wind picked up as we made our way ever southward. We reached Rio Gallegos around 8:30pm and the wind seemed to have driven everyone off the streets of the little city. We found a cheap motel and went for eats at a place called 'La Estancia', where we dined on some very good beef. We chatted with Guillaume, the owner, about life in the windy city. The ever-present wind is the main reason why so few people have settled in the region, one of the windiest places on earth. Many come but few stay. Calm days are rare; most days are fairly gusty and the strong winds interfere with just about every activity you care to think of. Hang washing out to dry and it will blow away. You can neither kick a football nor fly a kite. The wind blows seeds and topsoil away, destroys crops that do take root and when really stormy will demolish fences, roofing and even buildings with ease. We heard tales of people being blown off their feet, car doors being wrenched off their hinges and high-sided trucks being effortlessly tipped over.

It is a little known fact that Charles Darwin visited the region and noted how the sheep here have developed clawed feet to anchor themselves firmly to the ground. It is an even lesser known fact that this subspecies of 'Patagonian Wind-Sheep' provided him with the first inklings of his origin of the species theory. It is said that sheep imported here by the first settlers were simply blown off the land, caught in a vortex of Patagonian wind that deposited them hundreds of miles away in a river gorge in the Andes. The river froze through time to form the Merino Glacier, a moving slab of frozen mutton. So said Charles Darwin; or he would have if he ever did stand-up.

Guillaume also solved the mysteries of the strange shrines we had observed outside town. There seemed to be two types. One lot looked like a communal bottle dump and the other a collection of little red flags. I will return to the bottles later; first the story behind the red flags. On closer inspection these were made from red rags, pieces of red cloth and red garments attached to sticks and pieces of wire. Given that Latin America is predominantly Roman Catholic we presumed that the shrines were dedicated to some local saint but this was not the case. The centrepiece of each shrine was a little red hut and if we looked inside we would find neither saint nor virgin but a '*gauchito*': a little cowboy.

According to Guillaume, the *gauchito* was named 'Gil' (pronounced 'heel') and he fell in love with the daughter of a wealthy ranch owner, a young lady way out of his class. When the rancher learned of the affair, he had his men take the little cowboy out into the desert to murder him. Left for dead, the little cowboy managed to crawl back to the ranch, leaving a trail of blood, where he died in the arms of the woman he loved, hence the *gauchito* in the shrine with the red flags signifying his trail of blood.

Another version of the story, heard later, portrays Gauchito Gil as an Argentine Robin Hood, a deserter from the army in the late 1800s who stole from the rich and gave to the poor until he was caught and sentenced to death. Going out to meet his fate he told his executioner that when the man returned home that night he would find his son gravely ill. He told him to say a prayer in the cowboy's name and he would ask the Lord to intervene and save the boy. The *gauchito* was duly executed but on going home that evening, the executioner found the story was true. His son was terminally ill, so he prayed to the *gauchito* and next morning the lad was fine and the incident claimed as a miracle.

Gauchito Gil now has a massive following across Argentina, Chile, Brazil and Paraguay. Today there is a huge shrine to him at the place of his execution, near the city of Mercedes, where an annual pilgrimage drawing upwards of 150 000 people takes place every 8th January to mark the anniversary of his death. Visitors to the shrines leave the red flags and ask the little cowboy for his intervention in budding romances and to help with affairs of the heart.

From Rio Gallegos we drove west across the narrowed continent in a day to El Calafate, right at the bottom of mainland Argentina The Patagonian landscape remained enthralling as we approached the southern extremities of the Andes. The mountains re-appeared to bar our route, a saw-toothed, snow-capped skyline. The road turned to gravel and twisted and turned as we climbed towards the distant peaks and the domain of some serious birds of prey: a few small falcons to begin with and then a troop of caracaras, an eagle like bird with a very colourful yellow tipped claret and blue beak. We stopped to watch them shred a hare carcass. They seemed a little uneasy and at first we thought it was because of our presence, but a quick scan of the skies and we spied something resembling a small hang glider circling above us in the air; our first sight of a condor.

El Calafate is the gateway to one of the wonders of all of South America: the Perito Moreno Glacier. The Moreno is one of a number of monster Andean glaciers fed by the Southern Patagonian ice field, the third largest reserve of freshwater on the planet. It is quite special as it moves relatively fast, advancing several metres each day and is one of the Earth's few advancing ice fields. We spent a day at the glacier and it was a shock to the sensations. Sited in a National Park, it is reached by a twisting, turning road threading around lakes and into the mountains, offering at first only sneaky peaks of the glacier up ahead.

We parked the car and walked up to the viewing galleries. The approach is cleverly constructed so that the glacier remains hidden until the very last minute and you hear the action before you see it, rather like approaching the front line on a battlefield. First there was the odd distant rifle shot of ice cracking under pressure. Occasionally these would merge into a staccato of machine gun fire as a fissure formed when the cracks joined up. Finally, as we neared the viewing galleries, there was the furore of an artillery barrage, the farrumph of huge chunks breaking off the leading edge and smashing into the lake below. We stood awestruck and beheld wave upon wave of sharp ice peaks advancing in phalanx down to the lake to die in this spectacular fashion.

The main action runs along the 5 km long leading edge, where huge chunks of ice, the size of multi-storey buildings, continually break off and come crashing down into Lago Argentina some sixty metres below. The falling chunks explode on contact with the ice covered lake, sending shards of lethal shrapnel in all directions. The first impression was how vividly blue the ice was, with every shade and hue of the colour represented. The waves of ice are formed from individual peaks, each one elongated and holed, creating a series of crazy upturned snobby-nostrils poking out of the frozen river and into the sky as if sniffing for air. The galleries were deliberately built some way back to give a better overall view and prevent fatalities caused by people getting too close to the action.

Lago Argentina is 'L' shaped and the glacier stabs into the junction of the 'L' to bisect and dam the lake. The water in the upper section of the divided lake rises over time, making it up to thirty metres higher than the lower part. Eventually the water pressure acts on the ice dam, causing it to explode in a most dramatic and catastrophic fashion. The upper lake then drains into the lower to reach equilibrium once again, while the glacier moves in to build a new dam and the cycle starts again. When we visited Moreno, this had not happened for ten years (it was previously an annual event) and little did we know we were viewing the ice dam fully primed and ready to go. It finally exploded three weeks after we left, making national news headlines.

From El Calafate we drove back into Chile to Puerto Natales where we stocked up for a five-day expedition into Torres Del Paine National Park. In Puerto Natales we felt close to the edge of the world, and the origin of all that Patagonian wind. There is a rawness in the land and in the air of this bleak yet wondrous place. Everywhere we looked there were snow-capped mountains lapped by icy blue Pacific fjords and we sensed an air of expectancy around the town, as if the locals were reeling and catching their breath from the last storm while waiting for the next. Everything had a temporary feel to it and the dwellings resembled a shambles of low-lying, shot-blasted huts. There was nothing here that couldn't be quickly collected up and hammered back together again once the wind has passed and done its work. Laden with provisions, we set off into yet wilder lands, towards one of the most beautiful landscapes we have seen in our lives.

Torres Del Paine ('Towers of Granite') first appears as a shock of mountains on the horizon. It looks like the gods made an elaborate three-tier wedding cake from the finest rock ingredients available and then dropped it from a great height to splatter on the ground. There are layers of rock in every colour imaginable: sharp black granite running over softer bluey-grey slabs that melt onto a baked crumble of chocolate and amber. Vivid rusty red slashes form the jam in the cake, and the montage is crusted with a liberal icing of snow, with a huge slab off to one side forming the Grey Glacier. In the debris fields surrounding the centrepiece lie lakes aplenty and the whole area is teeming with wildlife: guanacos, rheas, condors and Patagonian grey foxes. The whole area is a hiker's paradise and the main trail, known as the 'W', takes three or four days to complete. The Grey Glacier forms the left arm of the 'W' which loops round to the Valle de Frances in the centre of the park and then loops on again to the Mirador Las Torres on the right.

We camped at the main Torres campsite for the first three nights and our first day took us on a ten-hour hike to the Mirador Las Torres, the 2800 metre high ice-smoothed Towers of Granite themselves. The trail followed a narrow snaking path deep into the flank of the mountains under a staggering ice-blue sky. It was breathless walking in the rarefied air with stops to chat with other hikers and to make way for the odd supply *gaucho* taking food up to one of the little camps by mule train.

A stop for lunch before a scramble up a sheer wall cascade of granite boulders and we crested the final rise for the land to suddenly drop away into a world of rock and water as the vast amphitheatre of the Mirador opened up before us. The Torres themselves grab the eye first, three sugar loaf projectiles lunging up into the sky. It feels like we are standing in the gullet of a broken giant jawbone with the Torres the only remnants of a set of gigantic dentistry. They run down over ice-polished rock, the texture of stretched elephant hide that sweeps down like a lunatic funfair slide into a cold grey lake of ice melt at the bottom. All around in the foreground broken rocks and rubble lay, tumbled down into the same lake. Other hikers make it up onto the crest and we smile in recognition at the shared sense of awe displayed on their faces. It is an enthralling sight and one that will remain with us for the rest of our days.

Evenings in the park are just as wonderful. The dusk sky fills with impossible science-fiction cloudscapes, shot through with pinks and salmons as the sun sets behind Monte Almirante Nieto. We are camped in the shadow of the mountain and once the sun has gone it freezes rapidly. The night sky runs to black crush-velvet and offers crystal clear views of diamond-studded heavens. We huddle together around a hot cuppa as we sit and stare agape at the limitless Milky Way, 'oohing' and 'aahing' at shooting stars as they slash through the darkness.

Over the following days we content ourselves with shorter walks around Lakes Nordenskjold, Pehoe and Grey. At Lago Pehoe we have the 'best campsite in the whole wide world', down by the water's edge with the impressive array of the snow covered Paine Grande Mountains and their massive 2500 metre *Cuernos* (Horn) formations lofting over the lake in the foreground. Each morning we rise and rush out of the tent to see what the mountains look like today. In that calm of dawn's early light we marvel at the majesty of these mountains mirrored to stupefying perfection in the lake before us.

We left Torres Del Paine on roads south. Just outside Puerto Natales, we stopped at one of the bottle-dump shrines I mentioned earlier and the second of the local legends may now be told.

70

Again the centrepiece is a little hut, but gone are the red flags to the *gauchito*, replaced now with row after row of thousands upon thousands of plastic lemonade bottles filled with water. This shrine is dedicated to 'Difunta Correa' and a peek inside the little altar hut reveals a cheap plastic effigy of a dead woman clutching a baby to her breast.

Back in the 1840s, Argentina was gripped in civil war. Not long after gaining independence from Spain, there was a struggle between Unitarians in Buenos Aeries seeking one nation and Federalists in the provinces who sought local independence. Men marched off to fight in the ad hoc armies, some willing, some pressed. For some women, such as Maria Antonia Deolinda Correa, there was no choice but to trail the army as camp followers. She set out with their newborn baby on a futile search for her beloved husband, a pressed man by the name of Bustos, who had been forced to fight for a local militia. She entered the hot arid desert to the north east of San Juan and, after a few days wandering around hopelessly lost, ran out of food and water at a place called Vallecito. Unable to continue further in these extreme conditions she climbed to the top of a small hill, bundled the little baby to her breast and died. A day or so later a passing mule train came upon her corpse and were staggered to find the baby still alive, sustained by its mother's milk.

When I first heard this story I took the two syllables of Difunta to be two separate words, with a 'Funta' sounding like it could be the Spanish word for a fount. After all, her body was the fount of life for her baby and the offerings of all the bottles of water left at the shrines today are there to quench Madame Correa's thirst. Difunta is actually all one word meaning 'defunct', a colloquial term for 'dead'. When the mule train discovered the corpse in the desert, they found a necklace around her neck that read CORREA. They buried the body and carved the name '*Difunta Correa*' on a nearby Carob tree. The incident was hailed as a local miracle and today Difunta Correa is a massive phenomenon. Many journeys in Argentina and Chile commence with an offering at the local shrine, resulting in these fantastic bottle dumps.

We parked the car just off the road and explored the shrine. The thousands of plastic bottles sat there in beautifully crafted symmetry all the more amazing considering each bottles had been hand set by individuals. Long wavy grass had grown through the arrayed bottles in places, softening the effect; all that could be seen were their rounded shoulders, with multicoloured bottle tops all nosing towards the altar hut at the centre, an obscure, fascinating piece of modern art. The site itself, looking back down a long road over Puerto Natales, was serenely peaceful and the impression not unlike that of visiting a First World War roadside cemetery in Northern France with the compact rows of white crosses replaced here by junk bottles. As we walked round the shrine neither of us spoke much, immersed in our own private thoughts. Observing local tradition, we added a bottle of our own to the pile. After the calamities we'd suffered so far on our own trip, we reckoned it wouldn't do any harm. Then the strangest thing happened.

Returning to the car, we both felt very calm and peaceful. I turned the key in the ignition and immediately my eye was drawn to the trip meter on the instrument panel; it had reset itself to zero. It was freaky and we both felt the hairs on the back of our necks rise. Resetting the trip was a fiddly and awkward process whereby you slot your hand through the steering wheel and press the little button. Previously it refused to zero and we had to twiddle with it, pushing the reset button lots of times, to make it function. We had refuelled a few days previously so the display had shown several hundred kilometres when we left Puerto Natales. There is no way either of us could have accidentally zeroed that trip meter. There was no one else around. An electrical fault in the car? Maybe, but how weird it should manifest itself here at this very place.

Leaving Torres Del Paine, we both felt totally revitalised and full of life. We had exercised with our walks every day and eaten extremely well: canned tuna with pasta in red wine tomato sauces as the staple, accompanied by lake-cooled beer and wine. The crash at Rio Mayo was well in the past. Ted Simon once said that it is only when 'the plan' goes wrong that a journey really starts. Our early disasters had opened these fabulous countries to us in hitherto unimaginable ways. On the road to Tierra del Fuego we looked forward with confidence to our trip continuing and ultimately being successful. Why not? Here, after all, was a sign from the gods!

Chapter 8: Into the Land of Fire

Maggie had the wheel and I rode shotgun, slumped in the passenger seat; reduced to that semi-somnolent state that only travelling long distance in a car can induce. The road was bumpy-bumpy-bumpy gravel and I was jolted left and right, to and fro, restrained by my seatbelt as the car slithered along. My mind was in free fall as I idly contemplated what we would find at the end of the world. For that was our next destination. To get there we had to cross over to Tierra del Fuego, the island at the end of the world. It ought to be something splendid, something rather special; a prize worth coming all this way for.

We left Punta Arenas under a heavy sky. Our fine weather had ended the day we left Torres Del Paine, replaced by a conveyor belt sky of murky grey stratus. It was cold too. A ferry ride took us across the Magellan Straits and driving off the vehicle ramp at the far side we were met by a sign bearing a skull and crossbones with the infamous legend 'Achtung Minen!' reminding us that in the past Tierra del Fuego has been an area of major dispute between Argentina and Chile. The border dispute was eventually settled by a third party arbitrator – The United Kingdom – who, according to Argentine sources we spoke to, sided heavily with its Chilean allies, giving them the best bits. Chile now owns both sides of the Magellan Straits and controls all the sea crossings from the mainland while the end of the road is in Argentina.

Tierra del Fuego: 'The Land of Fire', so called by the first westerners to arrive in these parts because of the plumes of smoke they observed rising from the campfires of the Yamana Indians. Early contacts with the natives were wild and ferocious, resulting in several deaths, and the Yamana gained a reputation as heathen cannibals. Combined with the inherent navigation hazards of the rock-strewn stormy waters, the area soon gained a fearsome reputation amongst seafarers. For many years the Land of Fire was an area to be avoided at all costs and ships stayed well out to sea rounding Cape Horn.

After only a few kilometres we began to seriously wonder why we had come here at all. It was a depressing place, with nothing to please the eye. Low rolling yellow-brown grasslands submerged along the blurry horizon of ground-hugging fug cloud to drain the soul and spirit. The sky yielded big splots of rain on our windscreen, rain that never came to anything; not wet enough to drive with wipers on, just big splodges that blurred the view and depressed the scene even more. And the land is still on fire, literally, although sadly they are no longer Yamana campfires. Instead, gas wells spotted across the landscape burn off massive exhaust flames, emitting clouds of curling black smoke, adding to the impression that we really have come to the end of the world, temporally as well as physically. It would make an excellent prison if the punishment to be meted included some sort of sensory deprivation. We drove past several sorry looking guanacos who stared back at us from soot blackened faces, common to the sub-species down here.

Crossing into Argentine territory we stopped for the night at Rio Grande, a fairly large city on the coast that lays claim to be 'the Garden City of Patagonia'. Anywhere that dubs itself a 'Garden City' reminds me of Greenland; so called to entice settlers to come and live there, when about the truth is the place hasn't really got much to recommend it. True, some effort had been made to brighten up the town with lovely little boxed flower beds up and down the streets, filled with marigolds and other blooms, but the effect was lost against the backdrop of derelict and crumbling buildings, battered no doubt by the wicked looking steel-grey South Atlantic. Still, we did find a warm and friendly hotel and our evening's entertainment was provided from a window seat in a restaurant where we dined on Patagonian lamb and watched a deranged, escaped guard-dog dragging a huge chain up and down the street in the pouring rain. He was a big lollopy mongrel with his floppy tongue hanging out and looked totally confused and bewildered at his newfound freedom.

We spent the rest of the evening contemplating the idea '*is this really all there is to the end of the world?*' It seemed as if the land had lost interest and was content to run itself out in this bland island wilderness of burning grasslands. Surely the end of the world deserves better: monster mountains; a vast chasm full of boiling lava; a cascade wall of water as it plummets off the edge of the abyss; some more fitting statement to mark the termination of the South American landmass.

Another string to Rio Grande's bow is that it is surrounded by some of the best trout rivers in the world, as celebrated by a huge lifelike statue of a trout marking the southern exit of the town. We crossed some of these rivers and they started to break up the previous day's dismal landscape and lend it more distraction. The ground rose and we departed those sorry grasslands, entering in their place a land of forest. But as we got closer, we realised there was something seriously wrong with the trees. They were dying, slowly being killed off by a grey-green lichen that hung suspended from dead branches like wispy battle flags after some particularly horrible medieval slaughter. Eerie, creepy, Hammer House of Horror stuff, black and white skeleton trees that surround Dracula's castle or maybe a haunted house. All we needed was a bed of mist and a driverless coach with blood-eyeballed, black horses snorting flames to complete the scene. We drove for miles through this weird land and then spotted the welcome sight of a few mountains up ahead.

The mountains expanded into snow-capped giants barring our path with the just discernable Ripio road our route through. The ascent clung to the side of a cliff face with breathtaking, crumbling drops off to the other side offering sweeping views over Lake Fagnano. We drove on into a mountainscape wreathed in dense Valkyrian clouds; splotting our windscreen once again with gel-like rain and somewhere in the gloom we swore we heard the 'hammers of the gods' at work. Now this is more like the End of the World! The noise, disappointingly, came from roadworks; an improved paved road was being laid, granting a smooth and gentle descent from the mountains to the end of our journey south. We coasted on to a welcome sign proclaiming *Ushuaia – Fin Del Mundo*: The City at the End of the World.

Ushuaia is set in a serenely beautiful location, nestled between the Martial Mountains and the deep blue waters of the Beagle Channel. The Argentine government has expended a lot of effort over the years to get people to come and live here, at first forcibly when it was a prison colony but more recently by grants to business and industry to try and create a thriving populous community at the end of the world. Locals became a little agitated if we pointed out that Chile has a settlement further south across the Beagle Channel at Puerto Williams, arguing that this is a government/military base and not a civilian settlement like Ushuaia.

We visited the Maritime Museum situated in the old prison. Ushuaia is a jump off spot for cruises to the Antarctic and the museum had a fine model collection of polar exploration ships from Scott's famous *Discovery* and Amundsen's *Fram* to the delightfully named French steamship *Pourquoi Pas?* (literally, the 'Why Not?' – a superb name for any adventurer's vessel). The museum detailed the visits of early explorers to the Land of Fire: Magellan of course, followed closely by Drake, who we now learned was a vicious, murdering English pirate, a description at odds with our own perception of him as a national hero; but most famous of all ships to visit this extremity is surely *HMS Beagle* (from whom the Channel takes its name), which brought Charles Darwin here on his famous circumnavigation that would take him around the Horn and up to the Galapagos Islands.

Today, Darwin's name is synonymous with the *Beagle*; a Royal Navy brig on a mission to chart the South American coast and make accurate chronological longitude fixings around the globe. The government encouraged the use of these voyages to make scientific discoveries; hence Mr Darwin's invitation to join the ship as a young, unpaid civilian naturalist.. A devout Christian (he had recently graduated in Divinity at Cambridge), he hoped to find scientific evidence to support biblical stories such as the Great Flood and evidence of the Earth's creation by the hand of god. He would find plenty of evidence, but little did he realise at the time that his experimental conclusions would tend to undermine rather than uphold the Bible's version of the Creation.

Also on board *Beagle* were three very strange passengers: Mr Jemmy Button, Mr York Minster and Miss Fuegia Basket. Robert FitzRoy, captain of the ship, had previously visited Tierra del Fuego, when he took possession of four locals, gave them silly names (Button was so named because he had been purchased for a few buttons) and brought them back to England where they were taught to 'dress proper' and speak English. Sadly, the fourth member, a man named 'Boat Memory', did not survive, succumbing to smallpox in England.

FitzRoy was a devout Christian who believed implicitly in every word written in the bible; the Lord created the Earth in six days, therefore everything on the planet could be simply dated to 4000 years BC. He believed it was his duty to bring God to these people; we are all sons of Adam and these poor wretches had merely wandered away from the 'true light' at some stage in their murky past. All that was required was some sound instruction in the good Christian way and they could be returned to the rightful path.

It must have been a wild experience for these Fuegians to travel so far from home and witness life in Victorian England. Fuegia Basket met the Queen, who gave her a bonnet and a purse to buy some good clothes, but what they thought of their experience is lost to history. The three unfortunates received some education (paid for by FitzRoy himself) with a view to returning them to their homeland on the *Beagle* to spread the good word. This would be accomplished under the eye of a young missionary, one Richard Matthews, an inexperienced young man abroad for the first time in his life, who was to be abandoned in this desolate place with his nucleus of three converts. The London Missionary Society supplied them with a stock of goods necessary to convert the heathen masses: essentials such as chamber pots, crockery, fine linen and wine glasses. The idea was that the locals would somehow immediately grasp the usefulness of these objects from the more civilised and righteous world across the ocean and throw away their stone-age existence overnight to become devout believers in the one true God.

The various tribes on Tierra del Fuego lived a Neolithic hunter-gatherer existence. They were very hairy and went naked but for a crude breechcloth of guanaco skin, relying on body grease and hair to insulate them from the ferocious chill weather. Paddling primitive canoes around the myriad coastline, they dined on the abundant local shellfish and built low sealskin huts, each surrounded by a growing midden of seashells and fish bones. When they had exhausted the local food supply, they simply moved on, dismantling their homes and leaving behind low, circular ramparts of shell. Through time these have become overgrown with grass but you can still see them around the island today, circular rings in the grass up to half a metre high, sadly all that is left of these people.

The expedition reached Tierra del Fuego in December 1832 after weathering some horrific storms on a run round Cape Horn. Darwin's first impression on meeting the locals on their home turf was that they were some sub-species, closer to wild animals than to mankind. He commented on their nakedness and resilience to the cold, observing a young mother in one of the canoes suckling her baby in a whirl of sleet, unfussed by the snowflakes melting on her exposed breast. To begin with, all went well. They landed near the home of Jemmy Button's own people and started work on a new settlement, erecting tents and making a start on a small vegetable garden. Matthews distributed gifts and wares to the natives, who regarded the strange proceedings with curious interest.

Beagle sailed on to further explore the channel, returning after ten days to find the settlement in chaos and ruin. It was a disaster. With the ship gone, the natives demanded more goodies, resorting to theft and menace when refused. Jemmy attempted to help Matthews but York Minster looked after himself, siding with the natives, while Fuegia Basket hid in her tent. Matthews could obviously not be left alone with these people, so he was taken back onboard *Beagle*, while all hopes for a Christian settlement were now invested in poor old Jemmy.

Beagle left Tierra del Fuego, spending the next year surveying along the Atlantic coast of Argentina back up to Montevideo before turning round to revisit the settlement on its way to the Pacific and the next leg of the voyage. The settlement had completely gone. York Minster and Fuegia Basket had reverted to their native ways and disappeared. Jemmy too had gone native and taken a wife who refused to come out to the *Beagle* with him lest they be kidnapped. After a final meal aboard the ship Jemmy returned to his wife and was last seen waving a sad farewell from the beach as *Beagle* left forever.

While FitzRoy was devastated at the utter failure of his endeavour, the episode made a big impression on Darwin. He realised that taking the Fuegians away from their home environment was a bad thing; primitive people could only survive if left to their own devices without outside interference. They had, after all, been successfully living in this inhospitable terrain and climate in a semi-naked condition for centuries. An obvious case of survival of the fittest; no doubt this and similar incidents were unsettling Darwin's traditional Christian views ever more as the voyage continued. Twenty years later another group of Christian missionaries arrived to find amongst the natives an older man who spoke some English. It was Jemmy Button. In 1859 this group was massacred, allegedly by Fuegians led by Jemmy and his family.

The voyage of the *Beagle* was a fantastic undertaking and the sights and discoveries must have been incredible as they unfolded. Where Europe has history, the Americas have geography in spades. Without the dictates of history, one can really focus on this geography all around. Consider Darwin's England, a land defined by history and tradition. In fact the story of Europe is largely dominated by the history of its peoples. Centuries of invaders and defenders, conquerors and kings, castles and palaces; for the most part, they totally overshadow the underlying nature and wildlife of the continent. What must it have been like then, to leave it all behind, the crowded towns and cities with perpetual war and strife and set sail on a dangerous lengthy voyage across the great ocean to lands comparatively uninhabited? To lands where the obvious things were not who owns what and how they acquired title to it, but free access to fantastic ultra-natural landscapes.

The land back home, especially in north-western Europe was mostly inert, with dead mountains standing silent and eroding. Consider then the Americas, with thousands of volcanoes spewing new mass to her thrusting peaks, with vast upheavals as the Earth's crust shifts back and forth along the overlapping plates of the Pacific ridges. Young lands with living, active geography, untouched by the hand of man and populated not by hordes of people but by spectacular creatures, big and small, bedecked in the brightest and most alien plumage. Still today, travellers coming from the crowded confines of Europe find alighting in the wide empty spaces of the Americas an awesome experience.

Sadly, in the local museum we learned the eventual fate of the remaining Fuegians. Later missionaries arrived and attempted to make them cover their shameful nakedness and to live in confined dwellings, contrary to the observations of Darwin. They were provided with Christian clothes; cast-offs from the poor houses of Europe riddled with typhus and other germs to which, like the North American Indians, they had no resistance. Populations fell dramatically from pre-contact tens of thousands until the age of photography, when the last known native was captured in print before he died in the early years of the 20th century. His photograph is now on display in the museum together with a few pathetic native artefacts, all that remains of the islands' original inhabitants.

A boat trip out on the Beagle Channel took us to visit a colony of cormorants with chicks all hatched, reared and ready to fly. These particular cormorants had beautiful white breasts, like gracefully refined and slimmed down penguins, and their colony was based on a large mid-channel rock, free from land predators. We arrived to see it under siege from patient and lethal avian predators in the form of a squadron of giant Black Petrels. Like overgrown soot-smudged seagulls, they bobbed patiently, paddling in the waters off the rock colony, scanning through beady black eyes for prey.

Fledgling cormorants readied for first flight, a feat that involved lots of standing around on rocky precipices, furiously flapping those stubby wings and plucking up the courage to leap into thin air, egged on by the chants of a thousand other youngsters all attempting the same trick. Most fall like a stone until, just before they hit the sea, their wings catch the air and they are off. After witnessing several successful flights, amused and at the same time awed by the effort of these young birds at mastering one of their elements, we were sadly to observe an unsuccessful attempt and precisely what the petrels were waiting for.

The young bird hit the water and for a moment it was all confusion and feathers trying to figure out what to do next. Having regained some co-ordination he set off, half flapping, half running across the surface of the sea. One of the petrels had anticipated this and paddled across to intercept, whereupon we were treated to the macabre spectacle of watching it drown the cormorant by grabbing hold of its neck, plunging its head under water and sitting on it. A brutal act of murder, but that is nature at work. There were thousands of fledglings and the petrels merely sorted out the weak and inept. We had unknowingly purchased front row seats at the Natural Selection show.

Driving back to Comodoro we decided we had better at least wash the car before returning it to the rental agency. On our travels, films of Patagonian dirt had stratified into a mantle of mud and the only parts of the original car now on view were the twin glass arcs left by the windscreen wipers. We found a garage with a hosepipe and washed the car back to the Silver VW Gol we started out with. It had been a good little charabanc and served us faithfully on our tour of the south. But a car is a car; a dull functional object that conveys you from A to B and arouses about as much enthusiasm in the process as when you realise that the jolly old fridge has kept the milk cold once again. Travelling by car is tedious; you are insulated and isolated from your surrounding environment, which scrolls by viewed through a glass barrier.

Bikes are altogether different and this is why they remain our transport of choice. When riding a bike the machine becomes part of you, an extension of your body as you take on the world and all it can throw at you. You are seated higher up off the road than most cars, giving better all round visibility and the impact of sounds and smells is so much more immediate and dramatic. Pull up in a crowded market place and you immediately become part of the throng, whereas in a car you remain cocooned in your metal shell. Our experience in poorer countries is that people have a very simple understanding of economics, so that they assume the reason you are on a bike is that you are not rich enough to afford a car and this makes them that little bit more amenable and hospitable.

The car was gone and we missed our bikes terribly. All we had to do was contact Lito to run us back to Rio Mayo. In Ushuaia we visited a hospital where Maggie had her arm cast removed. We entered a crowded waiting room expecting to be there for the day but were seen immediately by a doctor who instructed a technician to remove the Plaster of Paris. He told us to take it easy for another week or so and that was that. Our foray to the south was complete, Maggie's elbow was looking good and we had regained the confidence that we could reclaim our bikes and finish this trip. We couldn't wait!

Chapter 9: Oh Night Fever, Night Fever...

The next few days were spent relaxing in Comodoro. In any other country we would have found this soulless place a tedious halt to be vacated at the earliest opportunity but, as throughout Argentina, the people were warm and welcoming. Declining a visit to the Museum of Petroleum, we climbed Cerro Chenque, a 272-metre mini-mountain behind town with lofty overviews of the city and the Atlantic. We strolled the run-down promenade, stopping to look at the war memorial to the Falklands War. Comodoro is the closest Argentine city to Las Malvinas and was very much in the front line during the 1982 war. Many of the air strikes against the British flew from here. Before visiting Argentina we were wary of reactions from disgruntled locals under the misapprehension that *"Las Malvinas son Argentinos."* Thankfully the only evidence we saw to the effect that this sentiment might be true was the odd faded graffiti crudely sprayed on walls and war memorials dotted around the bigger towns and cities.

In 1982 Argentina was under the rule of a military '*Junta*' under General Galtieri. The country was enduring dire economic setbacks at the time and to deflect public attention Galtieri decided to mount a distraction; he would grab the Falkland Islands and claim them for Argentina. Initially all went well; the tiny British garrison of Royal Marines was quickly subdued and the success of the invasion relied on the fact that the islands lay at the other end of the world from Britain a faded world power who, while they might raise a storm of international protest, were never expected to challenge the invasion.

Early scenes of jubilation at the glorious triumph of the mighty Argentine forces gave way to consternation when they learned that, not only where the British not taking this lying down, but that a task force was ploughing south through the Atlantic. Within a few weeks it was all over. News footage showed ranks of surrendered, starved and dirty Argentine conscripts shuffling off transports in Uruguay on their way home at the end of the defeat. It was a disaster. Argentina's only claim over sovereignty of the islands was that they happened to lie off her coast. Galtieri ignored the fact that the inhabitants were all British and happy to stay that way. He had little international support for his venture, this hostile act of aggression.

On the few occasions when the topic arose, most Argentines we spoke to were embarrassed by the whole affair, denouncing Galtieri as a drunk who wrecked their country. Once they heard the British were on their way, most knew it was all over. On paper their defending forces looked formidable but from what we observed of the Argentine people, they are the most unwarlike race imaginable with a happy-go-lucky, devil-may-care approach to life that gears them more towards looking after each other and having a good time than to going out to cause trouble in the world.

Soldiers returning from the defeat were an unwanted reminder of the country's misfortune. Las Malvinas was a national embarrassment; the country had conscripted thousands of young men, mostly from the poorer classes of society, sent them to a bleak, frozen hell ending in death, dismemberment and defeat, and when they returned wanted as little as possible to do with them. Many turned to alcohol, drugs and crime, attempting to hide from or deal with what had befallen them.

In the years following the defeat scores of war memorials were built to honour the dead and commemorate their sacrifice. The one at Comodoro was typical, a selection of various brick and stone structures bearing commemorative bronze plaques overlooking the sea in the direction of Las Malvinas. Three statues depicting a soldier, an airman and a sailor stood to attention in honour of their fallen comrades. Adjacent to this assemblage was a stone cairn topped with another soldier statue, this time in an attack mode with his weapon levelled as he advanced on some unseen enemy position. Two rusting ancient cannon flanked the cairn.

I think war memorials in general are a good idea, 'lest we forget' and all that, but the embarrassment we encountered in Argentina over the issue of the Falklands War was manifest in memorials like this. First the location: a piece of waste ground on a quieter part of the promenade with all the rubble and dirt (cleared to make way for the memorial) simply pushed to one side and left there so that the site looked like a builders' rubbish tip. Then the statues: they looked like they were posed and modelled on some weirdly disproportionate GI Joe. Even worse they were made of cement, giving them a lumpy, sludge-coat finish, and all were starting to decompose. The advancing soldier had been crudely painted and had a metal pole sticking up his arse to hold him upright, which kind of spoiled any martial effect. His left hand had decayed to expose a wire hook and his weapon was broken, its barrel bent in shameful defeat towards the ground. Overall the memorial looked like it had been done on the cheap, a plan to build something grand and imposing executed by disinterested amateurs creating a sloppy mess that was thankfully not too public and would hopefully one day crumble back into the sea. How must veterans feel when they pass fallen shrines such as this - reminders of a nation's shame?

88

On a happier note, our return to Comodoro coincided with the city's 103rd birthday celebrations, marked by a noisy and cheery carnival. Afterwards we took a pleasant evening stroll to find somewhere good for dinner. A turn down a sleepy callé softly dimmed to dull ochre by the setting sun and we walk into a crowd of people on the street, doing the Tango, a display put on by the local dance school... They invite passers-by to join in and the street is a whirl of couples of all ages, from young kids to old aged pensioners, clutched in passionate embrace as they dance to the strains of Juan d'Arienzo.

We watch them all: the costumed professionals from the dance school as they swish-swash-stomp, their bodies lurching from one freeze-frame pose to the next. We smile at the little kids, putting on a brave attempt at emulating their elders and most of them holding their own. Finally a few older couples enter the fray. We are mesmerised by movement as they shimmy back and forth, an accomplished whirl of legs and heels, bodies arched, with swan neck arms. Stumbling upon the Tango danced in this raw and unexpected fashion reveals the sheer beauty of its movements, this sexual dance full of lust and desire. The music too, but we later find it is definitely music for a time and place.

Next day we picked up a copy of 'Juan d'Arienzo's Greatest Hits', thinking it might capture some of the magic of that Comodoro night, but oddly it doesn't work. Without the visual sensation of the dancers the music is screechy, flat and very, very depressing. I later read that during the Battle of Stalingrad in World War II, the Russians played non-stop tango across no-man's land as an exercise in psychological warfare, specifically to depress and demoralise their surrounded German opponents.

With a bang of the door, Lito arrived loud as ever in our hotel lobby right on schedule and we had another bumpy ride back to

Rio Mayo in his courier van, where we were greeted with a big warm smiley welcome from Teresa at the Viejo Covadonga. She ushered us into the function room where we disembalmed the bikes from their swaddling blankets. We spent the rest of the day sorting through our gear, looking for ways to pack it better, discarding anything that was excess weight. We gave a pile of stuff to the staff at the hotel and had another collection parcelled up to send home at the next post office. There were big hugs and kisses for Teresa and the folk at the Viejo Covadonga. We still feel quite emotional when we consider how they helped us, gently taking the pain out of our misfortune and soothing our woes, setting us on a path of healing without too much trouble.

For our first day back on the bikes, our immediate problems were bad roads. Right outside the hotel we were pitched immediately onto the gravel streets of Rio Mayo. Maggie was in a mild panic at the prospect. Here she was, with a tender, barely-healed arm and her first ride back on the bike was on gravel. I offered to ride her bike the mile or so out of town and back onto paved road but she declined. Her pupils dilated with mild terror, she put her helmet on and then simply took off. We wobbled uncertainly down the main drag, turning right onto the road out of town, the intercom alive with profanities as she cussed the bumpy road. Finally we hit pavement and set off up through Esquel towards Bariloche.

It's funny how a road can look completely different when travelled in the other direction. On the way south, this road had gradually peeled away from the mountains and out into the wild plains of Patagonia, open wind swept country, a tad tedious at times. Now riding north we had the same mountains but this time we were approaching them, watching them get bigger, before riding right alongside and into them, a spectacular distraction. We did 250 miles on our first day, with Maggie coping admirably well. Her only problems came at the few off road sections around the *Desvios*, those horrid roadworks we had to ride again where the bumps and grinds jarred and jolted her poor elbow. She was caught in a horrible no-win situation. To minimise the effects of the poor surface it is best to ride fast; that way the bike flies over the worst of the defects and the ride is smoother. However she now associated this technique with spectacular crashing, so took it easy, hitting and banging into every rock, lump and boulder along the way, with each shock pummelling that sensitive elbow.

From Bariloche we rode north into the splendour of the Argentine Lake District. Again we were awed by geography in action as we chased the Rio Conchico with stunning views over Oxbow lake formations in the valley below. This led us into Valle Encantado ('the enchanted valley') with hills and rocks tinted in toasted cinnamon cut through by one of the cleanest, sparkly-clear rivers we ever saw. At Junin de los Andes we stopped for gas and spotted a café restaurant called El Fortin.

I felt sorry for the waiter. He was a lively and upbeat guy offering us delightful food but we were tired and not sure what we wanted. It was late afternoon; should we wait and eat early dinner? We had a few more miles to go after this and then start looking for a place for the night. Maybe just a small snack? As we h'mmed and h'aahed over the menu the waiter interjected with a suggestion. He had a large trout, fresh from the lake. What about that between the two of us? OK? *Buenos.* Maybe a piece of fish between two would be light enough, so we agreed. We plonked ourselves down on some plastic picnic tables outside, so we could watch the bikes, and sipped iced water in the shade of a large sun umbrella, with medium to low expectations of our lunch that we didn't really want.

We sat for ages, watching stray dogs rummaging the gas station forecourt. Then it arrived. The Lunch. It came on a large oval platter, a magnificent plate of fresh, filleted lake trout fried in butter, served with lemon. It was overlaid with thin sliced fried potatoes, all sizzling, spitting and sparkling fresh from the pan. This was food to blow you away. Food surprise. Food to invade your sleep through vivid salivating dreams for months, nay years, to come. Food Heaven! So simple in ingredient, execution and presentation and I can tell you it tasted every bit as good as it looked. We both agreed later it was the best piece of fish we'd eaten anywhere in the world.

Leaving Patagonia, we stopped at a little mountain town called Chos Malal. The pace of life is great in Argentina, very slow and easy going. Locals generally don't set out in the evenings until around ten o'clock and several times we found ourselves lonely and obvious tourists dining at eight. The people in these regions have a degree of freedom that we really have lost back home. This evening there was a *fiesta*. They had cordoned off the plaza and a heavy rock band was set to play on stage around half past eleven.

At home this sort of event would be something to avoid unless you enjoy the company of drunken rowdy youngsters, wrecking the place, brawling and puking their guts up. Tonight the whole plaza was a delightful stew of the people of Chos Malal, all out enjoying the spectacle. Nine to ninety, if they can't walk in, wheel them in, as they say. We saw pensioners sat on park benches, arms propped on walking aids, smiling politely at the awful din emanating from the stage. By one in the morning there were packs of very young kids running amok, having a great time chasing round the park, playing the local version of tag. Headbangers lay siege to the stage, bopping away to the pretty appalling band, but even they were polite and considerate. What was noticeable by its absence was alcohol. There were no piles of abandoned empty beer cans, wine or cider bottles. No other litter for that matter. The police were there too, but only to manage traffic on the periphery and for the most part they loafed around smiling and chatting with not much to do.

For all that the band were awful, we had a great night's entertainment ahead. We were wearing our bike jackets against the cool evening chill when a local lad on an XL600 Honda spotted us walking around the plaza. He popped a big wheelie to the applause of some passing kids, turned round and popped another on the way back. Show Off! Then he parked up in front of us, leapt off the bike, flashed a million dollar banana-split smile and said 'hi'.

Felix could have been a stand in for a young John Travolta back when he did 'Grease'. He had dark slicked back hair and a ready smile but where John Travolta might be considered to be a man of the world, Felix was most definitely a man of Chos Malal. He listened to the tale of our journey so far and blew his lips and whistled at the mention of some of the places we had been. For you see my friends, the world outside Chos Malal is a dangerous place.

Felix was one of the most animated speakers I ever met. With most strangers, especially when they are speaking a foreign language, you concentrate on watching their lips and facial expressions to match movement with sound, as words are formed and flow into the conversation. Felix spoke with his whole body, especially his hands and his vocabulary was extended and punctuated by a series of sucking and blowing whistle sounds. These ranged from long 'phew-ees'- his exclamation mark response to anything startling - to a very short two-note 'hi-lo' whistle that signified 'Oh-oh, you don't want to do that, that's not good, could be dangerous!' Strange as it may sound, his choreography in all of this was immaculate and it was a delight to listen and watch him speak.

We started by telling him we had arrived in Chile. Short two-note hi-lo. Hand raised, palm up and out, stop; head shaking a strong negative, series of more short two-notes…don't want to hear any more.

"Chile? Chile??" He now quickly drew his right index finger from ear to ear under his chin, making a slit throat gargling sound, still shaking his head in the negative, lips pursed for the next whistle and then he explained... "All Chilenos are robbers and thieves. They come over here into Argentina to steal everything. They'd slit your throat too. Everybody knows that and you started there? Man, you are lucky to get out alive!"

We told him we were headed for Mendoza. More two-note hi-lo's, slit throat signs and this time he pointed to his bike, the fore and index fingers of one hand outstretched flat like snake fangs, while dragging his lower eye lid up and down with the other hand to expose its pinky fleshy inner. This was followed by a wrist slapping action, all of this combined to tell us, "Mendoza? don't go there, especially not with your bikes; lookie, lookie, they are, every one of them, robbers and thieves and they will steal your bikes for sure. You have to keep an eye on everything, otherwise it will most certainly be stolen!"

We said we had liked Bariloche. He paused, put his head to one side, then a two-note and a sad sorry headshake.

"Bariloche? Too many tourists! *Muy caro* ('too expensive'). You can buy the same things here in Chos Malal at less than half the price".

"Yes, but it's such a beautiful place. With all those mountains and lakes it is surely one of the most beautiful places in Argentina?"

94

Strong negatives, eye dragging and wrist slaps... "It's full of robbers and thieves. They prey on the tourists, you have to watch everything..."

At this point our conversation was interrupted by the arrival of a gaggle of smiling kids, who gathered around Felix. He immediately began a comic interaction with them in which he mimicked being lassoed, tied and shot several times but then he came back to life, managed to break out of his invisible bonds and chased them all screaming up the street, a monster on the loose. He was a caretaker at the local school and it was clear that the local kids adored him. But he was a small town guy who viewed everything outside Chos Malal with deep suspicion. It seemed at odds with his bike, a powerful 600cc off-roader, which he handled with expert ease. If I lived here with a bike like that, I'd be off exploring every road, track and valley in these marvellous surrounds and always wondering what lay just beyond. While Felix knew the local roads like the back of his hand he had this unfortunate mental block that forbade any further exploration and everything beyond his immediate locale was written off as dangerous, places full of thieves and robbers, where everything had to be kept under constant surveillance lest it be stolen.

On to Mendoza and our first taste of riding across the Pampas, the famous Argentine grasslands. Nearing the city, the countryside changed to pleasant farmland: fruit orchards and viticulture in the main. We rode along in the beautiful sunshine under perfectly-hued azulean skies, cruising down straight, quiet tree-lined roads with not a care in the world, looking forward to a taste of the 'big city' up ahead. The little traffic on the roads was mainly farm related: slow tractors and rusty pick-ups ambling along, easy to pass and causing minimal impedance to our progress.

I slowed for a particularly crabby looking open-back pick-up as we came into a bend. From behind, in silhouette, I could see all four tyres, a sure indication that the truck was bent hopelessly out of line. It sort of shuffle-ambled along the road in a spiralling, cork-screwy motion, the whole vehicle convulsing at the end of each motion with a shudder as the cycle repeated and forward progress was maintained. Once round the bend I passed him neatly and promptly on a short straight, pulling in before the next bend. Around the next bend, another straight and an ideal passing place for Maggie. She indicated, flashed him to let him know she was coming and commenced her overtake. Next thing the intercom was filled with a torrent of abuse. "Bloody Hell!!! You stupid %@$£££!!!! What are you trying to do? Kill Me? You !@$%!*!@$&!!!"

For a moment I thought she was off or had collided with the truck. I was now beyond the next bend and couldn't see what had happened behind. Maggie and I have been together for a long time and I love her dearly but one thing I should mention at this point is that she shares her birthday, 3rd September, with the outbreak of World War II. With a Stuka for a star-sign, when she blows, it really is best to retreat beyond a channel and let her calm down. Today World War II erupted in Argentina. I tried to call her on the intercom but you cannot broadcast when someone is already speaking and the connection was choked with screaming abuse, at least giving me the comfort that Maggie was still alive while also alerting me to the possibility that some poor Argentinian could be facing certain death. I did a U-turn and rode back to the scene of the crime.

Rounding the bend, my first sight was of Maggie pulled over at the side of the road, her bike upright on its sidestand by the truck. Good news; there hadn't been a crash. By the time I got to her she had vented her fury on the poor driver, suddenly finding the Spanish to cast aspersions on his parentage, driving ability, mental aptitude and manhood. The driver, a dozy looking fat bloke, had shrivelled into a submissive pose with both arms raised, open palmed, trying to bury his head like a turtle in his shoulders as he shook his head, while uttering profuse apologies. He had been transporting a large blue drinks display unit on the back of the truck, the sort of thing you see in gas stations made of tubular steel with five or six wire rack shelves for stacking large plastic drinks bottles. It was totally unsecured and had been merrily bouncing around to the lurching motion of the truck. Then on rounding that final bend, just as Maggie was pulling out to overtake, the lazy missile had made its bid for freedom and lunged off the back of the truck like a torpedo. Fortunately she saw it coming and managed to execute her best ever kung-fu kick, thwarting disaster by the narrowest of margins. As it was, it glanced the side of the bike and she had a swatch of blue paint down the side of her motocross boot. The poor guy was like a snail totally out of his shell, feeling all vulnerable and looking for somewhere, anywhere to hide. Spotting the rack on the road, he ran back to collect it, put it back on the truck and drove off.

We arrived in Mendoza without further incident. The fourth largest city in the country with just over a million souls, it was our first major city stop in Argentina. Pick up a bottle of Argentine wine in the supermarket and it will invariably be from the Mendoza region where over seventy percent of exported wine in the country originates. We were delighted to find that our arrival coincided with 'Vendimia', the city's annual festival to mark the wine harvest. It is one of the biggest public spectacles in Argentina and every year it makes headline news. The closing show, held in an open-air amphitheatre above the city, is the subject of a huge and elaborate television extravaganza. The centrepiece is a beauty pageant in which seventeen beauty queens (one for each department in the region) compete for the title 'Queen of Vendimia'.

Mendoza proved to be a pleasant city, graced for the most part with a cool, almost Mediterranean air, a feeling enhanced by the pavement café life around the plazas and callés. The main streets are lined with tall leafy trees that blot out nearly all the sunlight, providing cool arboreal shade. Only the presence of street kids reminded us that this was Latin America. They were a sorry sight. It was quite a chilling experience when we pushed away some unwanted sandwiches over a late lunch at a pavement café. Within about thirty seconds two little kids appeared, gesturing silently and without smiling, towards the leftover food. It was a shame to waste it so Maggie handed the sandwiches over and they ran off with them. We left feeling bad at the thought that we could sit and squander food, while a few metres away people were desperate, not knowing where their next meal was coming from.

On Friday night the city was choked with people in to see the *'Via Blanca'* the main carnival procession through the streets of the city. We joined the throng of well-behaved spectators lining Avenida San Martin, waiting under the tree-speckled illumination of a full moon for the action to start. We chatted to a lovely local woman and a young lass from Buenos Aires in the crowd in front of us and they explained to us what would happen and what we would see. They were keen that as foreigners we understood the significance of what was going on and that we should miss none of it.

Events kicked off at 10pm when a light cavalry band, followed by some lancers in Napoleonic dress, came trotting along. The horsemen heralded the arrival of the main procession, a series of elaborately decorated floats pulled by monster tractors, each one representing a different area or wine producer. The wine floats were festooned with vines, grapes, bottles, barrels and so on and accompanied by blaring music and flashing multi-coloured lights. They were manned by a galaxy of gorgeous young ladies, each float dominated by the winner of this year's regional title of *Reine* ('queen'), who stood high over her rivals. These regional queens would compete tomorrow for the supreme annual title of 'Reine de la Vendimia'.

The main duty of these delectable beauties is to look stunning, a feat they managed with great effect, all decked out in formal evening gowns, tiaras and sparkly wands. However, they were expected to perform a secondary role. Tottering on high heels on the wobbly trailers, they had to distribute small gifts to the eagerly expectant crowd: mostly bunches of grapes from the vineyards and newspapers from some of the sponsors. The comedy effect of wannabe beauty queens attempting to look poised and regal while chucking out sticky, messy grapes, terrified of breaking a nail, is a sight to behold.

The grapes were stashed in huge plastic buckets concealed about each float and the beauties flung them with a limp-wristed overhand girly action. As the evening wore on some of the girls, keen to discharge their messy cargo, gave up on any attempt at dignity and started hefting grapes by the bucketload into the crowd, where they exploded with spectacular effect in the upheld hands of eager catchers. For variety, some of the girls had apples and plums as alternative ammunition but we took cover when a float containing cannon balls opened fire. Looming out of the evening gloom like a ghost-ship man-o-war, its girlie crew carronaded the crowd with watermelons, shot-putting them into the mob.

The parade ended at midnight, when all of the floats had passed.

We went for a cool beer and then wandered up through a craft market set up on the main Plaza Independencia. The Mendocinos were out in force, enjoying this wonderful night. Around one o'clock a band began playing in the centre of the plaza. We took a perch on a wall in the park to listen to them playing a number of rhythm & blues songs that somehow suited the evening. As at Chos Malal, we were amazed at how well behaved everyone was throughout the evening. The police were a visible presence but again as at Chos Malal, they were mostly good-natured, staying in the background, enjoying the party like everyone else. At a quarter to two we finally wandered back through the dim tree-lined streets to our little apartment and bed. Outside, Mendoza partied on.

Next morning we loafed and lounged, happy to rest ahead of the *Acto Centrale*, the huge open-air extravaganza held in the evening just outside town. To get there we took the scariest taxi ride of our lives. Our conveyance for this evening was an old Peugeot 504 and all I can say about it was that it had all of the components normally associated with a motorcar. Where in a normal car these items - wheels, suspension, brakes, engine etc - all act in harmony to provide passengers with a smooth ride, in our taxi they had at some point had a serious falling out (about 25 years ago I'd say) whereby each component proceeded to act independently, happy to do its own thing and trying desperately to break away from the others.

To make matters worse, I seriously pissed off the driver when I slammed shut the paper-thin back door. So we set off, the driver avoiding our attempts at reconciliation, the car components doing the same with each other. With all these bits doing their own thing the net effect was that the whole assembly obtained a generally forward motion, accompanied by the odd sideways lurch that was quickly reigned in by the driver conducting this orchestra. Oh, did I mention too that the driver was a complete nutter? He was one of these guys who drives with raised elbows, power gripping the steering wheel, neck tendons visibly throbbing with tension. His left hand was never far from the feeble horn, as he mink-minked his way along the road, pecking, puffing and snarling at the other drivers who wouldn't get out of his way. In a twenty-minute white-knuckle ride we carved our way out of town, the whole time his head down and forward as he sought to peer out of the obligatory cracked windscreen.

The location for tonight's show was a superb venue for any entertainment. The 'Teatro Griego Frank Romero Day' was a grand open-air Grecian amphitheatre set in a natural bowl surrounded by hills, with an enormous stage comprising four overlapping circles shaped like a four-leaf clover. The show itself was performed under a full moon and told the story of the wine year and its traditions through the medium of song and dance. The impressive cast consisted of some 700 artistes, dressed as *gauchos* and pretty *Senoritas*, performing boot stomping routines that covered the whole spectrum of Latin American dance in a big stage production reminiscent of 'Riverdance'.

Yet the star of the show turned out to be a stray dog that managed to somehow get on stage between two of the acts. He was a scruffy old black mongrel with offset ears and a drippy tongue and appeared on stage from nowhere to the huge amusement of the crowd. Once he reached centre stage he stopped, looked up into the spotlights at the thousands of people watching him, decided it wasn't a good place for a wee doggie to be and left the way he came, plodding slowly off stage to a round of applause.

At the end of the evening this year's 'Reine de la Vendimia' was crowned from the beauty queens introduced at the previous entertainments (Miss Rivadavia won for your information). With the Queen crowned, the night ended with a grand fireworks spectacular, launched from the surrounding hills to a series of deep-drawn 'oohs' and 'ahhs' with the occasional 'wow!' from the crowd (proving that some expressions are universal).

It was in Mendoza that we decided to change our route. The plan had been to go back into Chile to Santiago and then ride the full length of the Atacama Desert before re-crossing the Andes into Bolivia, Lake Titicaca and Peru. This was a fairly direct route and would keep us on track to reach Alaska by late summer. Yet the ride up to Bolivia would be fairly quick, giving Maggie only a week or two riding on paved roads before we would be dumped back on dirt and gravel: insufficient time for her elbow to settle in. It made sense to stick to better roads to let her regain her confidence before tackling anything more technical. A second and perhaps more poignant factor was that we had both fallen head over heels in love with Argentina. This truly magnificent country with its great food and the loveliest people you'd want to meet anywhere. It seemed criminal to rush on and abandon it all.

As a bonus, our money was lasting well here. Previously the government had linked the Argentine Peso with the US Dollar, with one peso to the dollar, which proved a disaster; by the time of our visit you needed three pesos for that same dollar and the future looked bleak. Loans from the International Banks were now called in for repayment and the President of Argentina was bartering a deal with the IMF, offering them the choice of a lower return of 25 cents on the dollar or nothing as the peso tumbled. For us this meant our money would carry us a long way; we could stay in a

$100 hotel yet pay just $30 for the privilege.

Newly made friends urged us not to leave without seeing the Valley of the Moon National Park, the city of Cordoba and most importantly Iguaçu Falls. The problem with Iguaçu Falls was that they lie on the other side of the country, at the junction of her borders with Brazil and Paraguay, way off our track. To go there would mean goodbye to Alaska this year yet could we afford to miss it? Finally, we discovered that leaving Peru until May would guarantee better weather and avoid April rains. So we revised our plans to split the trip over two years, concentrating this year on completing Latin America and aiming at ending in Phoenix in the US by late autumn. We would fly home for winter, leaving the bikes with a friend, and return the following spring to ride the North American leg in year two. This decision took a lot of pressure off us and enabled us to approach the remainder of the year's journey in a more relaxed and laid-back manner. It meant a longer stay now in Argentina, with a ride to Iguaçu for sure!

Chapter 10: Miracles in the Desert

The roads out of Mendoza were as pleasant as the roads in. Arable land, mostly fruit farming that thinned out as we rode north to San Juan. From here we would ride past Vallecito and on to a place called Valle Fertil, where we planned to stop for a few days to visit the Valley of the Moon Provincial Park. You may remember Vallecito from earlier in this narrative; it is the place where Deolinda Correa died, giving rise to the Difunta Correa bottle shrines across the country.

The site where she supposedly perished was initially marked with a simple cross on a hilltop about a hundred years after her death. It has since grown into a massive shrine, spawning the small town of Vallecito. Looking at the clock, it was 3pm; time was getting on so we decided to ride on by, passing on a visit to the shrine and not bothering to refuel at Vallecito. After all, it was impossible to stop and see everything or we would never leave this wonderful land.

Our bikes would run for around two hundred miles before hitting reserve, which I reckoned conservatively to be an additional forty miles. We had covered 160 miles since leaving Mendoza this morning and the map showed a small town called Marayes about fifty miles further on up the road, so we decided to stop and fuel there. The desert was beautiful and we rode the gentle roller-coaster road to a backdrop of rocky dunes, chased by whirling little dust devils along the way. At Marayes, the road to Valle Fertil peeled off from the main highway and a blue sign with a petrol pump motif told us we would indeed get fuel here. Imagine our horror then when we rode into a tumbleweed-blown, dead-horse town, centred round the forecourt of an abandoned truck stop. There had been petrol pumps here at some time in the past but they had been uprooted; leaving only their little concrete islands with twisted, rusting mounting bolts as evidence of there ever having been gasoline here.

The only other structure visible was a pathetic low-lying bar establishment across the road. It looked like a stage set from a cheap spaghetti western and I'm sure there were rails outside to tie your horse up. We rode across and dismounted. I pulled my helmet off and entered the open door at one end of the structure. The bar was built of dismal grey block, with no attempt at rendering any kind of finish on it. Inside was dark and gloomy, illuminated by a few high, slotted skylights and by the ghostly light of a cold drinks machine, humming and sweating in the corner. The floor was unsealed dirt and a crude bar ran across the far end of the shack. On the rear wall another door opened into what must be the owner's living quarters, from whence a small round woman appeared. She wiped her hands on a dishcloth and responded appropriately to my *"Buenos Dias"*. Imagine the scene now from her perspective…

It is a quiet Monday afternoon. Busy weekend with a few truckers in. A bit rowdy at times but good fun. They've all gone now and peace and tranquillity resumes. She likes Mondays. The kids are all at school, the old man is at work and nothing much happens. It is a good chance to catch up with the washing, prepare some food for the week ahead and sit down for an hour or so in the late afternoon, get her tired feet up, have a siesta. She has just finished washing the lunchtime dishes. Not much to do, only a few plates and glasses from a passing road crew. Oh, and the plate from that *Bife Chorizo*, a juicy steak left over from a half dozen passed to her by a trucker friend. She had it fried with a green onion and a sly glass of Quilmes beer. Now she is looking forward to her afternoon nap when she hears somebody in the bar. Who on earth would be out and about at this, the hottest time of the day, disrupting the siesta? She looks at the clock. Just gone 4pm. *'Loco!'* she thinks and walks out, drying her hands on a dishcloth on the way.

The 'stranger' is very strange indeed. For a start he is heavily overdressed for the climate with a huge bulging jacket with lots of zips and pockets and padding on the shoulders and elbows. His trousers run into the biggest pair of boots she's ever seen in her life. 'Mad Frankenstein' boots with big metal clips down the side. Holy God, he must be a mad man, wearing this here in the *desierto*! He utters something weird that sounds like "Good day," but the words are poorly formed and badly pronounced. He is clearly cooking in his odd attire, stewing in his own juice like a *bife chorizo*. His face is all sweaty and his dark hair is damp and tangled, with bits of it stuck to his forehead. A *Gringo*, a foreigner no doubt! Still, he has kind blue eyes and is smiling; but looks nonetheless nervous. No, not nervous on second thoughts, more concerned.

"There is petrol here?" he asks furtively.

"*No hay benzene*," she tells him.

"But there is a sign on the street," he says, pointing out the door.

She laughs and tells him, "No, there is no petrol here. There was the truck stop across the road but it closed three years ago. Not enough business and the owners sold up and moved to town."

"Where is petrol near here?" he asks.

"*La proxima gasolinera es en Vallecito, cerca de 80km en el camino*," she says with authority.

He looks horrified. "No is petrol on road to Valle Fertil?" he asks with a hint of rising panic in his voice. She tells him there is petrol in Valle Fertil for sure, but that is over 100km and as she said, the nearest *gasolinera* is in Vallecito.

"Is possible to buy petrol here?" he asks, pointing to the ground.

"No, there is no petrol here," she tells him.

He thanks her, buys two bottles of cold water, paid for with a 100 peso note (she has to go to the box under the bed to get some change) and leaves looking thoroughly dejected. She follows him out the door and there are two yellow motorcycles outside, the other one driven by a *chica*, another crazy *gringa* dressed in the same crazy clothing in this heat. *Madre de Dios!*

One of the key lessons of the road we had learned was that all travel involves a certain amount of fate. I hold with no religion, simply accepting the fact that we are here because we are here. There is only one world; you have one life in it and the quality of that life will be what you make it. A certain amount of luck comes into it, but I have learned that you make your own luck, for luck is simply a by-product of hard work and effort. But now we were encountering 'Fate' and its hand impacting on our trip. That day it became apparent to us that there were certain things on this journey that seemed to be pre-determined. By this I mean some things that it seems would happen regardless of our own personal wishes on the matter. Today it was '*You will visit Vallecito.*' Outside we drank the cold water and considered this play of Fate slapping us across the chops and saying,

"Hah! Told you so. You will visit this shrine. It is ordained by the gods of the roads and you must obey!"

There was no other petrol to be had. The lady did say we could ask for some in Astica, about sixty miles down the road to Valle

Fertil, but we knew this was a small settlement and she already said it had no gas station, so even if by some miracle our bikes ranged that far we would have to rely on blagging some off one of the locals. As it was, I doubted our chances of making it even to Vallecito. My bike had flashed its reserve warning light eight miles ago and we had fifty miles to ride. I reckoned we would run out a few miles short of town. We'd have to abandon the bikes and hitch a lift, assuming we could find a passing car on this desolate road. Maybe we'd get lost and die on a hillock like Deolinda Correa. A passing truck would find us half dead with our bikes, suckling the antifreeze from their radiators in a desperate attempt to rehydrate. Maybe it would be enough and there would be a new cult: 'Difunta BMW' with lots of little motorcycle shrines and people would leave bottles of antifreeze at them, asking for safe passage.

The ride back to Vallecito was a nerve-wracking contest of time versus distance covered and best-guessing the fuel remaining. We rode at 40mph to get the best gas-mileage we could. Maggie's reserve light began glowing just as we left Marayes so maybe at least one bike would make it. We even killed our engines on several long downhill sections, freewheeling an extra few miles that could be the difference between running out in sight of the fuel stop and running out in the desert.

Half way we found a police checkpoint. We stopped and begged some fuel but the pock-faced cop was dour and unsympathetic. "*No hay benzene*", so we accepted the decision of Fate once more to continue back to the shrine. We asked if the policeman would look out for us in case we ran out but, although he nodded, we knew there was no guarantee of a rescue.

On with the last 25 miles and more of the same; briskly get into top gear, sit at 40mph and free wheel another mile and a half stretch downhill. I was sweating profusely inside my crash helmet and not just because of the desert heat. I was counting off the range on the bike, thirty miles into the reserve, then forty. After 45 miles I was waiting for the first slight chug, a misfire that would tell me the engine was dying of fuel starvation. I readied to pull the clutch in, hoping to freewheel as much extra distance as possible. Fifty miles into reserve; how was the bike doing this? We were really into new territory here and sure to conk out at any moment now.

Then, on the horizon we spotted thin black vertical lines wisping up into the sky: radio masts. Not another police check point but this time marking the site of Vallecito itself and surely only another mile or so to go! Then the first building to hove into view, the *gasolinera*! We'd done it! My bike had covered 57 miles on reserve when we pulled up at the pumps and was surely running on fumes for those last few miles. The owner must have thought we were crazy as we fuelled up and paid, grinning like a pair of loons all the while.

We followed the road off the main highway into Vallecito itself and parked at the foot of the main shrine. It was late in the day, the fierce heat of the sun gone, replaced by the first cool chill of evening. It seemed we had the place to ourselves as we set off to explore. The main location is the hill where Deolinda died and a stepped concrete pathway ascended to the sacred spot. We watched in awe as a bent and decrepit old lady crawled this on her hands and knees, stopping at each step to recount her rosary (some of the more extreme adherents crawl up these steps on their backs). The steps are open-sided but have been roofed and the upright supports were covered in Argentine vehicle license plates, thousands of them, left by grateful owners.

All around, the slopes of the hillock were covered in masses of little home made shelters looking like so many discarded bird boxes. Some were quite elaborate, like dolls houses and each left as an offering of shelter to Deolinda in return for her support. At the site of her demise we found a bronze effigy, slightly larger than life, of Deolinda dead, with the baby at her breast. Various parts of the bronze had been polished bright from repeated touches from adherents as they file by.

Descending the mound we meandered through the assortment of *capillos* (little chapels) that are another aspect of the shrine. Each of the seventeen *capillos* is furnished from floor to ceiling with mementos and *'gracias'*, themed or dedicated to a particular group of people, all associated in some way with transportation or motion. There was one dedicated to taxi drivers, another to truckers and yet another to race horses. Walls were covered from floor to ceiling in brass plaques, framed letters and dedications, race trophies and citations all thanking Deolinda Correa for aiding success in the appropriate venture. In the little museum chapel, there was even a car and an old motorcycle.

Whatever you think of the story of Difunta Correa, whether you consider it a tall tale of the Pampas or as miraculous evidence of some hand of God at work, there is no denying the sheer popularity of her cult. As her story and legend grew, millions have come to regard her as a miracle worker and when you visit the shrine in Vallecito or the water bottle dumps at the side of the roads, it is apparent what an important symbol she is in the life of many Latin Americans from Bolivia to Tierra Del Fuego. However, she is not a saint and at best the Catholic Church in Argentina regards belief in her as crass superstition. At worst, it has denounced her as contrary to church dogma and has even located its own church at Vallecito to combat the heresy. Their efforts have been largely in vain.

From a simple cross atop the desert knoll, marking the spot were Deolinda Correa fell, the shrine has grown into a small town complete with several hotels, a campground, restaurants, a police station, a post office, a school, souvenir shops and its own tourist office. There is no water here and I read somewhere that 2000 litres of water are piped in daily from the nearby town of Caucete. The whole site is administered by the *'Fundación Vallecito'*, a non-profit organisation that exists on donations from pilgrims and adherents and by recycling some of the items left at the shrine. Vallecito is a beautiful place, an oasis set in this most serene desert location. We were glad of our forced retreat to see it.

Back at the bikes we affixed stickers procured from one of the souvenir shacks. They were star shaped and showed the dead woman with her baby on a desert floor with a cone of heavenly light shining down on her corpse from the sky. They said *'Difunta Correa, San Juan, Gracias'*. We stuck them right on the point of our front mudguards. It seemed an appropriate place.

Our whole encounter with Difunta Correa had been a strange affair to say the least. First, the car trip-meter zeroing at Puerto Natales; and now our forced return to visit the shrine. For me personally, it is the only time in my entire life that I have had what could be considered to be a first-hand religious experience. As a child I dabbled with Christianity because my parents made me attend the local church and Sunday school, but rejected it all as I witnessed its hypocrisy in action through years of 'the Troubles' in Northern Ireland.

People are all mixed bags of fear and the biggest fear of all is the fear of death. This can be offset to a large degree by the acceptance that there is some prize to be gained beyond death and for most, that prize is a better place; heaven. It is a fear that is easy to prey on. In all my experience with religion I never felt spiritually moved and decided ultimately that it is all a question of faith, blind faith at that, acceptance of things that can never be proven. I grant you can equally argue that these things cannot be disproved; but blind faith is not for me. At the end of the day, that faith must be based on written words and who wrote those words? Man. They may have been written with good intent and other men may have verified they are the words of a 'god', but at the end of the day the involvement of people in the process is apparent and for me this is its downfall and why I cannot hold with it.

I have been repelled by the actions of organised religion throughout history, where the church has simply held sway and controlled knowledge and information, telling people what to believe and when to believe it. Where any deviation from this was severely dealt with. When they came up against an equally efficient but differing dogma it inevitably led (and still does lead) to war. Then, as information technology improved, first through the invention of the printing press and now through the internet, people could make their own minds up on all manner of things. Of more importance, new ideas and opinions could be circulated without the filtering influence of controlling organisations and thankfully we have reached the stage we are at today where most of the world is free-thinking or at least has some access to free thought.

So where does that leave me with my encounter with Difunta Correa? The answer is, I don't really know. Two weird events had now transpired on our trip, connected by this phenomenon of a woman dying, yet giving life to her baby through her corpse. Too much to be a sheer coincidence? Surely it couldn't be some mysterious 'Hand of God' at work? After all, the official church, God's representative on earth, denies the phenomenon, so why would He make some divine approach to us through a heretical agent? All I know is that these encounters with Difunta Correa sprinkled some magic on our journey and we each were glad to participate in our own way with the superstition, giving our thanks at the shrine and asking for a safe onward journey.

We reached Valle Fertil (or to give the town its full title 'San Augustin de Valle Fertil') without further incident, taking a little room at the pleasant 'Cabanas Dinosorio'. The town was a small, dusty, sleepy little place, extending a few blocks in every direction from a central plaza. Life is slow here under the furnace heat of the desert sun. This region is hostile with temperatures ranging from daytime highs of 45 degrees Celsius to cold nights with lows of minus ten. To the north lay Ischigualasto, better known as the Valle de La Luna ('Valley of the Moon') Provincial Park, our reason for being here. In the native Quechua language, Ischigualasto means 'Place where the Moon alights' and the park lies in a desert valley containing some of the most fantastic terrain on Earth, sculpted to an extra-terrestrial rockscape by the erosive actions of wind, sand and water.

It is incredibly old, dating back to the Triassic period (245 million years ago) and is one of the biggest fossil fields on the planet. Since the area came under the scrutiny of palaeontologists and geologists, numerous discoveries have been unearthed. Petrified trees (some up to forty metres tall), ferns and other vegetation have been found in abundance, giving a clear picture of an ancient habitat so different to the arid desert of today.

Back in the days before the formation of the Andes Mountains to the west, this whole area was a huge series of lagoons and wetlands surrounded by vast plains, lush green with vegetation. The land, until then only inhabited by plants and insects, became the domain of the reptiles, which , in the absence of any competition, flourished here. With the creation of the mountains, the prevailing climate conditions changed. Rainfall dropped off and the wetlands slowly disappeared. By the conclusion of the Triassic Period, the lush green valley had been reduced to a windswept desert inhabited by larger, more advanced reptiles. Over time these creatures too became extinct, their bones adding new fossil layers to those of their predecessors, buried and compressed in layers of volcanic dust and sediment until their relatively recent discovery in the 1950s.

Over the eons, wind and rain has eroded the rocks while periodic flooding from the mountains has deposited new sediment. The area contains coal deposits, made from all this compressed vegetable matter and it was in the search for mineral riches that the geology of the area and its importance was understood. Fossilised remains of some 63 different animals have been found, including dinosaurs. In fact the area contains some of the oldest known dinosaur remains and, perhaps the most significant observation on Ischigualasto, it contains a preserved fossil record in an undisturbed sequence right through the age of the dinosaurs up to the coming of the mammals.

The road to the park was eighty kilometres of dirt, good dirt at that, and just the sort of thing Maggie needed to regain some off-road confidence. The road ran through scrub-bush desert and we soon reached the park entrance marked with a couple of fibreglass dinosaur gate guards. A 40km circuit runs round the park and the idea is you travel in mini convoys with a ranger who explains the various rock formations along the way. A group had just left and we persuaded the ranger to let us catch them up rather than wait thirty minutes or so for the next. It worked out fine, since we reached the first stop point as the group were leaving and from there on we had the park to ourselves, the rangers content that we were sandwiched between two groups.

To begin with we couldn't see what all the fuss was about. Maybe you had to be into all this fossil stuff to appreciate the place but at a first glance it looked like more of the desert we'd just ridden through to get here. Distant 1000 metre-high bluffs surrounded the area and it all looked like so much rolling plains scenery from a fair-to-middling Wild West movie. Then we reached a little halt called 'Valle Pintado': 'the Painted Valley', a vast myriad of twisting and turning mini canyons, invisible from the road, sunk into the desert floor and stratified in diffuse salmon pinks shot through with grey and white streaks that constantly changed tone with the light. We found a rocky perch to sit awhile and watch as clouds teased the sun and the vivacity of the painted rocks alternated with the ever-adjusting brightness. It was one of those places you could visit a thousand times and every time it would appear different according to the particular light, time of day, time of year and so on. This was no ordinary rock garden.

Further on and the rocky scrubland gave way to sandy desert. In the distance we were starting to see slashes of raw red rock in stark contrast to the sand before us. The road too was transforming from a half decent dirt track into... well, into the landscape itself. Big boulders and rock clusters barred our way and the track ran a blurry path into them, through them, around them and over them. At times we had to stop and get off the bikes to make sure we were actually following the right path.

At one of these stops we realised we were no longer on this planet; the park was living up to its name and we really had strayed onto the moon. Only the blue sky with the billowy white clouds gave the game away. Our bikes became lunar landers as we bounced and jolted our way further into the labyrinth.

The rocks were now doing weird and wonderful things. The bright colours - salmons, whites, reds and greys - had now been joined by verdigris greens and smoky blues. The rocks had taken up acrobatics and we came upon successions of unwieldy and unlikely balancing acts. Huge boulders balanced on impossible pinnacles, formed over the millennia when a large hard rock found itself elevated by the erosion of softer surrounding and underlying substrate. Some looked like huge heads with eyebrows, equine noses and lips; others, such as the aptly named *'Hongo'*, seemed to be petrified giant mushrooms. At *'La Cancha de Bochas'* we left the bikes and wandered off into a world of dove grey sand and smooth, beautifully polished, round grey rocks. There was utter silence. There was no need to speak to each other as we marvelled in this wonderland. The slight wind had dropped. I lifted my foot and saw Neil Armstrong's impression on the Moon. The sky too had changed colour to match, clouds laminating in the distance to form a steel grey blanket; the smudge on the horizon below spoke of rainfall here in the desert, a small local cloudburst, common at this time of year.

Back on the bikes we rode past a nuclear submarine, stranded out here in the desert, where a long tongue of hard rock had been excavated and elevated by the action of wind and water. It even had a streamlined conning tower and a strip of dark round boulders ran the length of her hull, giving the impression of bilge tanks on this organic Soviet SSN. Further on, we wallowed through yet more soft peachy sand, leaving the grey moon with its nuke subs and magic mushrooms behind, exchanging it for planet Mars up ahead. Approaching a serrated red cliff wall, that marks the return part of the loop round the park, the rocks appear as if sculpted by a master stone mason. Pillars and columns buttress the wall and here and there the odd chimney stands out. Shadows cast on the rock face suggest doors and windows and the entire façade becomes that of the most intricately worked Far-Eastern temple. The Martian surface made for a better, more compacted track yet we rode slowly, heads held in permanent gawk to one side as we took in the detail and beauty of what must be one of nature's finest creations. On the road back to Valle Fertil we rode with a newfound inner peace and tranquillity. The Valley of the Moon had been a real jaw-dropper, its coloured palette landscape so soothing and revitalising, drawing us in and leaving us both sated. It really felt like this is as good as life could be.

The following morning a rude shock awaited us after our idyllic pastimes of the day before: it was pouring down with rain outside and had been all night. Yes, that's right; rain in the desert. Yesterday's cumulus sky with those billowy cotton-wool clouds had gone, replaced by a soggy wet blanket of dismal grey murk that was shedding its filth all around with no sign of letting up. The area receives little rain but today seemed like it was getting its annual downfall all in one go. We packed up and rode out of town back onto the dirt road towards the park, taking us on north towards Rioja.

Yesterday we noticed that the road ran across several gullies in the desert, river beds that filled with flash flood rainwater from the mountains. Where the road crossed, a section of concrete paving had been laid so the water runs off leaving no obstruction. After a good lashing of rain the gullies were flowing and the concrete sections were flooded under a few inches of water as the little streams burbled off across the plains. Around 40km from town I rode through one of these, the front wheel fan-tailing a spray of water over my legs and engine. The bike spluttered to a halt. She refused to restart, probably due to water in the electrics, so I spent the next hour and a half taking connectors apart, checking fuses, rapidly exhausting my (limited) knowledge of bike electrics, all to no avail. A new disaster in the desert!

What followed was one of the greatest acts of human kindness we ever encountered, an experience that gave us cause to forever hold the Argentine people dear for the rest of our lives. I took Maggie's bike and rode back to Valle Fertil for help. I wasn't overly hopeful as the place was small with no apparent major businesses; still, they had to have a *mecanico* somewhere. It was around lunchtime and the place was deserted but I noticed a *Gomeria* open, a little shack that does tyre repairs. The owner, a big chap called Fernando, was fixing an old truck tyre on a rusting wheel. He wore a dirty white T-Shirt over a pair of denim trousers, both smeared with the honest filth of his occupation; yet my attention was drawn to his smile, which grew bigger as I tried in my best Spanish to explain my predicament.

Bike; like the one outside, broke down on the road to Ischigualasto; wife with bike. Need *camionette* (pick-up) to recover bike to town. Can you help? Fernando didn't have a *camionette*, a fact given away when his smile turned to a brief frown. He shook his head, but then the smile returned as he remembered a neighbour with such a vehicle. Neighbour Juan readily agreed to take his old green and white Ford pick-up out to recover the bike. How would we get the bike onto the truck? He stopped at a street corner and whistled to a couple of loitering young guys. Quick staccato of machine-gun Spanish and they hopped up on the back, all smiles and thumbs-up. Juan's driving technique on the dirt was 'interesting' as he drove with one side on the road and the other on the side verge. 'For the suspension,' he explained.

Maggie was waiting patiently with the bike. A passing crew of road construction workers had stopped to see if she was OK and she explained that I was off to get help. They told her not to worry; she would be safe, they were working only a kilometre up the road. Any problems come and see them and they would take her back to town once they finished work for the day.

We hauled the bike up onto the back of Juan's pick-up and set off back to town and Fernando, who kindly permitted us a work space in his yard. Not only that, but he insisted on stopping his own work to help solve the problem. The investigation lasted over 5 hours into the early evening in the course of which we gathered a small crowd of on-lookers and passers-by, all of them looking more worried than me at not being able to fix the problem. There was a spark at the plug, but the engine would not start. We took bits off Maggie's bike and tried them on mine and vice-versa, but every time her bike started, while mine would not. One chap in particular, Pablo, seemed mechanically adept and I noticed that the others deferred to his suggestions and ideas.

Around 4pm a very pretty lady called Adriana Garcia arrived. She was the village schoolteacher and had heard some *Gringos* had a problem with a motorcycle; so she came to help, offering her services as a translator. She explained that Pablo, Fernando and another chap were the only mechanics in town. News had spread about our problem and they had all stopped by to help. All at once I realised what was going on and suddenly felt almost tearful at the kindness and consideration shown to us by these strangers.

When a bike breaks down beyond your personal means of repair, you know it will cost money and hassle to recover it and get it going again. I hadn't asked Juan how much his recovery would cost or agreed any prices with Fernando for his labour. At home I most certainly would have and then winced with pain at the expense of it all, especially if I had inadequate breakdown insurance. Here in Valle Fertil, it hadn't really crossed my mind. In fact it seemed crude to do so, although I made a mental note that I would at some point have to tally up and pay my dues for all services rendered this afternoon.

By late in the day we were fairly certain that the problem lay with fuel delivery. There wasn't any, which meant that either the line was blocked (we checked and it wasn't) or the fuel pump was faulty. The pump is inside the petrol tank and I was fairly certain it would be irreparable and would have to be replaced. The nearest dealers were at Mendoza or Cordoba. One of the bystanders, a tall thin lad called Jorge, piped in with the fact that he was going to Cordoba tomorrow in a pick-up, taking his mother and father there for a hospital appointment. Could he take the bike? He was a little reticent at first. We gathered that the truck was not his, maybe a company vehicle, and he was unsure; but Fernando and Pablo rounded on him, telling him we were in a fix and he had to help.

Now for the reckoning: I called next door and paid Juan a small fee for the recovery. Next Fernando; to our astonishment he point blank refused to take any money for his help today. He argued that he hadn't been able to fix the bike, so there was no fee. I insisted we had to pay something for his time, for taking over his workshop, but he was having none of it. If he had fixed the bike then we should pay. After a lot of arguing and at Maggie's insistence, he accepted a small wad of cash to go buy some beers and pizza with the others who had helped today.

This was a prime example of why we travel. Our best-laid plans had been completely undone by misfortune and our journey was about to set off in a totally new and unanticipated direction. Yet this same misfortune led us into a rich vein of encounters with some truly wonderful people, folk we would have probably walked past on any normal day. They had come together today magnificently, to effect our rescue and to enrich and invigorate our lives with a lavish bath in the milk of human kindness.

Jorge arrived at 6am next morning with his elderly parents in the truck. At a first glance they looked old and frail but we soon learned they were a tough and wiry pair. Maggie rode in the truck and I followed behind on her bike as we set off in the dark, and more heavy rain, along forty miles of red dirt road towards Cordoba. Jorge claimed this first section wasn't too bad. A short way out of town, we stopped at a little roadside shrine while Jorge's mother left some bread and water as an offering for our safe passage. I really needed it today and I was soon calling for Difunta Correa and any other saints or sinners who might help me survive this dire passage. It was a nightmare! They went tearing off in the pick-up and I was flying along hell for leather slathering through red sand and mud, trying my best to keep up. My visor quickly steamed up in the rain so I had to open it a little, letting in stinging cold rain and blobs of mud that blurred my vision. What was going on? This is supposed to be arid desert and there I was, tearing through it in the dark in pouring freezing rain!

On reaching the main (and finally, paved) highway the journey settled down to a more sedate pace across mundane, boring grassland, punctuated with several *Maté* breaks at little gas stations along the way. By lunchtime we had left the rain behind and at the next halt, Jorge's mum broke out a stash of Milanese sandwiches, delicious veal slices coated in breadcrumbs, served in fresh bread, washed down with yet more *Maté*. She had made extra for us.

Around 2pm we arrived at Falta, a city within the greater Cordoba vicinity, to find that Jorge and his folks would be staying with some friends there, ex-neighbours from Valle Fertil. They were an old couple and were keen to give us a tour of their very beautiful house. When the lady realised I had ridden another motorcycle here, all the way from Valle Fertil, she exploded with hospitality. I must be starving; I was led by the arm to the dining table, the old guy seating Maggie comfortably across from me. Some kerfuffling in the kitchen, oven doors banging open and shut, the rattle of cutlery being gathered and we were shortly presented with a platter of delicious home made *empanadas*, bite sized treats stuffed with meat and vegetables, melt in your mouth, drool from your tongue titbits to die for.

Expressing our approval of these savoury morsels was a big mistake… She disappeared once more into the kitchen and reappeared with a cold meat dish rolled in flaky pastry with a home made potato salad meticulously laid out on another platter. I wondered where all this freshly prepared food came from and then the peso dropped. Maggie had sussed it too and signed to me across the table that we were being served the dinner obviously prepared for Jorge's family. I was horrified. In unison, we protested that we had already eaten the excellent Milanese sandwiches and that no, no, the *empanadas* are enough. But she had already carved into the meat roll, so I just had to have a bit. At this point I was seriously wondering if these people would ever consider adopting me as their 43 year old kid, but politeness and the fact that time was getting on forbade further enquiry.

It was Friday afternoon and we wanted to catch the bike shop before the weekend so that any parts could be ordered and repairs set in hand. We bade farewell to Jorge's family, his parents and their friends with lots of hugs and kisses from people we'd only met this morning, all of them wishing us luck with our onward journey. Jorge's Mum seemed a little sheepish and unusually shy. She tiptoed up and whispered something to Jorge, who looked embarrassed. I asked if everything was alright, to which he replied, "Oh yeah, yeah, nothing's wrong, it's OK."

"Are you sure? Is anything wrong? Have we forgotten something?"

"No, no….well, it's just my Mum. She was wondering… could she maybe…I don't know how to say this, but she wants to try your crash helmet on."

I was flabbergasted! I quickly handed over the helmet and her face beamed into the biggest, toothiest, loveliest smile you ever did see. She was utterly delighted and quick as a flash popped it on her head.

"The gloves too, if you don't mind." She slipped the gloves on and stood there beaming from ear to ear as we took her photo. I was glad to have made her so happy and repaid some of her kindness with such a simple and unexpected action. As I drove off, I spied in my rear view mirror four very special elderly Argentineans stood on the pavement, hands raised high, waving an energetic goodbye. One of them stood just a little taller, smiled just a little broader, than when we had first met her that morning.

Chapter 11: Snakes and Ladders

BIG Motorcycles, the BMW dealer in Cordoba, quickly identified the fuel pump as the cause of our problem. Their mechanic, Ricardo, returned to work late on Friday evening, especially to look at our bike: just another example of exemplary service in Argentina. Even better, the warranty on the bike was honoured, so the repair cost nothing. A new part was ordered from Buenos Aires but would not arrive until Tuesday so we had an unexpected weekend to kill in Cordoba, Argentina's third city. We had now covered some 4000 miles on the bikes and 2500 in the car, so our interlude in Cordoba was a good time to meander sunny city streets, go window shopping and enjoy some fine food in some decent restaurants.

An invite arrived from Esteban and Consuela Sanchez, a couple we'd met when visiting *'El Mecanico'* in Rio Mayo. They had been holidaying in their car in Patagonia and came into the yard to have their brakes looked at just as we were leaving. Esteban had noted our website address off the bike and e-mailed us with an invitation to join their family for an *asado* (barbeque). We spent a wonderful evening at their home, guzzling *Quilmes* beer and Mendozan Red, tucking into an assortment of prime cuts of meat char-grilled to perfection. Dr Bernardo MD, a brother-in-law, had us smiling with his all too literal English translations of the cuts of meat (read 'body parts') on offer: "Have you had some glands, they're *delicioso*? Oh! And you must try the diaphragm!"

With the bike repaired, we left Cordoba on roads east, headed for a lazy afternoon ride to Paraná. We were off to visit the fabulous Iguazú Falls, one of the defining landmarks in all of South America, before riding directly west to Salta and back into Chile to pick up our original Pacific route through Bolivia, Peru and Ecuador. Today we exchanged dusty, desert, plains and grasslands for wetter, greener, lush exotic climes. Paraná, in its stunning setting along the milky coffee-coloured Paraná River, was a real treat; with beautiful old colonial buildings backing onto an impressive palm lined boulevard bordering verdant parkland along the riverbank. Having arrived at the Central Plaza, we scouted the excellent 4 Star Gran Hotel with the expectation of exorbitant prices. On looking at the bikes, the manager gave us a room for 74 pesos (£15) for the night. Dinner was another culinary marvel: tasty surubi and pacu, two of the local river fish.

Since deliberating in the last chapter about Difunta Correa, trying to make sense of possible otherworldly influences on our travels and destiny, one alternative we considered is that our journey is actually all just one big game of Snakes and Ladders, with the objective to make our way up the massive game board of the American continents. We had started with a few duff rolls that saw us stuck off the board in Paris but then the game came to life when we rolled a six to finally get going in Chile.

The snakes are more obvious: crashes, injury and breakdowns that have sent us back to find a different way round the board. Ladders are not always immediately apparent. Consider the impact on body and soul of a sojourn in a location like Torres Del Paine or Ischigualasto. You enter the location with a series of expectations and anticipations based on what you have read or heard about the place. The visit unfolds and you are presented with a series of encounters: landscapes, weather, wildlife great and small, chance meetings with other people, the digestive effects and lingering on the palette of what you had for lunch, olfactory assaults from stinky or sweet smells and the aural percussion of nature at work. When viewed after the event these incidents combine to an experience generally greater than the sum of its parts and construct a ladder that elevates and carries you on up the board; in fact they are little ladders you will carry for the rest of your life.

Encounters with people, fortunately, are mostly ladders. From the generous stranger's offer of a place to stay for the night to the fleeting, 'just for you' smile of a shy little child in a crowded market place, these experiences are memorable and uplifting and are particularly appreciated after a nasty snake fall! Sadly, though, some turn out to be serpents, out to take you for what they can; and our next encounter was with a viper.

One generalisation levelled at the reputation of Latin America is that, with the odd exception, all police and government officials are corrupt. Expect snakes and be pleased when this is not true. You can offset these encounters by doing a bit of homework. Where are the bent cops likely to be encountered? When should you be most on your guard and when can you relax? We certainly explored all this and took heed of warnings about police corruption in Peru and some of the Central American countries. In fact in Cordoba, we spent a morning at a colour photocopy shop making half a dozen laminate replicas of our driving licenses and vehicle logbooks.

The purpose of these was twofold. One: they prevent wear and tear of the originals, which can be kept secure and produced if really needed. Two: corrupt police officers will threaten to hold on to your documents unless you pay an 'on the spot fine', which usually goes straight into their pocket. If they have duplicate items you can feign protest and ride off, leaving them with the dummy items. Don't get me wrong, Maggie and I are law-abiding citizens and if we knowingly break the law and are apprehended we would expect to pay the penalty; but a dodgy cop expecting a big hand out for a minor traffic infringement is something else.

To date, our encounters with the law in both Chile and Argentina had all been pleasant, relaxed affairs, mostly at the roadblocks found outside major towns or on provincial borders. It is compulsory to slow down on approach and more often than not we were waved on. On the half dozen occasions when we were stopped, we were asked for driving licenses, vehicle logbooks and occasionally passports. The officers generally returned our smiles and were polite, interested in our trip and even on occasion offered advice on the best places to see and stay.

Leaving Paraná, riding east on Ruta 127 we were stopped at around four thirty in the afternoon at the police roadblock between the departments of Entre-Rios and Corrientes. I was immediately suspicious when one of the officers, in an unusually vigorous display of activity, sprinted across the road at our approach and flagged us down. He was joined by an older fat cop, and on producing our normal documents, we were asked for *'Seguro de Mercosur'*, apparently a vehicle insurance covering Brazil, Argentina and Chile. We didn't have it, having been advised that motor insurance was an obscure notion, non-existent in most of Latin America, so I tried to bluff him with a medical insurance document. He swiftly flung it back at me again, asking for the *'Seguro de Mercosur'*.

The two cops were a little frightening. The sprinter, a younger chap somewhere in his thirties, was tall and thin with fine Hitler Jugend blond hair. His face was unsmiling and instantly discomforting; a facet enhanced by a pair of cheap wrap-round imitation Ray-Bans and a knife slash mouth that was repeatedly insistent we hand over some proof of insurance. I had seen this guy before. He looked exactly like the ice-cold T-1000 Terminator played by actor Robert Patrick in Terminator 2 – Judgement Day. You know, the relentless killing machine made from shape changing liquid metal on a mission to kill the young John Connor. Picture the scene when he appears in the movie as a motorcycle cop and you'll have a fairly good idea of the man confronting me.

His buddy was his total alter-ego. A greasy slob with bad teeth, he hailed from Brazil and wore the remains of his lunch down the front of his fat belly uniform. He was smiley and easy going and struck up a conversation with Maggie about our home and travels. Meanwhile I would have to accompany the Terminator into his office while he explained a few things.

The checkpoint was nothing more than a small station house set back from the road with a few dusty police vehicles parked out front. There was a small, windowless hut by the roadside for the officers on roadblock duty. I followed inside, where I was given a rickety wooden chair, sat across a battered busted table from my interrogator. He sat back in his chair, stretched his legs under the table and clasped his hands together high above his head. OK, we have a problem, he explained. It was impossible for us to continue without a '*Mercosur*' policy. *Claro?* Impossible! So we would have to buy one, here and now. It would cost us $300 US. A pad of official forms, along with a tariff in a plastic wallet was produced from the table drawer and the $300 fee was explained on a crumpled type written sheet. I told him I didn't have $300 so he asked how much I had. I confessed to having 300 pesos (about $100 or £60). He smiled slyly and replied that would be fine.

Up to now I had been totally naïve, thinking these were honest policemen doing their job, when all along they were nothing more than corrupt cops on the take and here I was, lined up as their next victim. This realisation dawned on me, with all the subtleness of a sledgehammer arriving at a breakfast table, as I sat sweating in the little hut with this grim reaper demanding I pay up. I asked him to clarify: I pay the 300 pesos he would give me a *Mercosur* document for both of us? Sure. With a receipt? Of course; right here, he said, pointing to the folder on the table. And we would have no further hassle from the police? No, of course not; once we paid up, everything would be in order. I considered my options. What if I refused to pay? They might confiscate the bikes or drag us both up to the station house for a more persuasive interrogation that might cost us even more and not just money. I had stupidly admitted I had some cash, in fact I'd even told him how much.

It was one of those moments I would torture myself with, replaying it in days to come, kicking myself for not saying I had nothing or even having the sense to at least admit possession of a lesser amount. He even had my original documents. So much for being a clever-dick traveller! Our copies, so painstakingly created in Cordoba, were safely lodged in the bottom of a pannier to be unearthed later for use in really dodgy places like Bolivia and Peru, it never once striking us that we might need them here. I was simply and horribly cornered. In the end, I put the pesos on the table and they immediately disappeared into the drawer. The forms and tariff were put to one side and our names and vehicle registrations recorded on the back of a used envelope. It's all done 'on the internet' you see? And with that I was dismissed.

Outside, the other cop was chatting with Maggie, having a grand old time. It was just like all the other roadblocks, with him recommending where to go and what to see at Iguazú. I quickly told Maggie to mount up and she knew by my face that something bad had happened. I rode off feeling whipped, abused, defeated, ripped-off and utterly disgusted, both with the whole incident and my own performance. It had been so easy for him, like taking candy from a child. What hurt even more was that it should have happened here, in Argentina, a land we had fallen in love with, where so many people had readily taken us into their hearts and homes, rendering unheard of levels of assistance and co-operation when we had troubles with bikes and roads. To be mistreated and conned by such a despicable individual amidst this background of impeccable hospitality was all the more cruel.

Later we replayed the whole incident determined to ensure, if possible, that it would never happen again. We came up with a few plausible scenarios as to why we should be travelling with no money and agreed in future never to separate, where possible, as two can always maintain a better argument than one. We ensured that the copied documents were at hand for all future stops and used them all the way to Alaska without ever once having their validity challenged. We hit three further police checkpoints on the road to Iguazú. Each time we slowed, hearts racing, but the police were smiling and courteous, waving us through with salutes, advice and friendly recommendations as to the treasure awaiting us up ahead.

The ride itself now took our minds off our recent misfortune, a sensational journey taking us into masses of ever more jungly foliage, with huge palms and monstrous trees bedecked in creepers and vines threatening to reach out and reclaim the road. And what a road! A superb hard-top, alternating between sections of long straights and swooping bends that snaked and split-essed over and around the low hills of Misiones. We passed slashes of wonderful exposed red dirt, its hues of 'Burnt Sienna' clashing vividly with forty-shades-of-green jungle and the clear blue skies above. The light and colour here has an acrylic brightness and intensity and it is a painter's paradise. Even the wildlife was brighter. Gone were the ruddy brown twitter birds that had flitted around our wheels in Patagonia, replaced now by little Kawasaki green parrots that raced and chased us from the roadside vegetation.

We arrived at Puerto Iguaçu, a horrid tourist resort, just as it was getting dark and were immediately beset by touts trying to sell us everything from tours of the falls to accommodation. I chased them off and went into the local tourist information centre, where I was advised that accommodation availability was sketchy. The town was busy but we would probably find somewhere. Generally, when looking for a place to stay, we either checked a few of the recommendations from our *Lonely Planet* guide or we happened upon places by chance, our final selection based upon appearances, service, hospitality and price.

Outside, I found Maggie had been totally charmed by a young man called Gustavo. Incredibly polite, he adopted a gentle approach, merely presenting us with a selection of good accommodations that he could personally verify and backing off if he sensed he was annoying us or over doing it in any way. I asked about a place I had spotted in the Tourist Information office and showed him the leaflet. Yes, he knew this place but he assured us it was 'a dump' and went on to reel off comparable prices offering better value for money. In the end we took some of his leaflets and I gave him some small change for which he thanked us politely, wishing us a pleasant evening and success in finding a place to stay. The charm, grace and business ethos of Gustavo was all the more remarkable when you consider that he was a mere nine years of age! He was right too, my initial selection *was* an overpriced dump, but sadly his own recommendations were fully booked. In the end we found the beautiful Cabañas Leñador on the outskirts of town.

Right across the street was 'La Aripuca', a parkland entered through the stump of a giant dead rainforest tree that had been killed by termites hollowing out the inside to make their nest. Fungus had then set in to weaken and eventually destroy the tree, which had been brought here by lorry and worked into a magnificent gateway to what could vaguely be described as a museum of gigantic trees and woody things.

The owner, a big old boy with a beard and a smile, possibly of Germanic extraction, treated all visitors with an enthusiastic explanation on the origins of the site. We were shown an 'Aripuca', a Guarani Indian bird trap from which the park takes its name. The trap is set by laying some food on a trigger stick. The unsuspecting bird eats food off the stick, causing a small bamboo pyramid cage to fall, thus trapping the bird.

The centrepiece of the park was a 500-tonne 'Aripuca' made from entire tree trunks laid across one another in a hexagonal shape, like so many giant matchsticks. The result was a cavernous wooden structure that can be rented out for functions and special occasions. We walked in and stood twirling in the centre, looking up at the lofty ceiling of overlapped wooden roof tiles, feeling like two small birds in a very big cage. Beams of sunlight shot through the open slatted sides, catching specks of golden sawdust, glittering as they tossed and tumbled in the air. Add to this vision heady aromatic aromas of fresh cut exotic wood and the ensemble was that of a vast cathedral of the jungle, a place of earthly reverence and immense beauty.

Of our visit to Aripuca we can definitely say 'we never saw anything like it anywhere in the world'. On leaving, the owner left us with a reminder that we are all living in a global Aripuca. One day the trap will spring and it will be too late; we will all be caught like so many birds in a giant Guarani trap.

If Aripuca represented something we never 'saw the like of', at another Iguazú attraction we were told things that left us wishing we had never 'heard the like of'. Güirá Oga was a bird rescue sanctuary, an assortment of spacious cages set in natural forest that are temporary homes to an assortment of magnificent exotic birds. Many of the birds had been accidentally shot by hunters and brought in for veterinary treatment before recuperation and repatriation to the wild. Ricardo, our young ranger-guide, explained that some of the other inmates had been unwieldy pets kept by people under the delusion that these animals somehow reflected aspects of their own personality. For example, keeping an owl imparts an impression of sagacity or a predatory eagle, king of the food chain. But what sort of a statement was the individual trying to make by keeping a monstrous black vulture as a pet on a perch in a fifth storey apartment in Mendoza?

The saddest tales were the customs finds from illegal trading in endangered species. There were some talking parrots, beautiful bright lime-green birds, like the little Kawasaki birds we saw on the road into town. They are relatively common and of little value in the exotic bird trade as they are. However, put them in a bucket of bleach and dye them red to look like rarer related cousins and you can make big money. The birds of course die a few days after the sale is completed but by then the vendor has gone, disappeared with the cash. These parrots had fortunately been rescued before any respray was applied.

Most heart-breaking was the story of the Great Toucan. Toucans are one of the most beautiful birds in the world and we have a special affinity for them, coming as we do from Ireland where they have long featured in Guinness ads. The bird sat staring at us, an avian pint of the black-stuff, his blue-black coat shining in the dappled jungly sunlight that dazzled a stark white throat offset by a huge vivid yellow and red beak. On our approaching his enclosure, he hopped along a branch up to the wire, turning his beak side-on to the netting; allowing him to peer at us with a beautiful round blue eye, hoping we might have a tasty morsel for him. He looked sad and disconsolate and well he should be as the story of how he came to be here was simply appalling.

A passenger checked in for a flight at Buenos Aires airport carrying a thermos flask. Maybe he fancied some *Maté* on his journey but a thermos flask, even in Argentina, is a questionable article to board a plane with. And so it proved. He became tetchy and uncomfortable under questioning and customs were notified. On examination of the flask, they found its inners had been removed and the toucan stuffed inside to be smuggled out of the country for an overseas collector. Miraculously, the bird was still alive and sent to Güirá Oga where he now has a mate and will one day be released back into the wild. The apprehended villain is now stuffed up inside an oxy-acetylene welding cylinder, or would be if I were ever made governor of prisons in Argentina.

Iguazú Falls can justifiably claim to be one of the wonders of the world. The falls are the result of water cascading off the edge of the largest basalt lava field on the planet and are protected in a national park that spans the Argentina-Brazil border. Where the lava stopped flowing it has left an enormous seventy-metre precipice over which the Rio Iguazú spills. Consider your 'ordinary' waterfall; you have a river reaching some precipice over which it plummets like pouring water from a jug in a more or less controlled and directional manner. Iguazú is more like trying to pour water off a dinner tray; it just goes everywhere.

134

Its 275 different waterfalls make for a visage of aqua on a grandiose scale, the largest curtain of water in the world. There are single falls, double falls and multiple falls, curtains, chutes and rushes. Water in rills, dribbles, rivulets; spouts, sprinkles and sprays, trickles and tinkles. Whooshes of water in voluminous cascades, including the most impressive *La Garganta Del Diablo*: 'the Devil's Throat'. The surrounding green jungle canopy highlights the colours of the moving water, which is further illuminated by a world of rainbows, from big happy Noah's Arcs to little vapour bejewelled mini-bows each marking the gateway where a particular little spill falls off into the void.

The trail out to the Devil's Throat runs onto a metal catwalk that transports you out over the river with no hint of the deluge to come, until suddenly you are upon it, simply confronted with the biggest wall of water imaginable gushing straight at you; a scene of biblical proportions. This is what ancient mariners envisaged when thinking of sailing to the edge of the flat Earth, masses of boiling frothing green-blue water hurtling off the edge into some hellish oblivion.

In the afternoon we visited the 'lesser' falls that run between San Martin and the Salto Bossetti, an area of sub-tropical jungle that actually suffers occasional frosts in winter. Trails led us through the cool forest shade, suddenly opening to yield 'Lost World' vistas of the falls to blow our minds even more. A fast ride in an inflatable raft took us up towards the Devils Throat and into the deluge at the bottom of the San Martin cascades. Our long day at the falls ended with a walk out over the top of the San Martin and Bossetti Falls as the sun lowered in a blood orange sky, the evening settling like a pint of Guinness.

On the Argentine side you are very much in, on and around the waterfalls. A day trip into Brazil offered a different view of the cascades, with grandiose panoramic views and vistas over the park. On entering Brazil the customs officer on duty tried to wave us on through. He said if we were only going to visit the falls we could dismiss the border formalities provided we returned the same day. Still wary after our 'snake' encounter a few days previously we dismounted and insisted on the proper formalities. It took about forty minutes, while the officer puffed and pecked his way through triplicate forms for the bikes, but it was worth it.

Returning to Argentina we were not waved through as happy day-trippers but pulled over by different officers wanting all the documents for the bikes and ourselves. Inside the messy border checkpoint two guys handled all the 'ins' and 'outs' at one desk. The place was in chaos, caused by a group of Israeli kids who had thrown away their entry visas, sure they were useless bits of paper, and by a loud-mouthed Scot who had previously left the country at Rio de Janeiro without getting an exit stamp in his passport. Fifty dollar fines were meted out all around, along with a profusion of forms to be filled in and processed. All of this amidst howls of Jockish protests and abuse at the unfairness of it all:

"Where tae feck am ah gayin tae git fifta-dollars at this time o'the dae pal? Eh? Shure ah've no money in ma walt. Luke, see… nae money pal. Ah cam an go tae Brazil all the time an' ah've nivver had this kinda bo'er. It's no ma fault that some clampitt in Rio didna stamp ma passport is it? Can ya no just let me go an' ah'll send it tae ye in the post? Honest tae god ah will."

The Brazilian official unsmilingly told him there was a bank in town, it would be open at nine in the morning and he could go there to withdraw $50. Until then they would hold his passport. He should hurry too, as there could be additional fines if he lingered in the country without a valid passport. He suddenly 'found' $50 he had mislaid about his person, paid the fine and was processed out in a fug of 'fecks' and 'bastirds'.

From Iguazú we set out on a 1 000-mile ride across the Gran Chaco to reach Salta, where we had arranged to meet Peter Deck, the UN lawyer we met at Rio Mayo. Peter had made it to Ushuaia before heading north and like us became totally absorbed with Argentina. He had been visiting friends, John and Maria, in San Lorenzo near Salta, where they had renovated an old Italianate Castle, running it as a very exclusive hotel and restaurant. He had been riding up to see a renovated farmhouse owned by one of John's friends when he stalled his bike on the rocky track up to the house. Unfortunately he failed to get his foot down quickly enough and went over, smashing his hip on a protruding rock. It was a silly accident and underlined once again just how fragile any motorcycle journey can be. Peter was now convalescing and looked likely to be laid up for months, so he emailed us with an invite to come and stay with John and Maria.

The ride across the Gran Chaco promised to be a boring affair, a huge grassy plain that runs roughly across the bottom of Paraguay and the road on the map looks like it was drawn with a ruler, running straight as a die for some 600-odd miles. On the early stages the road was enlivened by spectacular grass fires all around, giving it the semblance of a battlefield after an air strike with huge columns of smoke drifting up into the afternoon sky, occasionally thick enough to blot out the sun. We had an overnight stop in Corrientes, a confusing jumble of a city but with a spectacular dawn ride out across the impressive General Belgrano Bridge, taking us back over the broad Paraná River for the last time.

Day Two on the Chaco was a bleak, straight-line ride on a deteriorating road, through tired and listless towns with depressing names like Pampa de Infierno and Rio Muerto implying hell and death. At one of these little towns, the slightly friendlier sounding Pampa de los Guanacos, on the state line between the Gran Chaco and Santiago Estera departments, we were offered a second chance to try our hand with the serpents in this game of snakes and ladders.

Again, the cop ran out to stop us, immediately alerting us that something was up. He was a chubby old cop with a Zapata moustache and slitty, beady eyes. We had obviously wakened him from a lunchtime siesta; his tunic was unbuttoned down the front and his police cap perched far back on his head, revealing thinning ringlets of greasy black hair plastered to his sweaty forehead. He licked his lips, then wiped them with the back of his hand.

He took our papers and looked over the bike and pointed vaguely at my engine, muttering the words '*Mata de Fuego*'. He shook his head and sucked his teeth, uttering '*Mata de Fuego*' once again, this time adding something involving 60 pesos per bike. When we failed to comprehend, we were taken inside the shabby checkpoint and an ancient statute book, that had been typed and photostatted some time ago, produced. We were shown the '*Mata de Fuego*' section and asked to pay a fine amounting to 120 pesos (around £25) for the two bikes. Official receipts were tabled and our details recorded on a scrap of paper. This time we were two to one and put into practice our new-rehearsed routine.

First we asked to speak with a superior officer; this was not possible, of course. We clarified that he wanted money, 120 pesos, before we could continue, then shrugged and told him this was impossible; we had no cash. He said we were Germans (probably from the BMW bikes and our riding gear) and didn't understand how Germans could not have cash (presumably they pay easily?) We explained we were from Ireland, therefore extremely poor and definitely not rich Germans. We were living on credit cards, as a cash machine in Iguazú had taken our cash card so, you see, we now have no money whatsoever. We were headed to Salta with nothing but two apples and a bottle of water to see us through. Would he like one of the apples? (Please bear in mind, this is all we have to eat all day). He dropped the price to 20 pesos; we stuck to our yarn about the cash machine.

Maggie was particularly good at playing this scumbag. She asked him over and over what on earth were we to do? Her lower lip was trembling as she ranted and raved about our 'dreadful' predicament. He became increasingly uncomfortable and this time it was him and not me who was squirming and sweating. She had obviously tapped into some nerve of macho bullshit whereby he could not stand to see a woman cry. He finally gave up, returning our papers to us, throwing them across the table in disgust and dismissing us with a wave of his arm.

We rode off and once out of sight of the checkpoint, punched the air in sweet elation at beating this low life. He never got past our first line of defence, the spiel about the cash machine. Our fall back was a dummy wallet with a few single dollar bills and a load of low-value coins from Chile but it was not even required. The taste of victory was a bonus laden compensation plus interest over my misery at being taken the first time. We later found that a '*Mata de Fuego*' is a fire extinguisher; the crook tried to fine us for not having a fire extinguisher on our bikes!

Salta on a Saturday was a hectic place for motorcycling with the most lunatic drivers in Argentina. Bomb alley streets lined with lime-washed walls magnified and focussed the heat of the midday sun. As we plunged into the narrow streets I felt like Luke Skywalker on a bomb run on the 'Dark Star' in 'Star Wars', dodging crazy taxi drivers, trying to shake maniac motorists off my tail. Maggie was my wingman, the intercom alive with dogfight chatter as we identified incoming threats, shouted out warnings, and yelled frustrations as we wove through traffic and rode past possible exits from this 'mélange of a melee'. Dried tongues stuck to parched-roofed mouths, yet permitted the taste of adrenaline to pass, like sucking on a rusty nail. Nostrils burned with car exhaust carbon monoxide and diesel fumes. No mercy; *No passeran!* Carve or be carved up. Hold the high road or die in the gutter. Plunge straight into multi-limbed intersections spewing traffic like so many metal filled paint tubes onto plaza palettes for mix and mash. We spent a nanosecond deciphering crazy unmarked road junctions, in the end opting for the line of least resistance, resorting to chicken run tactics just to get through.

We emerged from the downtown chaos onto a lovely four-lane highway that took us out of the madness and ran the few miles up into the nearby hills to the tranquillity of the delightful tree-lined streets of San Lorenzo. The *Alcalde* (Mayor) of Salta lives here, hence the extravagant expenditure of public funds on the best bit of road for hundreds of miles, all to ensure he has a good commute to work. A wide and gently winding side road led us up into the Quebrada (gorge) de San Lorenzo. The road turned beautiful through lush, exotic, flowering trees, massaging away the stresses of riding downtown. Right near the end we spied a profusion of tall palm trees, cascading like frozen fireworks, from which protruded the red tiled campanile of the castle. We pulled up and dismounted outside the black iron gateway. The click, click, click of crutches on sun-washed stone flags announced the hobbled arrival of Peter, who greeted us with a warm smile and a big hug. He looked relaxed and well after his mishap. He was accompanied by a tall, slim, extraordinarily beautiful woman called Maria. Long raven curls tumbled immaculately yet carelessly down over her shoulders, framing a face beset with the kindest eyes and the loveliest smile ever to greet us.

'*El Castillo de San Lorenzo*' was built some hundred years ago by Don Luigi Bartoletti, an immigrant Italian gunsmith, as an extravagant summer holiday home. He acquired the site through his marriage to a rich Saltanian lady. It was an expensive undertaking, with an architect especially imported from northern Italy to direct the work. Stones were brought by mule for the construction and dynamite was used for the first time in Salta to excavate the foundations. In the end it nearly ruined Bartoletti and sadly, in the early part of the 20th century, the house was abandoned and became derelict.

Twenty years ago John Johnston, a backpacker from Alabama, was hiking around South America with half an eye open for a haven that he could refurbish as a stylish lodge and restaurant. While in Salta he heard stories about an old 'Italian castle' in San Lorenzo a few kilometres outside town. John duly acquired the property and, with his Chilean partner Maria, renovated the place, first as a restaurant and later refurbished the bedrooms to open as a hotel.

One shouldn't really use the word 'castle', with its suggestion of imposing stone walls designed to keep people either in or out, to describe El Castillo. True, the walls are railed with old Remington rifle barrels, leftovers from the War of the Triple Alliance, which presumably old Don Luigi bought up as a cheap job lot, but they now have tasteful little decorative knobs welded on top such that you would never guess their original purpose. A palm shaded patio leads on to the grandiose arched doorway, inviting the visitor to enter the lofty main dining area, the castle keep, where a crew of efficient waiters are on standby to answer your every need.

Throughout the building, the stone structure is wonderfully warm and open. Soft red brickwork lines the arches and the stones themselves are selections from a palette of softer hues. Every good castle worth its salt must have a Beast. In El Castillo, his name is 'Beckham'; a one-year-old St Bernard dog, daft as a bog-brush, whose aim in life is to befriend everyone who visits.

Usually accommodation on the road comes in the form of a simple business transaction; you pay money and in return receive a service, a maintained room, bed, food, drinks etc. At El Castillo we were absorbed into the lives of John and Maria, who both went out of their way to look after all of their guests. Evening meals became dinner parties with other guests, lasting long into the evenings with excellent cuisine, far and away the best in Salta, and mouth-watering local Cafayate wines: the best in Argentina.

Our stay here was like a scaled down version of our visit to Argentina as a whole. From our original two-week foray to see Tierra del Fuego we had been so captivated by the diverse beauty and hospitality of the Argentine country and its people that we had been here now for nearly three months and it was looking like we might never leave. Likewise our stay at El Castillo, supposedly only to last a day or two, quickly ran to nine nights.

We had to prepare for the next stage of our trip. The bikes needed attention, fresh oil and new tyres and Salta offered the last opportunity to do this before heading into the desert altiplano regions of northern Chile, Bolivia and Peru. Part of our delay was forced by the fact that the bike tyres were not available locally and we had to order some from our friends at BMW in Cordoba, so they took a few days to arrive on an inter-city bus.

Another benefit of staying at the Castillo is its location. Since reaching Salta, we have felt for the first time on the trip that we really are in South America. Everything south of here had a distinctly European flavour, with predominant Spanish, Italian, German and even Welsh influences. The local Indians have been mostly eradicated or are minorities confined to small, remote areas. Even the scenery, awesome as it is, feels more alpine than altiplano. But it was in Salta that we began to encounter the Andean influence strongly for the first time. The city is sited on a vast plain, ringed by awesome mountains wherever you care to lay your eye. Take any road out of town and you are in mountain wonderland.

We ran in new tyres on a day trip out on the Ruta 68 to Cafayate. The last forty miles runs though the Quebrada de Cafayate, a tight, twisty hardtop road chasing a riverbed through a multi-coloured landscape of mountains, gorges and valleys on this 'Road of Many Colours'. It wasn't just the colours of the rocks, but the textures and shapes too that were so impressive. We trekked up the Quebrada de San Lorenzo, following the little gorge up into the trees for views back over the leafy suburb and spent another afternoon horse riding out on the 'Lomas Balcon', a vast grassland just outside town with sweeping views over the mountains and city.

The Lomas Balcon was the location for a big Holywood movie made here during the early 1960s: *'Taras Bulba'* starring Yul Brynner and Tony Curtis. Based on a short story by Gogol it is a tale of Ukrainian Cossacks struggling against their Polish overlords. Cossack chief Taras Bulba, played by Brynner, is an old war dog keen to initiate his sons into the Cossack ways by going on campaign against the Poles. His eldest son Andrei (Tony Curtis) falls in love with a Polish noblewoman and becomes embroiled in a conflict between patriotic duty, familial honour and romantic collusion with the enemy. The movie was filmed here with several thousand mounted extras recruited from local horsemen, all costumed and fitted out as Cossacks.

American Danny Liska rode a motorcycle through the Americas around this time and there is a great story in his book '*Two Wheels to Adventure*', telling how he obtained a part as one of the extras in the movie. The director wanted to shoot a massive cavalry battle scene so they split the horsemen into two big groups located out of sight from each other on either side of a hill. Both groups were directed to charge full tilt across the hill, neither aware of the presence of the other group doing the same. The idea was that they would clash, just like in a real battle, and the cameras were there to film the surprise and the mayhem. The result was sheer carnage, with many horses killed or destroyed and heavy casualties too amongst the riders.

Sadly, our sojourn at El Castillo had to end and the road once again beckoned. The bikes were ready and we needed to move on, to leave Argentina and make our way north. For our last evening John and Maria took us into Salta to visit 'La Caserna', a big old sprawl of a single story house with spacious rooms set around a tree-shaded courtyard. They served beer, wine and basic food but more importantly, La Caserna is a focal point where local musicians turn up to play.

We meandered through the various rooms, sampling music ranging from the typical Andean fare of panpipes and whistles to simple but haunting folk songs. A young lad, barely out of his teens, beckoned us join him for a while and be enchanted by beautiful melodies sung to airs plucked on his guitar. It was a mesmerising experience sat there staring at dreamy reflections of softish candlelight caught in the varnished wood of his guitar, listening to foreign lyrics sung in a strange tongue. Yet that divorce from literal translation allowed us to savour the spirit of each song, to focus on the passion of the singer. One piece in particular stood out (translated later by Maria) that told a poignant and tragic tale about a beautiful old tree cut down to make firewood for a rich landowner. I hoped for a final chorus in which some of the wood was rescued and crafted into a fine guitar used to tell the tale.

Our rounds of the music salons gained us introduction to Sammy, an Englishman who has become something of a local legend. A straight-talking gruff Yorkshireman, Sammy arrived a few years ago, took a room in La Caserna and never left. In his own softly spoken words, he has run up such a huge beer tab that he can never pay it and has become trapped here for all eternity. He sang us a simple folk song accompanied by the young lad on the guitar.

He was a more than passable vocalist and later admitted to having written a song about La Caserna a few years ago when it was closed down for a while by a temporary owner who had no interest in the music. His song told the story of the bronze bust of La Caserna's founder sited in the courtyard and how it stood guardian over the vacant dwelling. Silent and empty, the club became the playground of the 'Duende', the local 'little people'; Latin Leprechauns who tended it carefully until one day the sun would shine again and its doors re-open to the musicians of Salta. We left the club at 5:30am; the worse for wear with drink and lack of sleep but totally sated from this wonderful musical soiree.

Next day we overslept, as did the rest of the castle, waking late on Sunday afternoon. Sunlight streamed through the open window as I lay in bed trying to recollect the magic of the past evening and in particular this character Sammy. What a wonderful life he led; beer, bed and beautiful music all right there on his doorstep. I tried desperately to visualise what he looked like but today everything was hangover vague and misty. I remembered a battered slouch hat and at first thought it had a point like a wizard's. Was he some sort of Gandalf figure from *Lord of the Rings*, warning me of ring-wraith dangers on the road ahead? Or was that hat absent of point, a simple battered Fedora? From beneath its rim I recalled two piercing eyes, his most striking feature, dark and lively, illuminating a slightly hooked nose poking out from a wire-wool grey beard that probably had little forest animals living in it.

But now the memory clouds again and I cannot see the rest of him. There is just an indeterminate form draped in an old grey blanket poncho to keep out the chill of the night. He is hunched over the table with a hand clutching a pint and a soft-shod foot tapping a soft beat, the only visible extremities. His voice too was equally tantalizing. A low range, deep bass 'by-eck' Yorkshire mumble, yet when he sang he burst forth in strong, clear, resonant tones. And how did he get there? His presence defied all reason or logic, a Yorkshireman happening upon this place and given free beer and lodging. None of it made any sense at all. As I lay there contemplating these things, a strange thought came to me. Did I really meet this man, or was he some figment of my imagination given life by the heady infusion of alcohol and music supped in La Caserna? And then it struck me. Sammy wasn't real at all; I had conversed with the *Duende* of La Caserna.

Chapter 12: Atacama

The ride out of Argentina took us on the most spectacular roads of the trip so far, roads that led us through stark changes in landscape, altitude and people. Today the trip hit new highs, literally, as we discovered how both we and our bikes would perform under the lofty conditions of the Altiplano. We parted the Castillo with a tearful farewell and set out on a twisty morning road that chased the Rio Caldera over a green rain-forest mountain route to the city of Jujuy, whose local pronunciation always brought a smile with its high-pitched, owly, sing-song 'hoo-hooey'. Ascending roads north of the city led us into a dramatic transformation in the landscape from verdant greens to dusty browns and reds.

Both Salta and Jujuy sit at around 1200 metres altitude; Ruta 52 runs westwards and upwards to over 2000 metres and the little hamlet of Purmamarca, which surely has one of the most astonishing settings of any little town in the world. The immediate backdrop is formed by *'El Cerro de los Siete Colores'*, the hill of the seven colours, a slice of mountainside exposing a rainbow frozen in rock, burnished and shining brightly under the Andean midday sun. We wandered its sleepy plaza, lined with adobe dwellings, and selected a shady restaurant where we ate some excellent *cazuela* (a kind of stew) for lunch.

Today we once again faced the prospect of Ripio roads beyond Purmamarca but were delighted to find a new paved hardtop in construction. We whooped and hollered as we chased a fabulous liquorice bootlace of new tarmacadam that snaked lazily up through follow-on mountain scenery inspired by *'El Cerro de los Siete Colores'*. Switch-backs and hairpins interspersed with long straights that ran along mountain sides climbing ever on and upwards until we traversed the 4140 metre Cuesta de Lipan: 13 500 feet or two and a half miles high. Over the pass, we caught up with the roadworks advancing this road towards Chile and once through another *desvio* were dumped onto Ripio. For once, it was a 'good' bad road. The road haulage trucks delivering construction supplies had pummelled the surface so it was mostly compact with good going.

A white slash on the distant horizon announced the imminent arrival of the Salinas Grandes, Argentina's largest salt flats; ice cap white fenced in on all sides by a thin grey slash of mountain peaks while overhead the sun beat down from a cerulean sky. The road descended to a mere 3300 metres, returning to pavement and running off to a straight-line black apex pointing at infinity and contrasting with the sheer white of the Salinas on either side. We rode off-road for a muck-about-photo-shoot of the bikes on this blank canvas before continuing to Susques, our last stop in Argentina, having covered 190 miles today, every one a stunner, demanding a slow pace to take it all in.

Our first sight of Susques was the yawning gateway of a messy truck yard with a profusion of old and battered rusty hulks lining the road into town. Two unforeseen problems lay ahead, one for today, the other for the morrow. It took all of two or three minutes to circulate the bare earth streets lined by a few blocks of windowless single storey buildings, where our first problem was readily apparent: there was nowhere to stay. We asked around and learned there were indeed two hotels, a few kilometres on down the road to Chile. Both were fully occupied by road crews working on the new road so we rode back into town, hoping against hope to maybe find somewhere we had overlooked.

We were about to give up when I spotted a very small sign on one of the windowless shacks: '*Hospedaje*', a hostel cum B&B establishment. It was vaguely intimidating knocking on the door of this dwelling with no windows. From inside I could hear the treble-distorted blare of a TV set and some uninterested shouting from some kids along the lines of:

"Mum, there's somebody at the door."

"Well, go and see who it is."

"But we're watching TV. Will you go?"

And then an "Ah for goodness sake!" The door was opened by an incredibly large, incredibly dirty woman. Pigtails fell from a bowler hat down the side of a square-box face that would sour milk. Although bowler hats are stereotypically de-rigueur for South American ladies, this was the first on our trip.

"*Si?*" she asked in a voice at once gruff and unfriendly.

"*Tiene usted una habitacione doble por ese noche?*" I asked.

"*Si. Sigueme!*" she barked and, obeying the wave of her hand, we followed her into the darkness.

The door led directly into the living area of the house where a rabble of small grubby kids turned their heads away from the black and white TV set, craning their necks through 270 degrees like a bunch of little Damiens to look at us. They seemed to be all embarked on a competition to see who could accumulate the most bogeys on their top lip and the odd one or two sniffled and licked away some snot as we followed Mum out to a courtyard where she opened the metal door to the 'guest' room. Considering that last night we'd slept in a castle in an immaculately furnished colonial style room, on beautifully laundered white linen, the shock of what we were being offered tonight was all the more horrific: from castle to dungeon in one easy go.

Not that exquisite chambers in local castles were our normal dorm, in fact quite the opposite. Usually it was a cheap hotel costing a lot less than $30 a night but they were all clean and tidy. We had certain standards that demanded, as a minimum, a clean bed and a fair chance of not catching some unknown Andean plague. The woman stood over us as we gawked at her palace of filth. *Here's the room; take it or leave it, it's all the same to me.*

Before us stood a busted bedstead sinking in the earthen floor and covered with a filthy powder-blue candlewick bedspread in a cell of grimy bare-concrete block walls. Oh! And we could share the family toilet, a cesspit whose stench was just now permeating our nostrils; displacing the several other unmentionable odours already there to confirm that this was not a place conducive to our health and well being. We made an excuse about needing to be somewhere in Chile and left.

We returned to the two hotels to see if maybe we could camp in their parking lots but both refused. One of the receptionists suddenly remembered there was a lady in town that sometimes took people in. Not the *Hospedaje* we cried! The receptionist knew immediately who and what we were talking about; no, this lady has a respectable house near the old church. A phone call confirmed our reservation and so we met Doña Gladys who was waiting at her door when we arrived a few minutes later.

Doña Gladys was an angel and staying at her house was like staying with your best friend's mum. She was delighted to have us, made room for the bikes in her courtyard and showed us to an immaculate little bedroom. Dinner was included and we scoffed some delicious *tamales* followed by steak lashed in gravy with creamy mashed potatoes lightly spiced with nutmeg. There was pudding too, candied figs in syrup; and all the while Gladys fussed over us, making sure we had enough to eat and drink, that everything was warm enough and comfortable.

It was freezing cold in the night. Susques sits at an elevation of 3300 metres (11 000 feet) and the night time temperature on this edge of the Altiplano made us glad we were not camping. We now experienced the first effects of altitude on our bodies. At this elevation, due to reduced atmospheric pressure, there is only sixty-eight percent of the oxygen normally available at sea level so our bodies were running on roughly a third less oxygen. In real terms this causes a reduction in blood oxygen levels to around eighty-nine percent, which for some people can lead to headaches and nausea: early signs of Acute Mountain Sickness (AMS).

For most, simply resting will overcome the oxygen deficiency but in some instances the body refuses to adjust, leading to the onset of high altitude pulmonary oedema (HAPE). This is an acute, life-threatening problem and the condition can kill within hours. The general breathlessness due to the high altitude increases even when the person is resting as lungs are starved of oxygen and the blood vessels within start to constrict. The blood in these vessels is squeezed as the pressure goes up, forcing fluid out of the blood and into the lungs' air pockets. This stage is manifested when the sufferer's lips turn blue and they start to cough up pink frothy spit from their lungs.

To exacerbate the condition, dangerous and reactive substances form in the oxygen starved blood and these can damage the special membrane between the air and blood in the lungs, causing further fluid leak and worsening HAPE. The condition is best remedied by returning to lower altitudes as soon as possible. Exactly why some people should suffer drastic altitude effects, while for others the effects are minimal is not really understood. The lowest recorded altitude where HAPE has occurred is 2500 metres and there seems to be no correlation between external factors such as age, weight and general fitness. There are stories of seasoned climbers returning to Everest, only to be struck down by altitude effects and having to be emergency evacuated.

Fortunately we did not suffer any ill effect other than feeling a little breathless under exertion, such as pushing the bike. Arriving by motorcycle gradually exposed us to altitude, ascending over a period of hours rather than stepping off a plane and suddenly having to adjust all at once. The worst and most unpleasant manifestation of altitude effect for both of us came when we were sleeping. Breathing is a motor function, something your body does on autopilot without conscious instruction. While asleep, it is conditioned to breath at a certain rate to deliver the required amount of oxygen to the brain, which organises and regulates all the life systems. Normally our bodies were set to breathe at a sea level rate but now, sleeping in this rarefied air, our breathing was delivering an insufficient oxygen supply to the brain. Once our system reached a critical point the brain would kick-start the heart to pump more fuel, a horrible sensation causing you to wake with a nasty jolt, heart pounding in your chest as it hammered an emergency supply of blood to the oxygen-starved brain. This was followed by a spell of heavy rapid breathing before nodding off again; only to be jerked awake an hour or so later by the same thing.

In the morning an overnight frost slowly melted as the sun rose in a clear blue sky we now took for granted. We breakfasted with Doña Gladys before wheeling our frigid bikes out into the street, where we loaded up under the view of a small crowd of onlookers. Maggie mounted up, hit the starter and... nothing. My bike likewise refused to start; both bikes sounding tired and listless on turnover like their batteries were flat. We recruited some of the bystanders for a push start and eventually got both bikes running but it was a worrying turn of events.

I suspected a problem with the fuel injection system when cold starting at high altitude. To date, our little bikes had never faltered once and yesterday we had been glad for their fuel injection and its ability to auto-compensate for differences in temperature and rarefied air. On a carburetted bike we would be fiddling about with carburettor jets and needles to make this adjustment manually. Once started, the bikes ran smoothly for the rest of the day with no further problems. Just as well, for today's ride was almost entirely on Ripio.

The pavement ended just outside town and we set off on the dirt across a desert plateau ascending to the Paso de Jama where we would cross back into Chile. It was weird riding, as the road consisted of long straights of reasonably good firm surface, giving way to horrible soft red sand at every corner as it zigzagged across flat altiplano terrain ringed with a teased-meringue of mountain. I found I could clip along at a reasonable rate, getting up to 30 to 40 mph on the straights with confidence, but the sandy corners were horrible and I soon learned to respect them, slowing right down to waddle through. I was learning to read the road surfaces too. Perpendicular corrugations meant the surface was hard and bumpy but safe for speed. However when the corrugations changed and ran along the direction of the road, these ruts suggested a softer substrate and a warning to take it easier.

For Maggie the journey turned into a nightmare. A few early scares on the sandy sections forced her to slow right down. She was back in that horrid *Catch 22* scenario. Ride fast to minimise the bumps but possibly crash. Ride slow and hit every bump and grind on the road and take the shock of these impacts through that weak elbow. I took to riding ahead, checking out the road and looking for any particularly nasty sections. Then I would wait for Maggie to catch up. We had a flask of hot tea with us but had underestimated the time it would take to cover the distance to the frontier and carried only nuts and dried fruit for eats, when we really needed something more substantial. We made slow progress, inch-worming our way along this dusty, desert road. It took seven hours to cover the seventy miles to the border checkpoint crossing at some unmarked point on the road, the Tropic of Capricorn.

The surrounding mountains were breathtakingly beautiful and that day, for all its difficulties, stands out as one of the most awesome journeys we ever accomplished on a bike. At the border, a desolate outpost, the customs people were courteous and efficient in stamping us out of their homeland. We thanked them profusely for having such a wonderful country, giving us such a rich and rewarding travel experience and we both really choked with emotion as we mounted the bikes for what we realised was the last time in Argentina. Five kilometres later over a rocky pass, an overhead gantry heralded our final return to Chile. The reappearance of pavement was very much appreciated by Maggie, now nursing a horribly battered elbow.

A further 85 miles lay between us and our destination, San Pedro de Atacama, on a road that would take us across the 4600 metre Paso de Jama, our highest elevation of the whole trip. The sun was showing an interest in calling it a day and on the shady sections where we rode out of its warming light it was bitter cold. We stopped to put on one-piece wetsuits for added insulation and the effort at this altitude had us both wheezing and coughing like sixty-a-day smokers. Up here the oxygen level had now dropped to fifty-seven percent of sea level amounts, so we were running on half fuel. Distant salt flats ran to streaky red mountains congealed to blood by the setting sun, giving the impression we were circumnavigating a Martian ice cap. Huge volcanoes darkened our evening horizon, notably the 6000-metre monster Licancabur, offering us our first views into Bolivia, whose border the mountain straddles.

Using San Pedro as a base, we made excursions through arid salt flats around Lago Chaxa leading to briny lakes dotted with pink flamingos, catching and reflecting crazy snow-capped volcanoes. In the evenings we dined on llama and sipped freebie Pisco Sours, a tout's enticer to get us through the door that worked every time.

The bike's cold start problems were manifest again; it seemed that at any elevation over 2000 metres we were going to have trouble. San Pedro sits at 2400 metres with cold nights and dewy mornings so we were well into the no-start zone. While tinkering with the bikes outside our hostel, we attracted the attention of a big Chileno riding a big BMW GS 1100 with the Romanesque name of Julio Cesare. He was convinced our 'cold starting malady' was due to the battery not having the oomph to start the bikes, but we explained we had already examined these and they seemed fine. An obvious remedy was to park the bikes in the blazing heat of the sun, first thing in the morning. Once warmed they would start and, once started, run all day.

We rode down to the coast to visit the two northernmost cities in Chile: Iquique and Arica. The journey took us into the Atacama Desert, the driest place on Earth. To date, all our deserts had been dainty, fine landscapes painted from the finest ingredients and mixes on Mother Nature's palette, with saddle views easy on the eye. Hot and dusty for sure but serene and tranquil; vacant spaces where you can empty your mind and let every care and worry drift away on the desert sands. Our ride through the Atacama was something else. Pretty to begin, as we extracted ourselves from a maze of Andean peaks and volcanoes, the road then descended and straightened out with all the contours and colours of those high deserts flattened and bleached to a plain of grey rolling dirt and the ugliest, most boring road on the planet.

We picked up twin lines of power pylons and a run of telegraph poles that pointed our way to oblivion where they apexed with the road at centre horizon, this dead-sterile-grey environment an exercise in sensory deprivation. We could have rigged the steering on centre lock and gone to sleep for the next few hours and not missed a thing. We searched vainly for something to look at. There was no wildlife so, apart from a few stick plants, the only objects of interest were the odd vehicle track in the dirt running alongside the road.

By mid afternoon tedium reigned. Little stony heaps now joined the landscape, grey of course, and I have no idea how they got there or what they were for. Possibly spoil from holes dug for pylon or pole footings? They made a messy place look even untidier. It all looked like the builders had been and gone, leaving this litter trail of waste tips.

Fortunately, the final 60km into Iquique was a tad spicier, taking us over some coastal mountains, the road winding up and over arid hills and then running along a seaside cliff face with the city of Iquique perched impossibly on a coastal shelf below. It was a spectacular view with the sun setting in the early evening sky. We stopped for some photos. It is a big city (around 200 000 souls) and we could see a modern central business district complete with glass and steel high-rise buildings. Most eye-catching were the monster sand dunes that sit to the north end of town. Bigger and taller than anything manmade they formed an intermediary backdrop between mountain and city. From our lofty perch we considered this weird amalgam of sun, sea, sand and habitation when we heard another motorcycle approach. It was Julio Cesare. He knew the city and offered to help us find a place to stay. He also knew a place where we could buy some new batteries for our starting problem.

We followed JC into the city and after a while were fairly certain that he did not really know Iquique. We shot around and through narrow streets and alleys checking out a number of accommodations; his recommended place was fully booked so we set off into an older seedier part of town. We declined several small hotels that proved to be pricey and grubby with no parking for the bikes.

Stopped at some traffic lights we looked on as a bunch of street urchins took delight in setting off a car alarm by jumping on the bonnet. Not content with this, three of them climbed up onto the roof, using it as a trampoline, bouncing in time to the wailing alarm; to which, as with car alarms the world over, no-one paid the slightest attention. By the time they were finished, the roof panel was stoved in and they bounced off down the street looking for new opportunities for mayhem and destruction. I finally stopped at the better-looking *Hotel Las Dunas* and we picked up a clean room for $19 with secure parking off the street. JC seemed happy enough and booked in too.

JC was a really decent chap. He was tall, fair skinned, thick browed with a slightly bulbous nose and a big Ernest Borgnine smile complete with a mouthful of milestone teeth. He ran a business in Santiago selling computer games and DVDs but had recently split with his wife. By his account she was trying to tie him down: wear nicer clothes, get rid of the bike, comb your hair sort of stuff; he got fed up with it and left. He told us this over dinner and a bevy of Pisco Sours at a local Chinese, while we regaled him with tales of our travels to date.

Both Maggie and I are very much social animals; we enjoy the company of others, especially motorcycle travellers on the road. These encounters are great opportunities to exchange experiences and advice (especially on what lies ahead) from locals or from people travelling in the other direction. It is refreshing too to find new company but after a few days we generally found that both parties become eager to split by mutual consent, hopefully invigorated and informed from the encounter. People are generally keen to be helpful too when you have a problem but occasionally this can become mildly irritating when they insist that their solution or remedy is best and don't listen when you discount their course of action; so it was with JC.

In the morning his bike had gone, so we settled down to breakfast. He reappeared with a big grin on his face and armed with two pieces of information. First, he'd located a battery shop where we could buy two new batteries. Second, he'd spoken to a local traffic motorcycle cop called Manuel, who rode an F650. Even better, Manuel had agreed to take us to the police bike mechanic to check our bikes. I put him off on his first count, politely reiterating that there was no way we would be changing the batteries until I had positive proof that they were the cause of the no-start problem but a chat with a police mechanic sounded good and we thanked him for putting himself out to try and help us.

Back at sea level, the bikes started enthusiastically at the first push of the starter button. We rode out to a police roadblock at the termination of the road off the mountains into the city, not far from where we met JC the day before. This road is a big fast dual carriageway plunging down the mountainside, ending at a roundabout that splits off into town. The cops had set up a speed trap and were pulling over car after car for speeding, so easy to do on this piece of road. Manuel's green and white F650 sat by the roadside with two or three others. He ran over to us and apologised. Could we wait for ten minutes until he had his quota? Then he would take us to see the mechanic.

JC laughed. They have to nab so many cars in a morning before taking a break! Three tickets later, Manuel handed over the hair-dryer speed-gun to another cop, mounted up, adjusted the set of his Ray-Bans and signalled us to follow him; so we set off on a breakneck pursuit through mid-morning traffic. Manuel knew that everyone would brake for the green and white police bike; so he rode into the heart of busy intersections, stopped dead, sirens and blue lights flashing, palm raised to stop and open traffic jams like a bike-cop Moses parting the Red Sea of vehicles. By this time the three of us had caught up and whizzed through, shortly to be overtaken by Manuel speeding on to dissect the next junction.

I had been under the misapprehension that we were headed for some police motor pool or workshop but Manuel took us to one of the city's outermost housing 'projects' near the big sand dunes. We rode into a street of two-storey blockhouses, painted in the brightest pastel colours that utterly failed to mask the fact that the place was a slum. Gardens spilled refuse out onto the street, wheel-less cars sat around on piles of bricks and all of the houses had steel bars welded over their doors and windows. Security was obviously a big issue here, as further denoted by the three or four heavy locks fitted to every home's front door.

The mechanic's house was even scarier. He had a single storey iron bar cage fitted over the front garden like he maybe kept lions or tigers. Manuel had to rouse him and he came out yawning and scratching his balls, a tall lanky man with a thick mop of hair. Manuel registered our shock and whispered to Maggie: "Don't worry; as a *mecanico*, he is *excellente!*"

And so it proved. He tested the charging systems and found that everything was running perfectly. JC asked about changing the batteries. Well, we could do that but he didn't think they were the problem. It was something to do with the engine management system and how it was set up to deal with cold temperatures in thin air with reduced oxygen. JC went on…but we could check the batteries? No, you have to go to the battery shop in town to do this. In the end we agreed that I would ride with JC to get the batteries checked; we would shortly be heading up into the altiplano in Bolivia and Peru for weeks or even months, so it was important we checked out all possibilities just to be safe.

Maggie would stay here with the dead bikes and we wouldn't be long. Manuel returned to his police duties and the mechanic disappeared for a hospital appointment. Before leaving he padlocked his place like it was a Houdini escape trick and told Maggie to leave nothing lying around, as it would be stolen for sure. She was horrified but sure we would be back soon.

We were gone for over two hours. First, JC's sense of direction was atrocious as usual and we couldn't find the shop, even though he had been there that morning. Having located the shop up a small back street, the guys checked the batteries, found no problems with them but recommended we leave them on charge for the afternoon. JC dropped me back at the hotel and went off to get Maggie.

160

Left alone in the slum, she sat reading with the bikes while strange people came and went from one or two of the houses to the clatter of locks being unlocked and doors being unbolted. She was convinced that this was what a crack den looks like, a neighbourhood of crime. American gangster cars rolled by, blackened windows lowered as they slowed to take in the bikes, the girl, and then took off. She was going to be kidnapped for sure. Then, after an eternity, JC arrived and she wanted to punch his stupid lights in as he came off with this cock and bull story of life in the battery shop. No, better still, wait until the hotel and then punch my lights in for being so stupid as to leave her in such a dangerous place!

After a short lunch of scallop and cheese *empanadas*, over which I managed to calm Maggie down, we were ferried back to the bikes (me first) and JC went off to do some shopping and collect the batteries. He arrived back having left us for another two hours in which time I experienced first hand some of the panic Maggie felt in the morning being left in this 'lovely' place. Batteries installed, we rode back to the hotel feeling aggrieved at having wasted so much time today on this wild battery chase. At dinner that evening JC announced he was leaving tomorrow, off to see some friends who lived nearby. He was a decent, amicable big fellow but at times we felt a little railroaded into doing things that were, in hindsight, against our better judgement. Still, as with all fellow travellers, it was sad to say goodbye when we parted.

We spent an extra day alone in Iquique and had our first haircuts of the trip ($10 for both of us and a fine job too). We mooched around the pleasant city centre and old town boardwalk areas and were bemused by a huge vulture hanging around the doorway to a rather elegant department store like a ghoulish commissionaire. I checked the internet, where I discovered that the cold start problem with our bikes was not uncommon and <u>was</u> all to do with thin air and low temperatures. Later, speaking to some contacts at BMW, we found amazingly that the bike had not been tested properly for these combinations during development.

From Iquique the Ruta 5, the road north to Arica, took us on a pleasant morning's ride through scorched grey river valleys back into some grandiose mountains. By early afternoon we descended a broad dry valley to Arica, one of the driest inhabited places on Earth with an average annual precipitation of a mere 0.8 mm (0.03 inches). We mooched the shady and colourful market near our hotel and took a morning stroll to climb the Morro de Arica, a steep hill overlooking the city. At 140 metres above sea level, it was the last bulwark of defence for the Peruvian troops defending the city during the War of the Pacific and the gun batteries there now form a museum with elevated views over the city and the wild Pacific Coast.

At El Morro, we met a group of Austrian bikers on KTMs and participated in one of those afore-mentioned traveller information exchanges. Where we sang the praises of the beautiful country lying in wait up ahead, they had only tales of woe for us. First, they enquired in clipped English, had we heard of the disaster at Machu Picchu? A train had crashed with seven people killed, leaving thousands stranded in the mountains. They were not sure if it was even possible to visit the ruins now.

But before we even got that far there was turmoil fermenting in Bolivia and a blockaded bridge up on Lake Titicaca in Peru. This had forced them to make a detour of several hundred kilometres out into wild open country, far from road or track and navigating with GPS, all to find a ford across the river. They were travelling on lightweight, unladen bikes, on a package tour, with all their kit

162

in a heavy-duty support vehicle sweeping along behind them ready to pick up any casualties or breakdowns.

We pondered our future as we walked back to town. The road forks at Arica and we could choose to continue on up the coast, away from these reported troubles. It would be a relatively safe route but promised to be a boring continuation of the dismal Atacama road, an ugly road all the way up to Ecuador. The other fork leads into the Andes, Bolivia, La Paz and on to Lake Titicaca. Following the lake's western shore we wanted to visit Puno, jump off for trips out to the reed islands on the lake. Beyond this lay the fabulous city of Cusco, gateway to the Inca Trail to Machu Picchu. To miss out on this would be to miss the lands of the Incas and the essential South American experience, so it was a clear 'no contest'. We would head for the hills and take our chances with whatever came our way.

Our last rest in Chile was in the sleepy little town of Putre, a recommended acclimatisation point for travelling beyond to the High Andes. We spent my 43rd birthday in the nearby Lauca National Park that runs on to the border with Bolivia. High Altiplano grasslands skirt snow-clad volcanoes as far as the eye can see. Every peak is a volcano, most of them well over 6000 metres (knocking on four miles!) high. At their feet, melt-water flood plains are filled with flamingos, heads buried in water as they dredge for shrimp. Lakes shiver and shimmer, mirroring the mighty snow covered domes.

Centrepiece is Volcan Parinacota, a Fuji-esque piece of symmetrical beauty with Lake Chungara laid at its feet. Riding a short way round to change the perspective and a second peak looms out from behind, Parinacota's Siamese twin, joined at the hip, Volcan Pomerape. Both stand there nobly at over 6200 metres tall while way off in the distance we spy Volcan Sajama, at over 6500 metres, the highest peak in all Bolivia.

With volcanoes everywhere we look, what is incredible is that we stand amongst them alone. Apart from the park ranger at the entry gate and some tourist stalls at the main halt at Lake Chungara, there is no one here in this most remote and beautiful wonderland on the planet. Just us. At 4500 metres the air is thin and we really feel it today. Wildlife abounds. We chase herds of *vicuña*, a smaller version of the *guanaco* and the lakes and water are full of ducks, geese, giant coots and flamingos.

We stopped at a place called Las Cuevas to visit the hot springs there and saw our first *vizcachas*. These are a large rabbit-like animal with a thick bushy tail and we ran across a whole colony of them inhabiting a rocky outcrop near the springs. They seemed unbothered by our presence, allowing us close enough to take photographs without the use of a zoom lense, and then went back to playing their games, jumping in and around the rocks. The soak in the hot springs at Las Cuevas was sublime. A little stone hut had been built to cover the naturally heated spring. Stripping off in the altiplano chill, we were frozen; but plunging into the hot water was heaven itself and rounded off what I now consider to be my best birthday ever.

And with that, our travels in Chile and Argentina are at an end. The easy part is over and, if we are to believe the stories, more difficult roads lie ahead. We found out some more about our likely travails: the train wreck at Machu Picchu was caused by a mudslide from heavy rain and they are working round the clock to re-open the line. Of the strikes and blockades in Bolivia and Peru, they are random but may occur at any time, in any place, so we will wait for more current local information and take appropriate action as the situation demands. The bikes are performing well again; ensuring they are out in the sun seems enough to get them going in the morning.

At the frontier, we followed the usual procedure getting the bikes and ourselves stamped out of Chile. The police officer involved was an old guy with a roly-poly face, wearing one of those Russian fur hats with ear flaps buttoned together at the top. He was smiley all the way and asked us what we thought of Chile. We loved it; the people, the volcanoes, the Pisco Sours. He asked us to wait a moment and popped into his station house, returning with a small gift that he presented to Maggie. It was a small wooden handmade key ring cut from a section of tree. On one side was a condor, on the other a little Andino man and woman. 'Bienvenido de Chungara' it said. Bienvenido and adios to Chile!

Chapter 13: Bolivia

The grandly titled 'War of the Pacific' was fought in the late 1800s. It started with a dispute over the Atacama region, which was then part of Bolivia. As we found riding through the area today it seemed to hold little of interest so Bolivia wasn't too fussed when Chilean prospectors began nosing around. Of course the area is one of the richest mineral veins on the planet and when the Chilenos starting digging wealth out of the ground the Bolivians tried to tax them. It all escalated into the War of the Pacific with Peru siding with the Bolivians.

It was a mostly one sided affair with Chile giving the other pair a fair pasting. Bolivia lost most, ceding the mineral rich province of Antofagasta to Chile, losing her coastal access forever and thereby dooming the nation to become the poorest in South America. Chile built a railroad connecting the Bolivian capital of La Paz with Arica and guaranteed freedom of transit for Bolivian commerce through Chilean ports and territory, yet there remains a lingering animosity towards the Chileans for 'stealing' their coast.

Bolivia insists to this day that the lost coastal provinces should be returned and this has remained a major point of contention between the two countries, escalating periodically to breaks in diplomatic relations. In 1974, the Act of Cochabamba identified the question of a seaport as the issue of greatest national importance to all Bolivians. Land-locked Bolivia retains a navy of around 6500 men and a variety of small boats up on Lake Titicaca. They have a proper sea-going vessel, the *Libertador Bolivar*, docked in Argentina, where she travels up and down the River Plate. But their most important mission is keeping the dream alive of a return to the sea. On 23rd March the country celebrates the *'Dia Del Mar'* (Day of the Sea), an annual public holiday that underlines that dream.

We arrived at Tambo Quemado, our crossing point into Bolivia, early in the day. There was a five mile altiplano no-man's land between the Chilean and Bolivian customs posts. The Chilean 'half' was patrolled by two men in a small Toyota pick-up truck, wearing high visibility boiler suits and rubber gloves. Their task: to pick up litter and they had several plastic bins full of it in the back of the truck. The Bolivian 'half' was filthy, with shredded plastic bags everywhere. As we approached Bolivian customs we rode into the source of the litter.

The post was a huge truck yard where several groups of bowler hatted Indian ladies were fully occupied hoking the bins. Customs proceedings were a tad untidy too. Gangs of officers hung around doorways waiting for something to do, staring at us balefully as we approached. It was a trifle intimidating as their intent was not clear but on chatting with them, asking where to go and what to do, several of their faces lightened up as they sprang into action to sort us out. The sight of your smile reflected is generally a good sign that people are going to be alright. We sorted our passport stamps, organised the bikes and were slightly alarmed when at the end of the process we were instructed to go to a booth to pay money. The officer sensed my tension and explained that the road on to La Paz was a toll road; in the end it cost pennies.

With an *adios* we left and set out on a beautiful afternoon's ride across Sajama National Park, the Bolivian extension of Chile's Lauca National Park. The road circumscribed the lofty Volcan

Sajama and pierced another of those painted deserts we love so well. Soft salmon sands with raspberry ripple rock, all laced with lashings of good hard top. Sit back and enjoy the view. The road was virtually empty, with no habitations until Patacamaya yet there were people around. We would suddenly come upon little old women seemingly wandering about in the middle of nowhere, miles from any habitation with only their bowler hat for company. We saw this phenomenon years ago in Morocco (minus the bowler hats of course) and it remains one of the great mysteries of travel as to what these people are doing out in such backs of beyond. We came upon a single dwelling along the road: a small Mormon church that looked like it had blown in and been deposited here from someplace else.

Riding towards Patacamaya, speculating on the occupation of vacuums, our progress was blocked by the Serrania de Sica Sica Mountains, harbouring a wall of evil-looking black cloud up ahead. We stopped short of the storm to put on waterproofs and then... into the fray. It lashed out of the heavens, raining re-bars. Throw in the percussion of just-behind-you thunder claps and wicked too-close-for-comfort lightning strikes and this brew is sassy. Turbulent winds bitch slapped our bikes and we were riding a storm and a half. It lasted a good half hour and was terminated by the biggest, brightest, stained-glass rainbow in the world.

Bolivia was proving such a contrast to our Panamerican experience to date. The people were nearly all Quechua or Aymara, Andean highland Indians, and we rode past miserable hovels where they subsistence farmed, dependent on the animals they grazed and on what they grew in the ground to keep them alive. Likewise in the little towns, roads decayed to rutted dirt streets immediately on leaving the main highway. We drifted along the high plains under

168

dramatic post-storm skies, distant snow-capped mountains adding a touch of menace to the scene. According to my trip-meter, the capital city La Paz lay a few miles up the road but mysteriously it remained invisible. Then we hit shantytown.

Grey tarmac, stained bloody muddy by a wash of squalor from a world of cardboard and wooden dwellings. People thronged along the edge of the road by the thousands. Cops directed traffic at the odd intersection or stopped the flow at pedestrian crossings. It seemed more African than Latin American and the thought of trying to find a place to stay in this mess of humanity was more than a little daunting. This was *'El Alto'*, the High One; La Paz's notorious slum district sited along the top of the canyon in which the city lies. 750 000 people live here, mostly Indians from the country trying to make it big in the city and mostly getting stuck here in the fastest growing township in South America. Suddenly the chaos opened up and a line of tollbooths blocked our path. We paid up, rode through and were immediately presented with the canyon rim itself.

The first sight of the city of La Paz is one of travel's great shocks. We pulled over, totally flabbergasted by the sight in front of us. We trembled as we got off the bikes, shakily reaching for the camera but where to start to capture the scene before us? Imagine the Grand Canyon. Line it with a ring of snow-clad mountains and volcanoes, so tall their peaks are wreathed in clouds. Then throw a city of over one million people into the canyon itself, complete with skyscrapers, sports stadiums, parklands, domestic habitations, all the paraphernalia that goes with big city life, and you will have some idea of La Paz.

Free of the tollbooths that shut out the shantytown, we followed a big modern dual carriageway that gently descended via a series of hairpin bends down into the city. They say it is impossible to get lost in La Paz. Just head downhill until you can go no further and you will be on the main thoroughfare, the Prado. We hit rush hour. A young chap on an old FT500 Honda befriended us at some traffic lights and offered to show us some hotels. We set off in pursuit as he flung his bike through the evening traffic. Heading right off the main drag we plunged into a hive of narrowing cobbled streets, following a one-way system onwards and up. A short ride along the canyon on level road ended with us plummeting downhill into an area full of hostels and cheap hotels.

"This is a good hotel, very cheap, very clean. My friends stay here when they come to visit me in town," he said.

"It looks very nice but how are we supposed to get off the bikes?" I whispered to Maggie. My bike was almost standing on its head, held there by the front brake. I tentatively put my kick-stand down but realised the bike would roll off immediately. It would be quicker if I just jumped off and let it crash to the bottom of the hill, then ran down and collected all the bits. Maggie was shouting at me to move on, her bike was slipping on the smooth cobblestones and she had her hands full trying to hold it upright. Our buddy interpreted this as a sign that we thought his accommodation too down market, which was not the case and so took us off to find a more luxurious dwelling. He left us at the Hotel Europa, a 4 Star joint downtown but with the bonus of a flat street outside. I thanked him and walked up the red carpet, past the top-hatted commissionaire and enquired at the very-posh-reception if they had a not-so-posh room for evening.

"Yes, the room rate will be $175 per night". I explained to the receptionist that we didn't want to buy the room, only rent it for a few nights. She was really sweet and gave me a map of town, recommending a small hotel down near the university. The Hotel

España proved to be pleasant, cheap and had a little courtyard off the street where we parked the bikes. It was fairly central too so we washed, changed and set off to explore the city at night.

Outside the city buzzed. Walking along the Prado we could have been in London's West End, strolling with the affluent, bumping into tourists, were it not for the bowler hatted ladies selling everything from Kit Kats to shaving foam. They squatted on the pavement with onion-layered skirts spread out across laps as a table cloth to display their wares. In a startling culture clash, one chubby Aymaran lady was selling the very latest blockbuster movies on DVD, pirate copies of course, all for a dollar. We bought two big Kit Kats, our first chocolate from home on the trip and one of those things we didn't realise how much we missed until we were offered some right there on the street.

The Kit-Kats proved useful as mouthwash later on with a cup of tea back at our room, as we tried to displace the taste of *Chuño*, a Bolivian delicacy we had tried that night at dinner. *Chuño* is a potato dish made by alternately freezing potatoes overnight and then leaving them sitting in the sun all day, while trampling them to extract all the juices. This cycle is repeated over a period of days and the thus preserved potatoes can last for years, a useful foodstuff in these harsh climes. They are absolutely disgusting. One of those foods that leaves an aftertaste well out of proportion to the minute quantity held in your mouth for the few nanoseconds it took your tastebuds to mutiny as you realise this stuff tastes truly awful.

We were increasingly fascinated by these bowler hats or '*bombin*' as they are known locally. How did this most English hat come to be such a fashionable item of millinery in a far away place like La Paz? The first bowler hat was designed in 1850 by James Lock & Co. of St James's Street, London. The hats were requested by Sir William Coke as a piece of protective headgear for his game wardens to wear when patrolling his estate on horseback, to safeguard against low tree branches. The new Lock design was manufactured by hatters Bowler Brothers, whose family name would be forever synonymous with the new style. The story goes that when Sir William turned up at the Locks' premises to take delivery of the first bowler, he decided to see how robust the new hat was by throwing it on the floor and stomping on it. He picked it up, examining how sturdy the design was before stuffing it onto his head. A satisfied customer, he promptly paid his 12 bob and left with his new, somewhat battered, headgear.

The bowler broke down class barriers in England. Traditionally the upper classes wore top hats and the lower classes soft flat caps. The bowler was something in between and was adopted as a uniform chapeau by all manner of businessmen from bankers and city brokers to fish sellers and carpenters. It went out of fashion in the 1960s, probably due to the explosion of the motor car in society, which made hat wearing superfluous.

Bowlers made their first impression on the South American market in the 1920s when a Bolivian outfitter accidentally over-ordered on his stock of bowlers. He decided to market the surplus items as women's wear and they went down a treat, especially with the indigenous people, who believe the 'bombin' enhances fertility. By the 1930s they proved so popular that one Italian millinery firm, Borsalino, began making bowlers specifically for the Andean market and they remain popular today.

Nearly every 'bombin' we saw in Latin America looked two or three sizes too small and perched impossibly on top of the wearer's head rather than sitting snug on it. Apparently that original over-ordered batch was mainly small sizes, which the milliner, obviously a good salesman, declared was the fashionable way to wear these items and the under-sized style stuck. Yet how are they held on? There was no strap and try as we may we couldn't see evidence of any hat pins. Maybe they are glued on? Is there such a thing as Bolivian Hat-glue?

A more intimidating form of headgear was the sudden appearance of a group of kids wearing ski-mask balaclavas. You know the ones that completely cover the face with only two holes for the eyes and a third for the mouth, so favoured by terrorists and paramilitaries the world over. They were really scary until we realised they were only shoeshine boys wanting to clean our boots. Next day we saw dozens of these kids dressed in the masks. I read somewhere that they wear them to hide their face in shame at the menial work they are doing, but I reckon they were just a group of kids who found a common identity dressing up in the same regalia.

The next day we spent wandering city streets, starting at the fabulous Plaza de Los Heroes and the Iglesia de San Francisco. A steep ascent took us up Sagarnaga into a maze of colourful winding alleyways with markets selling all manner of tourist souvenirs from pan pipes, great and small, to vibrant, colourful stripy llama-wool ponchos and bags. Sadly, they had no Bolivian Hat-glue. Our meanderings took us on through the Mercado Negro with its more utilitarian stalls selling everything from new washing machines to wood screws and on into the *Mercado de las Brujas*, the 'Witches' Market' with its charms, potions and llama foetuses.

The star attraction of the day was a trip to the Coca Museum. Coca leaves have always been an integral part of Andean life. Archaeological evidence shows their use in early civilisations dating back as far as 2500 BC. Chewed or simply boiled as a tea, the leaf provides a mild stimulant effect, much like caffeine, in these hardy climes. The leaves are stripped of their coarser veins, to make them softer, and gently chewed to break the cell membranes and form a pulp. After about ten minutes, once the half crushed leaves are sufficiently dampened, the chewer adds an alkaline agent such as sodium bicarbonate, which provides a medium to maximize the action of the alkaloids from the leaf. The activated pulp has an anaesthetic effect in the mouth, throat and tongue and is useful in the alleviation of pain for a wide range of ailments such as headaches, toothaches, and stomach problems. The absorption of these alkaloids is rapid and it also eliminates fatigue, staves off feelings of hunger, introducing a mild feeling of euphoria and general uplifting of the spirit. The effect of chewing disappears progressively and it is necessary to refresh the leaves to maintain the effect.

Intensive users, such as miners and farmers, chew the leaf up to four times a day when work is hard. For centuries the native people cultivated the leaf and it occupies a central role in their lives, a staple that has always been there, like the snow on the mountains and the llamas on the plains. Although not attracted to the idea of chewing a bunch of raw leaves mulched with baking soda, we did try coca leaf tea and found in it a fantastic remedy for altitude sickness and a great general pick-me-up in the way that a cup of mid-afternoon strong sweet coffee can get you going and lift you out of those post-lunch doldrums.

If this was all there was to the story of the coca leaf then we could happily end here by saying "so that's where your lovely cup of coca-tea comes from, you know that refreshing alternative to tea and coffee we all take each morning to get us going for the day." Remarkably it is illegal today to bring coca leaves into either North America or Europe.

After the Spanish Conquest the Catholic Church, examining native practices, declared the use of coca as unholy and in 1569 decreed its eradication, declaring that the plant had satanic powers, starting a narco-inquisition. There was, however, one big problem with this: miners working the silver mines at Potosi used the leaf extensively. Output fell markedly when the coca leaf was withdrawn, prompting a rapid U-turn in church policy. The Church lifted its prohibition, established taxes on coca and eventually included the leaf as part of its own proceedings. King Philip II of Spain himself declared coca a product for the welfare of the Andean natives. Control the leaf, control the people.

In the late 1800s pharmacists began exploring the anaesthetic properties of the leaf. In 1859, a German scientist succeeded in isolating cocaine as the active anaesthetic component. When the substance was applied to a nerve trunk, it either blocked or reversed the passage of nervous impulses that transmit the sensation of pain to the nerve centres of the brain, without loss of consciousness in the patient. In other words, a ground-breaking local anaesthetic had been discovered. Soon, cocaine derived solutions were applied to dentistry and even eye surgery. It also found its way into a range of pain relieving pills, creams and ointments to treat everything from earache to haemorrhoids. So far, so good.

In 1886 Dr John Pemberton, a pharmacist in Atlanta Georgia, produced a soda-syrup made from a blend of coca leaves from the Andes and cola nuts from Africa. Mixed with carbonated water at a soda fountain, he produced a refreshing, invigorating cold drink. Pemberton sold his shares in the product to entrepreneurs who took Coca Cola on to make it a worldwide brand. They also realised they were inadvertently selling 'The Real Thing' and extracted the cocaine from the drink way back in 1902.

In addition to its anaesthetic effects chemists examined the stimulant effects of the extracted cocaine. Coca leaves were now elevated from a slight pick-me-up gained from chewing a few leaves or drinking the tea to the source of a major narcotic substance. The rest is history, sad history for all concerned. Demand in the developed countries outstripped supply. Poor locals living in Third World conditions were given the opportunity to cash in on the situation. The abundant supply of coca leaf could be taken and the cocaine and its derivatives, including crack, extracted and the poor get rich. Leaves grown in Bolivia and Peru are taken to Colombia for final processing and shipment north to the United States.

In return the US has retaliated with their War on Drugs, which to date has cost billions of dollars with no lasting impact on the trade. Some of these efforts are pathetic. Back in Argentina we dined one evening with an American chap working for the UN who had just been to Colombia, where he was working on a forestry project, trying to persuade local farmers to grow exotic trees, producing hard and precious woods in place of coca. The whole idea was ridiculous. The trees would take years to grow whereas coca was an instant cash crop. The guy said himself it was crazy, a token attempt to do something rather than nothing.

The US, unable to stifle the market for drugs on its own streets, seeks to eradicate cocaine at its source and thus the humble coca leaf has been vilified. At one point it was estimated that eighty percent of the world's cocaine was derived from coca leaves from Bolivia. The US tried to persuade the main growers to halt production and even pressured the government to outlaw the leaf but these are dangerous politics in Bolivia, an unstable country at the best of times. There have been hostile reactions from the locals who resent American intrusions into something that is such a fundamental part of their lives. From their perspective, the coca leaf never did anyone any harm until a white man came along, looked at the leaf, took it apart and sowed the seeds of a nightmare on the world. Now he is reaping the whirlwind.

Over half of Bolivia's population is Indian and a further thirty percent is Mestizo (of mixed Indian and European blood). This leaves a small minority of Criollos (white descendants of the original Spanish conquerors), making around fifteen percent of the total populace, who for years have held all the high and important positions in the country. Spice this up with an overdose of corruption and inefficiency and the country is a tinderbox.

Having lost its coastal access in the War of the Pacific, Bolivia is the poorest country in South America with some seventy percent of its population living in poverty (according to Christian Aid sources, over a third of the country lives on less than $2 a day). The country has always been rich in natural resources such as coal, tin and gold but these resources have been repeatedly exploited by foreign ventures making enormous profits while Bolivia struggles on.

In the year 2000 in the city of Cochabamba, locals took to the streets in protest at the privatization of the city's municipal water supply. It was a crazy scheme, selling a public utility to a private company in such a poor nation (the fact that engineering giant Bechtel of USA held a twenty-seven and a half percent interest in this company didn't help as it was perceived that foreigners were coming in to 'lease the rain'). After weeks of blockade and violence, the Bolivian government ended the water privatization.

Then in 2003, as we planned our trip, the country erupted in a series of violent confrontations over the exploitation of the country's gas reserves. Bolivia's natural gas reserves are the second largest in Latin America (after Venezuela). The cash-poor, state-owned gas company was privatised after which exploration by the new owners found that Bolivia's natural gas reserves were some 600 percent higher than previously thought. A consortium called Pacific LNG was formed from big name gas concerns including BP and Repsol to exploit the newly discovered reserves. A plan costing US $6 billion was drawn up to build a pipeline across the 'lost provinces' in Chile to the Pacific coast, where the gas would be processed and liquefied before being shipped on to Mexico and the United States. To the locals, this whole thing smacked of corrupt politicians selling their national resources for a fast buck.

By October there were widespread demonstrations and civil unrest. Protesters demanded the immediate nationalization of the gas reserves so that all profits could be kept in the country and used for the benefit of the people. They sought clarity in coca laws, the resignation of the president, Sánchez de Lozada, the release of jailed political leaders and justice over the abuse of power by the police and the military. Hundreds of thousands of farmers, coca growers, students, union workers, and ordinary citizens protested, went on strike and constructed extensive road blockades across the country.

Protests were particularly violent in El Alto, where the escalating situation resulted in the declaration of martial law. At 10am on Sunday, 12th October a heavily armed convoy of gasoline tankers escorted by military and police tried to pass through the blockades to carry fuel supplies to La Paz, where the shortage of gasoline had brought the city to a standstill. The protesters in El Alto stood by their blockades. The escorting security forces opened fire from the ground and from the air, where they had a helicopter presence, indiscriminately shooting into the protesters and nearby dwellings. Over seventy people were killed and many more injured. Sadly, the casualty list included a number of children.

178

The next day in La Paz, nearly twenty more protesters were killed in confrontations with security forces but these heavy-handed measures were now drawing international condemnation in addition to uniting the opposition groups. On 17th October, Lozada fled the country, hopping on a plane for Miami. The vice president Carlos Mesa took over with a promise for a national referendum on the gas exportation issue. He also appointed several indigenous people to cabinet posts and promised that no further civilians would be killed by police or military during his presidency.

Such was the state of Bolivia when we arrived in May 2004. At the time we were not aware of all the details, only that in October some 200 people had been killed across the country in violence that would later be dubbed Bolivia's 'Gas War'. In fact the British government had briefly included Bolivia on the Foreign Office list of proscribed countries, places it recommended its citizens avoid, such as Afghanistan, Iraq and Colombia, but by the end of the year it was back off the list. Latest reports indicated the unrest had largely subsided, so we felt it was safe enough to travel there. Now walking around La Paz, we sensed unease and it made us uncomfortable. There was tension in the air. Outside La Paz University, across from our hotel, we saw lots of students lurking around the grounds. Why weren't they at class?

Late in the afternoon we retired to the Café Berlin to grab a quick coffee and rest our feet, tired from padding the pavements of La Paz. We had just ordered the coffee when we were joined by an old man who introduced himself as Fernando Bueno. He sat himself down at the end of our table and asked us where we were from in gasping rasps that gave away the fact that he had smoked all his life. Burnt pork sausage fingers confirmed this as he clasped his hands together on the table in front of us.

"We are originally from Northern Ireland but we currently live in England", we replied.

"Ah! Whereabouts? I know England very well."

"It's a little town called Stevenage…"

Before I could say 'not far from London' he said, "Do you know Dane End?" Of course we knew Dane End; it was a quaint little village near our home and we cycled there frequently over the summer. It turned out he had lived there for a number of years; in fact he was quite a traveller, having spent time in Canada, Australia and London.

Fernando was a fascinating character, fond of the sound of his own voice and we were content to sit there, sip coffee and listen to him. He was a tubby little guy with a round face, podgy round nose and bright round eyes that bulged on their stalks as he talked. A grey-white fringe surrounded his bald, sun-browned pate. He had thick lips and separate nicotine stained teeth that seemed to jump around independent from the rest of his mouth when he talked. He had made the mistake of returning to Bolivia ten years ago and got by now doing occasional work as a technical translator.

"Why do you regret coming back?" we asked.

"The place is a shit-hole," he replied. "Bolivia is a crazy place. Loco. Everybody here is crazy. Country has no infrastructure. Too many poor people, mostly fucking Indians, do nothing but piss and shit in the street and stand with their hand out for a free dinner. I tell you, only ten percent of the population pay taxes. Then, by the time the politicians take their cut, there is nothing left to do anything with. You see the students by the university?" We nodded. "They standing round all day doing nothing. Why? Because there is no money to pay for the university and I don't just mean the teachers' wages. There's no money to pay for heating, maintain the buildings, cut the grass, nothing. Fuck all. Poor bastards haven't been in class since January so they hang round the streets all day and join the protests and strikes. Like the one coming Thursday."

"Sorry, a strike on Thursday?"

"Yes" he replied. 'The new government raise the price of petrol so the transport workers union call a one day strike. Wait and see, the students'll join in and the whole place will come to a grinding halt. Like I said, Bolivia is crazy!"

We tried to change the subject and asked him about where he lived, his travels and life in other places. Fernando liked only to talk about himself and his present world and what a shit-hole Bolivia had become. I tried to lighten things a little by asking him how the Indian ladies keep their hats on their heads, mentioning our invention of Bolivian Hat-Glue. He frowned and said, "I tell you how they keep their hats on their heads... Don't fucking wash. Never fucking wash and anything will stick to your head!" By now we were tired and uncomfortable listening to this incessant racist diatribe so we said our goodbyes and left.

Although he had been annoying, what Fernando said about a strike on Thursday was troublesome news. It was clear that Bolivia was still very much in turmoil and we had a restless night. Outside on the streets students, were throwing the occasional firecracker and we nodded off to their distant pops and cracks. Then, in the small hours of the morning, we were disturbed by bigger explosions. Coming from Belfast we know the sound of a bomb in a city. Later we found that the protesters like to liven things up by tossing sticks of dynamite procured from the miners. In the morning we went down, gritty eyed from our night of unrest, for breakfast. There was an armed policeman at reception.

"What's he here for?" I asked.

"For your protection," the receptionist replied.

"Sorry? Why do I need protection?" I asked, a little alarmed at this.

"For the protest tomorrow. We recommend you don't go far today, but go and buy some food and water, maybe enough for two or three days. Tomorrow it is best if all guests stay in the hotel. The policeman will be here and it is *'peligroso'* on the streets, especially for *gringos*."

Considering out options, we remembered passing the British Embassy the day before and decided to go there and check for advice. They were useless. Staffed by local Bolivians, they took our names and passport details with the address of the hotel we were staying.

"To inform your next of kin," the girl said. I thought this was a joke but she was deadly serious.... "In the event that anything happens." Mild panic set in. We tried to find out if this protest bore any commonality with the events that led to the violence last October. "Well it did start the same way but this is Bolivia, you can never tell what will happen next."

We could try and sit out the strike here in La Paz, but it didn't seem a clever idea in the event there was any escalation as the focus of any unrest would undoubtedly be centred on the capital. Our options were twofold: retreat back to Chile, or ride north to Lake Titicaca and the border with Peru. Walking back to the hotel we stopped by an agent who organised mountain bike, river and hiking tours out from La Paz. The guy was brilliant and calmed our fears now bordering on full phobia since talking to the Embassy staff. He told us that we could travel safely today. Tomorrow, we should definitely not travel or go sightseeing during the protest march scheduled for midday. Apart from that it was a relatively minor dispute, even if it was nationwide, with only the transport union and the students and should blow over. In the end we packed and left for the lake. Out of the hotel we rode past the university, the pavement lined with hundreds of police and military with shields, CS gas and riot sticks at the ready, faced off by a phalanx of students now wearing ski-masks or scarves pulled up over their lower faces. We rode though the silent stand off. Time to get out of Dodge.

Regarding the outcome of the Gas War, on July 18th 2004 the referendum took place. Voters were asked to choose yes or no to five questions concerning the gas issue. They included increasing revenue with a new plan, using the gas to regain access to the sea from Chile and looked at how profits from gas exports could be used to develop schools, hospitals, roads and jobs. The referendum split the opposition. The main workers union and the farmers union were opposed to it while the coca workers and socialist movement supported it.

When it came to referendum day seventy-five percent of the voters said 'yes' to all five questions, a surprising result. The opposition claimed that most voters did not understand the convoluted wording of the questions, which were loaded to confuse the uneducated voter into making a 'yes' vote. More crucially, the referendum had sidestepped the all important issue of re-nationalization of the gas as an option, leaving the door still open for corporate exploitation.

In May 2005 a new Hydrocarbons Law was enacted, raising government profits from the gas from sixteen to thirty-two percent. It was not enough and the protesters took to the streets once more by the tens of thousands. Mesa resigned and was replaced by Evo Morales, the first indigenous president of Bolivia. On 1st May 2006, Morales finally signed a decree stating that all gas reserves were to be nationalized. He also halved his salary and increased the wages of teachers and health workers. He gave foreign companies a six-month 'transition period' to re-negotiate contracts or face expulsion but taking care to state that the nationalization would not involve confiscation. By late 2006 negotiations between the Bolivian government and the foreign companies had reached agreement, giving the government massive revenues from the gas fields. The government profit now stands at over sixty percent and it is estimated that the government's energy-related revenue for 2007 will rise to $780 million, a nearly six-fold expansion from 2002.

We rode back through El Alto and took the road to Copacabana. For Maggie today was a red-letter day. All her life she'd harboured a burning ambition to go to Lake Titicaca. What is it about that name *Lake Titicaca*? A funny name for a place for sure, mildly rude in a comedic double-entendre sort of way, yet managing to sound exotic, a proper ultimate destination, a remote goal far off the everyday map. Maybe it's the fact that it is the highest navigable lake in the world that is the attraction, a geographical 'summit' to be attained?

It surely sits with that pantheon of exotic places with alien names like Timbuktu, Serengeti and Kathmandu, dreamy Xanadus that can only be reached by travelling dangerous and adventuresome paths. Destinations that fire the imagination and ignite passion in the minds of all travellers. Places we must all strive to one day reach. Whatever the attraction in the name and in spite of all the trouble, today was a dream come true. Just an hour from La Paz and we were there and my girl was the happiest girl in the world. She confessed later to having the odd tear in her helmet as the lake hove into sight and we rode along its shores.

But unknown to both of us in this state of lakeland euphoria, up ahead lay the scariest twenty minutes of our lives. Actually, the water before us was not the main body of the lake but that of its major subsidiary, Lake Huinamarca. It is separated from the main lake by a narrow strait at a place called Tiquina. Our road map showed a connection across the strait, maybe a bridge or at least a ferry. We rode into the little village and there at a lakeside ramp was the ferry waiting. Even better there was a funny little old man, wearing a nice red baseball cap and a big toothless smile, to wave us on to the ferry, a small flat barge open at one end and big enough to carry one small bus or two cars. It was already loaded with a little Toyota Hi-Ace minibus.

"Room for two more, this way if you please…"

I was so preoccupied with following the directions of the pleasant little ferryman that I failed to pay attention to what I was getting onto. We mounted the ramp and onto… The 'deck' was formed from sun-dried, sea-weathered, splintered planks thrown loosely over the ribs of the boat's hull. Between the planks were huge gaps… Holes big enough to lose a wheel down! We each picked the widest available plank and rode onto the barge. We were now fully loaded with the Hi-Ace van up front and our two bikes behind, side by side. It had gunwales on three sides, reaching about eighteen inches above the loose plank deck. The only good thing I can say about the ferry was that it was painted in that nice blue colour.

Once onboard, we couldn't get off the bikes. There was nowhere to put a sidestand down and we couldn't dismount without falling into each other on the inside or falling overboard on the outside. The deck planks were bowed too, so the bikes wanted to roll forward and we had to keep our front brakes on. Looking down, a big gap on my left begged me to put my foot in it just so it could snap my ankle off when the bike toppled. Oh, and if the bike toppled it was going to keep going right overboard to be lost at the bottom of Lake Titicaca.

Just as we had come to terms with our teetering predicament the real fun began as the ferry cast off and started moving. We crossed the narrow neck of water broadside on to the waves, so it ploughed across, bobbing up and down and side to side like a crippled arthritic turtle. If you have ever sat relaxed on a bike and somebody suddenly grabs the rear end, it induces the most horrible panic that you almost dropped the bike. That's how this ferry was, the whole way across. Twenty minutes that put years on both of us.

I managed to get both feet firmly planted but still, the weight of the bike was constantly shifting and the ferry was working on this to try catch me off guard. Maggie, she was screaming good, some of it even in Spanish… *"Señor, Señor, socorro! socorro! peligroso, peligroso!* Will you please grab my bike! I'm going to fall over the side, Ayeeeee!" The wee man with the red cap appeared, as if by magic, smiling and having a good old chuckle. Probably seen it all before. He grabbed the front end of her bike to steady it, assisted by the driver of the Hi-Ace.

By now my own eyes were closed tight. The Hi-Ace van was bouncing around like crazy. It started as a minor oscillation, down one side, up we go, down on the other and so on. But by mid-crossing the amplitude had increased to the point where the vehicle was travelling to the full run of its suspension, up and down, up and down. The next stage would see it start bouncing on its tyres, maybe bounce back over us? Best keep those eyes shut.

Finally a bump and a final lurch (I screamed louder than Maggie this time) announced we'd arrived at the far side. Panic over? Well it would be once we got off the ferry and to do this we had to go back the way we came on. The bikes had to be pushed backwards and down a ramp. To add spice, the ramp on this side was more of those crappy planks with added scope for falling off or breaking that ankle. Ferryman and Hi-Ace driver helped me waddle off, where I dismounted and returned to get Maggie off.

Back on dry land we prised her off the bike and then had to restrain her. A crowd of German tourists crossing on a little bus on a similar ferry had circled round to watch the fun. I looked up to see them all stood, hands in their pockets, smiling. Not one of the swine came over to help us in our moment of extreme distress. Luckily for them there were no missiles nearby or she'd have had them. They probably wrote later in their travel journals that they saw something 'very interesting' at the ferry today.

Beyond the terror on the ferry lay a just reward, what is known in motorcycling terms as a great 'scratching' road. It climbed away from the water with gorgeous overviews of the sun-spangled lake and took us bending and twisting over green hills reminiscent of the mountain section at the Isle of Man TT races. We took off, whooping and swooping until some unfilled pot-holes right on the race line reminded us these roads were dangerous and best to slow down.

We arrived in Copacabana mid afternoon and, leaving Maggie with the bikes up in the plaza, I set off to find us a room. My grin on returning to the bikes told how I had just secured a beautiful lake view room with a balcony, the best room in the house, at the Hostal Leyenda. The building was a basic concrete block built three-storey structure fronted with arched balconies. The outside walls and archways were festooned with rustic Inca decorations, characters and statues, cast in concrete to create a wonderful if kitschy Andean atmosphere: a pretty garden out front and Titicaca just across the street.

When Maggie saw the room her face lit up with delight. She was at her dream lake with a room to match. A huge bed faced out towards the balcony so we had the delight of sunsets over the lake from the pillow. The room also harboured a sofa styled like one of the traditional lake boats made from totora reeds and a pair of cane rocking chairs out on the balcony. Copacabana was a treasure and a place we would find hard to leave. At 3800 metres we even felt acclimatised to the altitude and settled down for a dreamlike stay at our new found Nirvana.

The strike affected Copacabana only in that the roads in and out of town were closed. Otherwise the place seemed oblivious to the protests. Fortunately in La Paz the proceedings passed peacefully, the clash between the military and the students defused with no serious casualties reported. We were up on the lake now and abandoned all plans to go back into Bolivia. The country was beautiful but for us, at this moment, a little unruly; we would press on to Peru. It seemed too that we had *'saltado la sartén por dentro el fuego'* (think levitation, frying-pans and fires). Latest reports said that the bridge we heard about back in Arica was still blocked, our next obstacle up the road. But for now we could forget the strikes and the blockades and settle down to enjoy the lake.

Chapter 14: The Lake

We spent five nights in the little town of Copacabana up on Maggie's Lake. The bikes were secured in an enclosed grassy yard belonging to the hostel, with a few hardy Andino sheep for company. The little town was full of backpackers and fellow travellers so there was plentiful company and tall tales at dinner. The centrepiece and main draw for this little town on the lake is the Basilica of La Virgien de Copacabana, patron saint of Bolivia. The virgin in question is Mary and the Basilica contains a 16th century, four-foot high statue of the lass made of plaster and maguey fibre. The effigy is dressed like an Inca princess robed in gold with jewels on her neck, hands and ears. The famous resort in Brazil was named after this Copacabana, when a replica of this very Virgin was installed at their church.

It is a beautiful building, blindingly white outside with Moorish tile work trimming arabesque doors and archways. We padded the cool interior of the basilica, watching silently as little hunched-over women prayed to the Virgin for assistance and the spectacle reminded us instantly of others we had seen enacting similar rites at the non-secular shrine to Difunta Correa in Argentina. I have to confess, all this idol worship sits uncomfortably with me, coming as I do from a Protestant household. Why should the church condemn one of these idols yet build a huge basilica to house and glorify the other? The people seem to worship at them with equal conviction, so I guess they both service a need.

Bizarrely, you can also get your car serviced at the Basilica. Every Wednesday and Sunday the Basilica is the site of the bizarre spectacle of 'La Benediciones de Movilades' (the benediction of the vehicles). People arrive from far and wide with their cars, vans and minibuses, freshly washed and all decked out in flowers and ribbons to have them blessed at the home of the Virgin, a sort of divine tune-up and MOT. We strolled through the Sunday morning proceedings, watching a taxi from Peru and a private car going through rites that appeared more pagan than Christian.

An old shamanesque woman started the proceedings as she leant over the open bonnet of the taxi-cab waving a smoking incense burner, mumbling a strange incantation and ching-chinging little finger cymbals, thus blessing the exposed vitals of the engine. A man followed her, chanting prayers, sprinkling holy water and flower petals on the said components while the old woman moved on to do the wheels, brakes and body work of the car. When the car had been purified, cleansed of evil-spirits and the patina of divine protection reapplied, the family and friends all celebrated by spraying Paceña beer, champagne style over the driver and his wife. Then everyone piled into the car and drove off to the lakefront, where we later saw them picnicking at the end of their grand day out. All very colourful and curious, but I was horrified by the thought that the 'blessed' vehicles can presumably now be driven without regard and essential vehicle maintenance ignored, as surely these are mere trivialities compared to the protection offered by the Virgin of Copacabana.

With the last vehicle 'benedicted', we mooched around the various stalls outside the cathedral selling effigies of the Virgin: medals, stickers and the like. Quite a few of the stalls were well stocked with toy cars, miniature houses and toy money, the idea being that you take one of these into the church, have it blessed by the Virgin and then surely some time soon you will get the real thing: a new car, a new house, or loads of money! One stall sold toy soldier packs and toy guns. It makes you wonder, who on earth would want a blessing on artefacts such as these? Some of Bolivia's up-and-coming politicians?

Copacabana is overlooked by Cerro Calvario, standing 400 metres above the town and topped by a little chapel reached by an ancient stone stairway. We took a late afternoon climb up the long 'stairway to heaven', instantly shattering the illusion that we had somehow acclimatised to the altitude. At the top we settled down, finding our own little space amidst a party of rather fat nuns to contemplate the views over the little town before the sun turned Titicaca into a tureen of blood. The lake is fringed with a frozen froth of mad whipped mountains and we espied the Isla Del Sol.

We took a day long boat excursion out to explore the island, taking a breathtaking (both literally and physically) three-hour walk along the Camino Inca, an old stone road that crests the island, stopping to mooch the various Inca ruins along the way. The Incas believed the sun was born on the island and it was from here that Inti, the Inca Sun God, ordered Manco Capac, the first Inca ruler and his sister-wife Mama Ocllo, to emerge from the depths of the lake near the island and travel north by means of underground caves and tunnels to found and establish the city of Cusco, heart of the Inca Empire.

Our tranquil holiday in Copacabana came to an end. Unfortunately, for all its lake-town delights, Copacabana suffered from that Bolivian blight of dodgy politics. We saw a crowd ranting in the plaza outside the cathedral on Friday evening, a throng of blaring loudhailers punctuated by the vicious snap of firecracker bangs. On enquiring what the problem was, we found out that there had been some trouble with the *Alcalde*, the local Mayor, allegedly something of a crook. According to the stories circulating round town, he had recently been tried for his sins by the local jurisdiction and sentenced to four years in jail. Eluding jail, he was currently holed up in the town hall where he had broadcast on local radio to his supporters in the surrounding communities for help. He had also thrown a bit of money around and events had escalated to the point where the people of Copacabana, the biggest community in the region, were now aligned against the Mayor's supporters from the surrounding area, hence the protests in the plaza.

A similar dispute with a mayor existed in Ilave up the road in Peru; only the people there had advanced to more direct action, blocking the bridge on the main road, the Pan-American Highway. Ilave, next stop on our ride north was the place those Austrians on the KTMs back in Arica had warned us of, where they made their lengthy desert detour.

The road skirted Lake Titicaca from Copacabana across the Peruvian border, where it ran all the way to the River Ilave. Here a long trestle bridge spanned the river and deposited the road into the town of Ilave itself on the far side of the crossing. Since arriving in Copacabana we had been closely monitoring the situation. In the beginning protesters had blocked all access to the town; travellers took the bus from Copacabana to the blocked bridge where they dismounted and had to walk through the blockade, over the bridge and through the town to pick up the Peruvian bus on to Puno at the other side of town. It was a seven-kilometre walk and entrepreneurial locals exploited the situation, hiring themselves out as porters.

The protest was now in its fourth week and the blockade at the other side of town had been removed; travellers now only had to cross the bridge itself to collect the follow-on buses waiting at the other side. On enquiring for information on the situation at Ilave and whether it would be safe for us to go there, we were presented with a hundred different scenarios. Everything from the roadblock being some light, barely manned affair that we'd be sure to be waved on through, to a wall of steel that spelled death for all *gringos*. The facts were that the road was blocked and we probably couldn't cross the bridge, but we might be able to ford the river in some way. On our last evening in town we chatted with some bus drivers, who seemed to be the best source of information. They gave us cause for optimism: the protest was nearly over and the bridge could even be open tomorrow.

Monday morning, we set off for the eight-mile ride to the border. Customs formalities were quickly sorted, with the Peruvian officers warning us that we might well be turned back. Yesterday we'd met two Argentine guys on a Honda and a Kawasaki. We felt bad as we ruined their day by telling them about the likely fun up ahead (they had no idea of the situation and had just finished a pleasant lunch on the lakefront when they met us). The Peruvian customs guy said sure, they came through yesterday and hadn't returned, which could be a good sign? We had sixty miles to mull over this information as we rode round the lake.

It was a beautiful morning ride under a top-of-the-world cloudless sky with the blue lake sparkling on the horizon. The Peruvian countryside seemed a lot more orderly than Bolivia. People working the little farms seemed happier and waved to us as we rode along through pleasant lakeland fringed with soft green mountains reminiscent of a beautiful Scottish Loch. The road was empty; hardly a surprise considering it was blocked up ahead. It was a perfect day for motorcycling until a litter of rock chicanes and burned out tyres across the road announced that we were approaching Ilave. A short incline led into a log jam of buses and vans setting down or extracting passengers from an infusion of baggage porters, hawkers (all those grannies selling drinks and snacks) and townspeople just down to watch the fun. We became helplessly caught up in the press of flesh and metal until a path opened for us onto the dirt track by the bridge.

Clear of the melee we dismounted to survey the situation. The bridge was a simple steel I-beam construction of four or five sections made of stark red-leaded chunky girders that shone brightly against the backdrop of blue sky. It rested on a number of concrete trestles across the wide but shallow flowing river and looked more like a rail bridge than a road crossing. One thing was for sure: we were not going to ride across. The town of Ilave lay on the far side, an untidy sprawl of whitewashed dwellings that spilled down to the river.

We chatted with the two guys about trucking the bikes across. They confirmed that they had successfully ferried the two Argentines the previous day and I went off on my foray with the deaf and dumb guy to explore the road under the bridge, the one blocked by the artic' as related in the prologue to this account, to see if we could get the bikes down off the high earth embankment.

Meanwhile, Maggie chatted with a group of kids, who asked her ceaseless questions about the bikes. 'Where are you from?' We come from Ireland. Do you know it? Maybe you heard of it in school? 'What's this for?' That's the horn, see... mink, mink. 'How fast is your bike?' Oh, on a good day it does about 100 mph 'Wow! Whose bike is the quickest?' Oh, definitely mine. My husband is tubby and his bike is much, much slower. 'What's your name?' Maggie, what's yours? 'How old are you?' Oh, let me see now, last birthday I was seventeen...

The bikes had by now gathered a smattering of colourful stickers accumulated from the various places we had been and the kids were fascinated by them. One very serious looking young chap introduced himself as William. He was eleven years old and asked about the writing on the panniers. 'What does it say?' Maggie read it out to him, pointing at the words... *'Pan-American Adventure 2004! From Chile to Alaska for Cancer Research UK'*. Maggie explained our journey, where we had travelled, where we planned to go and that we were doing it all to raise funds to help sick people get better.

I had just returned when Ilave erupted with the crowds of angry protesters rushing for the bridge. We joined the general evacuation and fled along the dirt road. Arrived at our new halt the other bystanders, mostly women and small children, seemed friendly and, sensing our unease, told us we would be safe here with them. They were fed up with the whole business and it was good that things were coming to a head today. They didn't care much for their mayor, a guy called Robles. It seems he was a bit of a crook and had refused to resign, so the bridge was blocked and had been for the past 25 days.

William reappeared. He told us now about a ford down towards Lake Titicaca, maybe we could cross on the bikes? We asked the kids for more information and received the full gamut of responses from the gloomy pessimism of *'Oh no señor - Esta muy peligroso'* (it's very dangerous!) to the smiley, optimistic *'Oh si, si, si! En Moto, No Problemo!'*, leaving us with the impression that this second crossing might be anything from a shallow ford that we could ride safely across, barely getting our tyres wet, to a raging, rushing white-water torrent ready to send us and the bikes to some horrible watery end. At this point one of the adults intervened to end this nonsense – the ford was clearly impassable for motos. William, having been dismissed by his elders, wandered off.

Ilave seemed to have emptied its population onto the bridge and we could hear the distant garbled din of lunatics wailing on loud hailers, now and again drawing cheers or hurrahs from the crowd, along with enthusiastic bouts of stick, flag and placard waving. After about twenty minutes or so of this, it all got a little boring and our little crowd of bystanders slowly dispersed. A figure on a bicycle approached from the bridge. Daniel was fifteen years old and stopped to give us a 'thumbs up' and a big smile when he saw our bikes. He wore blue work jeans and a blue sweatshirt with the trademark logo 'CAMP' written large across the chest. All of his clothes were filthy black with what looked like honest dirt and we guessed maybe he helped out at a Gomeria.

He told us it was crazy on the bridge; everyone was very angry and it was best to stay back here until it all calmed down. We mentioned the ford. His face lit up and he said, "Sure there is a ford and you could easily get across on your bikes." He offered to show us the way. A hasty council of war and we agreed there was no point in lingering any longer. We were trapped and the crowd on the bridge showed no signs of dissipating. We could at least go look at the ford and decide for ourselves whether it was to be our salvation. With a big smile Daniel led the way, elbows out, legs pounding the pedals, as he showed off on his bike. We struggled to keep up on our fully loaded motorcycles, as they bumped and bounced along the track.

The track ended, spilling onto descending farmland that ran for at least another kilometre down to the river. A path seemed to run into the river and out the other side so it looked like there was indeed a ford. But to get there we had to traverse a series of ploughed fields where a number of women were at work with rakes and hoes. Daniel assured me that there was a route through and we could get the bikes down easily. It looked risky so Maggie waited with one bike while I took the other on a test ride down to the ford.

We zigzagged down narrow little footpaths that bordered the first couple of fields. I rode slowly, in first gear all the way, feet down paddling on occasion to shift the heavy bike through muddy and rocky sections. Then we traversed one of the fields, the bike crashing and battering its way across a sastrugi of dried mud furrows until we picked up a smoother, sandier path, the last obstacle before the river. This led into a big sandy rut, like a bunker on a golf course, flanked on either side by tall grass-topped embankments that reached up over my head. I took a run at it and slithered and slathered out on to soft white sand. About half way across the bike stalled and sank up to both axles. I sat there, sweating like an adrenaline-fuelled bastard, totally exhausted by my exertions, but the stuck bike was the least of my problems.

Suddenly there was a burst of angry shouting from the embankment above my head. I looked up to see a sharp-faced, stringy, mean-looking man, who I took to be the landowner, standing over us, his vicious appearance enhanced by the curled cattle whip he fingered in his hands as he raved. I tried to talk to him, to calm him down and explain our predicament but he told me to shut up. Having claimed to speak only Quechua, I listened to him rant. There seemed to be an awful lot of Spanish in his diatribe, in which he berated Daniel for bringing us to the ford.

Crazy farmer wanted to know how much money we were paying. Daniel protested his innocence, saying he was only trying to help. I dismounted, the bike stuck upright in the sand, not sure what to do next. Should I negotiate a price for crossing the man's land? He now flung his arm out in the direction of the bridge, veins throbbing on his spindly neck and flecks of white spittle flying from his lips as he insisted we turn back. He seemed upset at the fact that Daniel was helping us break the blockade. Maybe there were principles involved here? Offering money might only inflame the situation.

He was now hopping from one foot to the other, fidgeting with that whip in his hand, looking like he was getting ready to come down and deal with us, when the strangest thing happened. From out of nowhere the young boy, William, appeared up on the grass embankment beside the man. He explained to the angry man that he had to help us. The farmer raised his hand as if to strike the youngster who recoiled but held his ground. He reiterated that the man had to stop this and help us cross the river. Why did he have to help us? he fumed at William, why?

William explained, slowly but clearly, that we were 'medicos' working for a Cancer Charity, that we were good people and he had to help. "Is this true?" he asked me. I told him yes and pointed to the pannier stickers, the ones that Maggie had explained up at the bridge. With that the man's whole demeanour changed. He dropped the whip and jumped down into the bunker, indicating that I should get on the bike and he would help push me out. I fired her up and, with the aid of Daniel, William and a mad farmer, made it through and down to the entrance to the ford.

Meanwhile Maggie had been waiting with her bike. She had watched my nightmare ride across the fields and saw me disappear into the sand bunker. Some of the women working in the fields had shouted at her, telling her to go away and she was a tad anxious. Eventually I reappeared on foot and my smile gave away the fact that I had made it to the ford. We got the second bike down and made preparations to cross.

Unlike at the bridge, the river here was quite deep. The mad farmer sat back and watched as William and Daniel helped us ride across. I had read a little of river crossings prior to the trip and to be honest was keen to have a go. However I had imagined riding through a bubbling little brook, the bike making a nice little splishity-splash, parting mountain-fresh waters that just about covered the wheel rims, as I rode smoothly across just getting my boots a little damp. The reality now was that I would be riding through water that came over the top of those boots, almost up to seat level on the bike.

Daniel and William had stripped down to their undies and led the way, showing me a safe path. It was about 300 metres across the river and the ford ran in an arch shape. My bike first and I proceeded slowly across guided by the two boys, staying in first gear with my feet down, ready to catch the bike if she should stall and using the clutch to pull her across bit by bit. The bottom alternated between slippery smooth round stones, that had the wheels slipping and sliding, and soft sandy sections that grabbed at the wheels, trying to make the bike stick fast. I also had to counter the force of the fast flowing water that pressed ferociously against the bike, especially when broadside on to the flow.

Near the far side I stalled in a sandy hollow and lost my footing, nearly dropping the bike. But the aluminium panniers helped to steady things, acting like floats to keep the bike upright. The two kids rushed over and helped me regain my footing and the bike restarted to pull me on and out of the river. Crossing on the second bike was easier as I had a little more confidence and used more power on the ride across. Maggie meanwhile had been ferrying our baggage across. It was exhausting work as the river reached up to her thighs and threatened to topple her at any time. Getting ready for her last crossing, she had a tap on the shoulder; it was the angry farmer, who proceeded to carry her across on his back.

Pausing to empty the river from our boots and wring out our socks, we were elated. We bade farewell to William, that brilliant little kid who had saved the day. He stood there all serious looking and watched as we rode off, following Daniel on his bike. On crossing the river Daniel looked worried and insisted on guiding us around the outskirts of Ilave to the road, all the while casting anxious glances in the direction of the town centre and mumbling something about it being wise to avoid there today. He took us around the broken back streets of this shabby and desolate place until fifteen minutes later we were back on tarmac that would take us to Puno, with the bridge at Ilave safely overcome and well behind us.

The short ride to Puno was completed with some slight discomfort at the wet feet from the river crossing but fortunately we suffered no further delay. Today's adventures were well rewarded with a lovely little hotel in Puno, the 'El Lago', with smiling friendly staff who helped us unload our bikes and put them away safely for the night. The manager sent up a pot of coca leaf tea and we certainly appreciated its revitalising powers that afternoon.

That evening over dinner in a snug warm restaurant we felt ten feet tall. We had run up against a formidable obstacle and managed to circumvent it. Reliving it all over a bottle of wine I felt like I was some kind of Indiana Jones, outwitting the evil baddie with the whip before plunging on my bike into the river, now magnified to a raging torrent and probably half full of Piranha. I replayed the story, half riding, half swimming across the croc infested waters to barely make it alive to the other side. Undoubtedly our journey would next lead us to the discovery of some fabulous lost Inca treasure, requiring us to negotiate and disarm a series of cunning traps involving pointed sticks and large boulders, and eventually fight off a bunch of secret Nazis before claiming our reward.

In truth the whole success and forward progress of our trip had depended today upon the actions of two children. It is almost unbelievable that we entrusted our whole trip to the hands of an eleven and a fifteen year old. If someone had told me beforehand, 'you will reach an angry protest at a blocked river, but don't worry, two kids will see you through alright,' we probably would never have left home. William and Daniel shine as two of the brightest stars of our Pan-American adventure. There was an honest sincerity in both these young boys, who behaved and acted at all times out of a basic desire to help strangers in need. We were both close to tears when we said an emotional farewell to Daniel. Contrary to what the farmer may have thought, neither he nor William asked for any payment or reward for their help and we had to forcefully insist and press some money upon them when we parted.

Today was also the first time that our Cancer Research fundraising impacted directly on our journey. When William told the angry farmer about our cause and what we were doing, he transformed instantly and remarkably from a deadly opponent to our best friend and ally. I have never witnessed anyone undergo such a rapid U-turn in personality and demeanour. William was stretching the truth when he said we were doctors. We used the Spanish expression '*un fundación contra cáncer*' to describe the Cancer Research charity and I guess to the simple workings of a child's mind it is doctors who work to fight illness and disease. More importantly, he recognised us as two caring souls trying in our own way to make a difference in the world. The angry farmer saw that too; we were no longer just two 'rich *gringos*' out for a bit of a holiday.

In the morning I awoke, still on a high, and we showered, dressed and went down for breakfast. A lazy day around Puno after yesterday's excitement sounded good. No bikes, no protests, no rivers, no playing Indiana Jones. We sauntered downstairs, strolling outside to briefly look in on the bikes before breakfast. The hotel manager was outside having a cigarette and we nodded and exchanged *'buenos dias'*. The bikes were fine but looking around I noticed that the national flag over the front door was flying at half-mast, as was the flag over the post office across the street. I asked the manager what the occasion was. "It's for the *Alcalde* at Ilave," he replied. "The people there, they kill him yesterday." We froze as the shock horror of this dreadful news sank in.

"But we were there yesterday. It was just a protest at the bridge," we explained.

"No. Not just a protest. The people dragged the mayor out and beat him to death. If you were there yesterday you are very lucky to be here today."

After breakfast we went out and bought a newspaper. The large headlines read *'Fue Una Masacre!'* The cover picture was of a naked dead man on a stainless steel mortuary table, his face swollen horribly, his body beaten black and blue.

The dispute at Ilave was settled that Monday morning, 26th April 2004. Frustrated at the stalemate at the bridge, the protesters decided to force the issue. A crowd estimated at between ten and fifteen thousand people, mostly Aymara Indians and including many people from surrounding villages who were camping in the town for the duration for the protest, gathered in the town plaza to demand Mayor Cirilo Fernando Robles resignation over allegations of corruption and failure to deliver on campaign promises. Robles was captured in town along with some of his supporters. They were severely beaten, after which Robles alone was paraded through the streets and further beaten until he collapsed outside the town hall. His body was then carried down to the blockade, to the eye of the storm, where it was thrown from the bridge.

After lynching Robles, hundreds of demonstrators laid siege to the main police station where three protesters, suspected of inciting violence during the blockade, were being held under arrest. The fifty besieged officers fired off all of their riot ammunition, rubber bullets, CS gas etc to stall two separate attacks. They maintained a panicky radio contact with the interior minister in Lima and asked what to do in the event of some horrible final onslaught. Their last orders were not to surrender their weapons, to 'Do what you have to.' Then, the radio went dead. In the end, the mob succeeded in gaining entry to the lower floor of the police station and released the three prisoners. The police officers retreated to the second floor before heavy reinforcements arrived and dispersed the crowd with tear gas.

We wandered the streets of Puno in a state of shock. The crowd we had seen rushing out of town onto the bridge obviously contained the mayor's killers and they had his body. Then the assault on the police station; this was all in progress while we were negotiating the river crossing, yet we knew and heard nothing of it until after the event. Small wonder Daniel took us on such a circuitous route around the town. It was as if he knew Ilave was a bad place to be that day and now, in possession of the full story, we are even more indebted to those two kids for saving us.

Peru was in a state of national shock and the story remained in the headlines for days. We asked around, enquiring if Robles was a bad man. Was he corrupt like the Bolivian mayor of Copacabana? Most people we spoke to claimed he was no better or worse than any other small town politician and certainly did not deserve this fate. He was a duly elected public representative. There did not seem to be any major scandal associated with the man and he was Aymaran, so racial prejudice was not the issue. In Ilave, heavy police and army reinforcements arrived and broke up the blockade, dispersing the protesters. The following day, the bridge re-opened.

Further research after the event tells a sad and sorry story. As mayor of Ilave, Robles governed the surrounding province of El Collao, a rural area up on Lake Titicaca, encompassing 180 mud-walled villages. An orchestrated campaign had convinced the peasants that their mayor had stolen public funds (a charge never proven) allocated for projects to rebuild a collapsed bridge over the Ilave River and construct roads linking the town with some of their villages. They blocked the bridge, welding road signs to form their impassable barrier and demanding Robles resignation.

The Aymara have a strong traditional community ethos: steal from one, steal from all sort of thing, so any perceived criminal intent is met by a group response. Entire villages emptied, coming to town to enforce the blockade at the river. They were joined by all manner of external trouble makers, including Bolivians promoting Aymaran nationalism, old 'Senderistas' from Peru's Shining Path terrorist movement and others associated with unsuccessful uprisings elsewhere in Peru. Throw in some personal rivalry in the form of the deputy mayor, Alberto Sandoval, a rancher who had been a rival of Robles since the two men were in college together and who now wanted him removed. It was alleged that Sandoval plied the peasants with alcohol and coca leaves to keep them in town, all the while stirring up hatred against the mayor.

The protest escalated and Ilave radio stations inflamed the anti-Robles hate campaign. Two weeks previously, Robles had already fled from the hostile crowds in Ilave to Puno, the regional capital. He was warned by a colonel of the National Police not to return until tempers cooled. Some of the more level headed residents tried to draw the attention of mediators and government to the escalating crisis. Eventually, a delegation went to Lima, where they were refused admission to the doors of the National Congress and turned away at the office of the President. No one was interested in these petty squabblings amongst some bunch of Indians in some remote backwater far away from the capital.

Meanwhile, the brains in Ilave came up with a strategy to remove Robles. By law, if he failed to attend three consecutive council meetings, his position could be declared vacant. Five members of the council opposed to Robles quickly convened two meetings in his absence. Before they could hold the third, Robles announced he would return to Ilave and hold his own session at his sister's house with the five council members still loyal to him. He arrived at his sister's home just before dawn on 26th April. He was doomed.

He felt he had to return to prove he was not a crook and demonstrate that he had done no wrong. When the protesters realised Robles was back they were inflamed, whipped to a fury by a local radio station broadcasting news of the council session and urging everyone to prevent it. Hundreds gathered, trying to break down the door to the house while masked men climbed onto the roof before breaking in. The mob rounded up the pro-Robles council members found hiding under beds in a neighbouring home. They were assaulted and taken to other villages, where they were later released. Robles was found hiding in a closet. He was beaten and then dragged around town past his various works projects, including the collapsed bridge he had promised to replace.

Back in Puno Robles' wife, who had been in contact with his sister throughout the morning and was fully aware of the assault on the house, frantically phoned authorities in Ilave and Lima for help. The police commander in Ilave told her he had not received authorization to intervene and his officers remained in the police station throughout, guarding members of a government reconciliation commission that had belatedly arrived in town. Witnesses said the mayor already looked half-dead when the mob brought him to the plaza. He had been beaten to a pulp, by some accounts stabbed, and another individual was seen whipping him with his own belt. They forced him to walk up the steps of City Hall and placed a microphone in his hands and demanded he speak. He stood up, uttered the words "I'm sorry, forgive me," before collapsing, his head making an audible thud as it struck the concrete steps. The crowd then took the lifeless body to the river and dumped it by the broken bridge.

The individuals within the mob that day, captured on video beating the man to death, look unlikely to see any retribution for their actions. Forty two people were formally charged with killing Robles. It was difficult to pin a murder on any one individual; how do you prove who inflicted the killing blow? A year later, only Sandoval remained in custody, under open house arrest.

The problem is that the whole town is complicit in Robles' death and police are reluctant to make further arrests. The head of the National Police, when questioned on this failure to arrest suspects, said the police are 'waiting for the appropriate moment' to apprehend them. On top of this the government is trying to play down the whole incident, in fear that the town will explode in violence again. Even the mayor's small band of allies believes, reluctantly, that none of those indicted will ever be convicted.

From the perspective of our trip, the bridge at Ilave was a traumatic experience. For the next few days we relived it over and over, this time with the added knowledge of those horrific events going on elsewhere in the town as we made our river fording. We had witnessed, first hand, human beings at their best and at their worst. Death at the hands of a mob is an especially horrific way to end a person's life. It happens in Europe; occasionally you hear about a soccer fan caught in the wrong place at the wrong time, kicked to death by gangs of rival supporters. Back in March 1988 we had spent a normal Saturday afternoon shopping in Belfast. Coming home we were debating what to have for dinner when I switched the TV on to catch the afternoon's football scores. There was a newsflash with some story about two off-duty British soldiers accidentally driving into a republican funeral procession in West Belfast. TV cameras recorded the soldiers being dragged from their car, beaten by the crowd, and then shot dead by the IRA. These were brutal images and shocked the world and the good people of our home city to their core. How can 'civilised' people turn so savage so quickly, to set on and tear apart a fellow human being, whatever their beliefs and loyalties?

In Peru, the 'what ifs' haunted us. What if we had arrived half an hour earlier and made it on to the lorries in the river? What if they got us across and unloaded us to ride straight into the mob? What if the kids hadn't been there that day to show us the ford? What if we had arrived a day later? The protest would have been over and the bridge would have been open. What if every town up the road in Peru turned into an Ilave? On this last point we were reassured by the shock-horror reaction of everyday Peruvians that this was not a normal occurrence or something they endorsed. At the end of the day we had ridden unknowingly into what amounted to an inter-tribal feud, a power play between two rivals that had gone completely out of control. For all the horror of the day, it was a local issue and thankfully it was all behind us.

From worries and troubles in La Paz, we had fled to a peaceful haven at Copacabana, where the wheel of fortune rolled on, dumping us into the mayhem at Ilave. Now at Puno things were on the up again. We finished our time at Titicaca with a day trip out to the Islas de Uros, the famous reed islands of the lake. This group of some forty floating islets is home to the Uros people. Welcome to reed world. Everything substantial on the islands is crafted from reeds: houses and furniture, sunshades and shelters, the watercraft that sail the lake and not forgetting the very islands themselves beneath our feet.

The islets are made of a dense mat of totora, a reed native to the lake. They must undergo constant maintenance, since the islands exist in a perpetual cycle of decay and replacement as the bottommost reeds dissolve and rot; meaning new reeds must be added to the top to compensate and maintain the mass of the island. Legend has it that the Uros created the islands to flee from the Inca, who dominated the area at the time, taking to the lake where they could live undisturbed by mainland events. There are an estimated 3000 descendants of the Uros alive today, of whom a few hundred still live on the islands. Although the Uros live off the lake through fishing and hunting, a substantial portion of their income today is from tourism.

Our lake cruise-guide gave us a run through the daily life of the Uros, which can be harsh and severe. Living in proximity to so much water is a cold and damp existence and most of the older folk (read 'middle-aged') suffer horribly from rheumatoid and respiratory conditions. A chubby lady approached our guide.

She was beautifully dressed in a geranium pink frock with a blue shell jacket embroidered with tasteful little multi-coloured collar, epaulettes and cuff bands. She sported a soft brown bowler, again perched impossibly on a mass of inky-black pleated hair with no visible means of attachment (not even a glue line barely visible just under the rim). She offered to be our steerswoman for a short boat ride on one of the totora reed craft.

Fourteen of us clambered aboard something that looked like a big floating banana made of bits of straw tied up with string. The lady clambered aboard at the stern where she wielded a huge oar-rudder in a sweeping motion that propelled and directed the course of the boat. It felt like we were putting to sea on a burst sofa. Back on straw land, several of our party needed to pee and were directed to a flat extremity of the islet with a low woven fence for privacy. Poos are retained, dried out and burned rather than pooping into and polluting the lake.

From Uros, we boarded our tour vessel and sailed on to Taquile, a substantial lake island, 45km from Puno and our destination for lunch. Taquile was part of the Inca Empire and its remoteness made it one of the last locations in Peru to fall to the Conquistadores. The Spanish colonists banned the wearing of traditional dress and the islanders adopted the Castilian peasant dress still worn today. On landing we ascended a horrifically steep Inca staircase, a flight of stones that climbed up the hillside, taking us through terraced farmland and into the little village community at the heart of the island. Here we lunched on delicious quinoa soup followed by some Pejerrey (Kingfish) from the lake.

The island life is again harsh and somewhat abstract. The women do all the heavy, backbreaking menial work such as digging, weeding, tilling the land and so on. The men, well… all they seem to do is sit around all day knitting and weaving. As we walked into the village we passed small groups of them, sitting on sun-kissed stone benches, nattering amongst themselves, enjoying the *craic* as they knitted away. They were turning out mainly *chullos*, those zany little Andean earflap caps, for the collective craft market in the plaza. What a life!

It took three hours for the boat to return to Puno, three hours of sunshine cruising on the highest lake in the world, this most fantastic destination. Titicaca is beautiful and our visit here will certainly be memorable. High waters, high anxiety, high expectations and high jinks all rolled into one. We dozed a while on deck, nudged into slumber by the gently swaying motion of the little boat, faces smothered in sun block, snuggled up in warm fleecy clothes. The highest lake in the world. A while later the boat changed direction, heading back into the reeds that mark the approaches to Puno and a changing wind awoke us from our snooze. We looked across at each other and Maggie smiled, just for me. We had been married for over twenty years and she didn't have to say a thing. She knew, that I knew, that she knew, we were living the best days of our lives.

Chapter 15: On the Trail of the Incas

From Puno it was an easy day's ride to Cusco. The road ran north leaving Lake Titicaca and by mid-morning we were riding through the hustle and bustle of Juliaca, a colourful little market town along the way. Beyond Juliaca the road ran into increasingly desolate wild mountains imbued with an ancient atmosphere that sang to us of our Celtic homeland. The road climbed up and on, past snow-capped highland peaks, hauling us over the Abra La Raya pass at 4338 metres (14 200 feet or 'three and a bit' Ben Nevises, gauging it against the highest mountain in the British Isles).

Riding through steep terrace-farmed valleys we reached the huge Inca gateway at Rumicolca, engineered and built by the Huari, predecessors to the Inca, who dominated the lands of Peru from around 500 to 1000 AD. Originally an aqueduct, the Incas converted it into a massive gateway barring the major southern route to their capital. It remains an impressive sight. Red stone walls run from the sides of the valley to link three imposing stone towers blocking the central course.

We left the bikes standing dwarfed at the foot of the towering gateposts and set off to explore this formidable obstruction. The towers were squat five-storey terraced-pyramid structures around forty feet tall and they stood there like sentinels guarding the approach to some Jurassic Park. The stonework was warm and ancient, easy to differentiate the original crude Huari walls from the smooth mortarless stone cladding applied later by the Incas.

Rough stones had been left protruding diagonally up the walls, forming a steppy-stone stairway ascending to their narrow grassy-terraced tops.

Sat atop the biggest tower, we enjoyed commanding views up and down the valley and lounged in the sun awhile to wonder at this most definitive barrier across our route. The wall and towers must have taken years to build and it seemed like an awful lot of effort to block just one of many valley accesses to Cusco. It looked like it was built to keep something awful out; maybe an Inca King Kong or some other such monster once roamed the land around Titicaca. Either that or the Incas were just real show-offs and built the gates to impress travellers heading north into their heartland. The gates certainly worked their magic on us and we rode on awestruck with heightened expectations as to what other Inca treasures lay ahead.

Legend has it that Inti, the Sun God, gave Manco Capac a golden rod up on Lake Titicaca and set him off on an Andean quest to found a new city. Manco journeyed high up into the mountains and after a period of fruitless searching he came upon a spectacular location in the Huatanay river valley. When he tested the ground the golden rod was immediately consumed, a sign from the gods that this was the site for his new capital. Successive rulers expanded the city state to its climax around the early 1500s when the Spanish arrived. Pizarro's men described the city as being as fine as any city existing back home in Spain. One of its palaces was said to contain a garden where every single tree, flower petal and blade of grass was made from solid gold (which was quickly melted into ingots and carted off to Spain to engorge the royal coffers).

We arrived early on a bright and sunny Thursday afternoon, greeted by streets lined with soft Inca stonework supporting limewashed low dwellings that radiated the warmth of the sun.

212

Sagging terracotta roofs slung from gable ends like lazy hammocks, inviting us to slow down and slouch. We liked the place immediately. The city had a 'let's get ready for the weekend' feel to it as we bumped our way down cobbled callés trying to orientate ourselves in this cauldron of over a quarter of a million people set high (3400 metres) in the Andes. We found a room in the 'Hostal Palacio Real' where we were met with the warm smiles of Victor, the manager, who ran the place with his family. We rode the bikes into the glass-fronted reception and parked them in the cool and cavernous dining room where they would stay for the next week or so as we set off to hike the Inca Trail.

It took four days to formally process the access passes for the Trail, giving us time to acclimatize in Cusco. We spent lazy days wandering the labyrinth of twisting ascending alleyways and narrow streets, taking pleasure in getting lost in the Inca capital. Every now and again the cobbled streets spilled out into sleepy plazas lined with churches, museums and galleries. The architectural styles were a blend of mainly colonial baroque interspersed occasionally with soft fine rounded Inca stonework. In some places colonial upperworks were simply plonked on top of an original Inca base.

Across the city a profusion of red-white-red banded Peruvian national flags fluttered idly in the light breeze interspersed with what we initially took to be the gay pride banner, that rainbow-striped flag that announces just about every gay bar in the world. We found out later that in Peru this rainbow flag is known as the 'Tawantinsuyu' and is the modern banner of the Incas and city flag of Cusco. This bright and vivid flag is a fine representation of the Cusqueños, who we found to be a cheery lot, whether we were declining ludicrous offers from smiley shoe-shine boys to polish our canvas and rubber walking boots, or issuing 'no-gracias' to the toothless old women trying to flog us knitted water bottle carriers, belts and *chullos* all embroidered with little llamas, condors and other Andean imagery. Millinery too had undergone some subtle changes. Gone were the drab black and brown business bowlers from Bolivia. Retaining the bowler design, dazzling chalky whites and soft light browns were the chapeau of choice for the ladies, while for the *señors* white cowboy hats were all the rage.

Cusco is pleasantly blighted with all the trappings of a big tourist city, with Irish Bars, English Pubs, Italian Pizzerias and American Burger Joints but we found they complemented the atmosphere rather than dominated it as they do on the Spanish Costas. Our first night in the Plaza Des Armes saw it choked with people, most of whom turned out to be touts for various bars, clubs and restaurants. On arrival of 'fresh *Gringo*' they descended like a plague of flies and we readied ourselves to fend off their enthusiastic onslaught.

The first wave was loud and vocal, thrusting flyers and handouts onto us, at the same time trying to out-shout each other to gain our patronage for their particular 'best in Cusco' venue. They brought us to a halt and we were quickly surrounded. Next, the second wave from the restaurants; the heavy bombers armed with huge menus shouting out the dish-of-the-day, 'cooked specially for you with the cheapest prices in all of Peru'. Menus were thrust over the heads of the flyer crowd and we were ducking and diving, slowly buckling under the onslaught. Quick thinking, I shuffled my armful of flyers, picked the brightest and most colourful and began counter-touting, trying to force leaflets back on the touts, mimicking their cries of '*Buen Precios*' and '*Muy Barata*', confusing them long enough for Maggie to cut a break and take flight across the plaza.

I hastily followed with a tail of touts hot on my heels. They had just completed their second encirclement when I caught sight of two familiar, friendly smiling grins heading our way. The crowd parted to admit two tall and incredibly pretty girls, who set about instantly taking their pick from the handouts, dismissing the rest who retreated broken and defeated. It was Corinne and Alison, two of the backpackers we had met on the Isla del Sol up at Copacabana. Travelling through South America, Corinne from Washington DC and Alison from Oz had met shortly before arrival at Lake Titicaca and teamed up for this leg of their respective journeys. They had arrived several days before us and were waiting for their trail passes. Of more immediate importance, they had sussed how to deal with the touts. Alison explained that some of the handouts were for complimentary drinks and definitely not to be refused. The girls had been living it up, touring the bars and clubs, getting inebriated on free booze including our favourite, Pisco Sours. And there was I, an Irishman, refusing free drink!

Over the following nights we hit these Cusco hot spots and rather than training hard for our forthcoming trail, we instead worked studiously on getting rather drunk, rather a lot. In the lively company of back-packers like Alison and Corinne, in a range of rowdy establishments all serving cheap (when not free) Pisco Sours, it was difficult not to. On an early visit to the Plaza Des Armes I was contentedly scanning the facades of the buildings that line the massive square, taking in the myriad of arches, embellishments, portals and finely festooned *fenêtres*, when I spotted a 'Norton' motorcycle logo. This led us to the 'Norton Rats Tavern'. Run by an American called Jeff, a biker and Norton aficionado, the 'Rats' is a weird joint: a biker bar in a city with no bikers. Large cc motorcycles are prohibitively expensive in South America, where they are taxed as luxury items. All of the bikes we had come across on our travels to date were invariably ridden by other foreigners or super-wealthy locals. The bar itself was lively, with dartboards, pool tables and a claim to serve the best burgers in town. The walls are covered with fading photos from Jeff's own two wheeled travels round the globe. The best seats in the house are out on the slim balcony tables where you can sup suds and peruse the Peruvians on the Plaza down below.

One night, while quaffing in the 'Rats' with the two girls, Corinne let out a yell. "Hey look you guys, it's the Pirates!" She disappeared into the crowded bar, leaving us to wonder just how many Pisco Sours it took to produce this effect and what on earth she was on about. All was revealed when she returned to the table trailing two sun-bronzed and finely-muscled young men. We were quickly introduced to Mattheus and Martin whom the girls had met in an Irish bar the previous evening. As introductions were made and we cleared a space for them at the table I took in their dress. Both sported black leather waistcoats, double breasted with twin rows of snazzy silver buttons, over black and white stripy long-sleeved vests. This ensemble topped some long black pants and scruffy boots. Spotty neckerchief headdresses, loopy gold earrings and stubbly beards completed their costume. Corinne had been absolutely spot-on in her initial description: they were indeed two pirates.

Mattheus and Martin were from Germany and members of an 800 year old brotherhood of craftsmen. Since the Middle Ages, German craftsmen have gone *'auf der Walz'* (taken to the road): a working-pilgrimage that artisans make after completing an apprenticeship with a master craftsman. These travels last for up to four years and one day (depending on their chosen craft) and are meant to teach the apprentices all about work and life. While on the road, they are not allowed to return to within fifty kilometres of their hometown. Each journey can take these young, trained craftsmen and women anywhere in the world. On their travels they have only their '*Zunft Kluft*' (their tradesman's uniform, the 'pirate' outfit) with a small backpack containing their tools and their trademark '*stenz*', a handmade walking stick. They earn their keep on the road by applying the skills of their chosen trade and must take care to uphold the honour and tradition of their craft at all times.

Over a few drinks in the 'Rats' we found Mattheus and Martin to be charming, witty and very sociable. Their main draw was their costumes and they delighted kids everywhere, pretending they had lost their pirate ship full of treasure and enquiring as to whether anyone had seen it? We found ourselves smiling at them all the time like a couple of kids ourselves, totally taken in and mesmerised by their dress and adornments, believing that we were somehow talking to a pair of roughtie-toughtie pirates over a bottle of rum, rather than a couple of guys off a building site. Their every move held fascination. Even when they paid for drinks we all double checked to see if they paid in silver doubloons or 'pieces of eight' and were mildly disappointed when they used Peruvian '*Nuevo Sols*' like the rest of us.

Mattheus was a carpenter and Martin a joiner, complementary skills enabling them to travel and work as a pair. They built houses, Mattheus doing all the big jobs; doors, stairs, windows, wall partitions, etc while Martin did finer work, such as furniture making and detailing. Since leaving Germany over three years ago, they had worked on projects in Switzerland, Austria and Norway and now their journey would end in a few months time, here in South America. They looked forward to their homecoming; neither had seen their families since they had been away. They obviously relished their travels and their training must surely be one of the best foundations for any life. They stayed with us for a few drinks before drifting off to the next bar on their nightly tour of Cusco. When they left I pondered what mysterious convolutions these travels take us through. Here we were sat in a biker bar in a city with no bikers, high up in the mountains a long way from the sea, making idle conversation with two German Pirates with no ship. Who would ever believe it?

Alison and Corinne set off for the Inca Trail a few days ahead of us and the bar seemed emptier without their lively presence. This was probably a good thing as it made us concentrate on our own preparations to get ready for our hike to Machu Picchu. Two days before we were due to set out, we had a practice walk to explore the various Inca ruins outside the city, taking a 20 km hike out to the old fortress of Puca Pukara. We began by climbing up ever narrowing, ever steeper streets of the city to reach the remnants of the zigzag stone battlements of Sacsayhuamán, the huge Inca fortress that overlooks Cusco. Sadly, today only the lower parts of the great walls remain, together with a large grass parade ground, that is still used for festivals and open air concerts. The Spanish dismantled their uppers to (a) obtain materials for the churches and dwellings they built in the city and (b) remove a potentially dangerous fortress from their midst.

During the conquest of Peru the Pizarro clan at one point found themselves cut off in Cusco, under siege by a vast Inca army. The beleaguered Spanish decided that their only hope of salvation lay in capturing the fortress. Juan Pizarro, one of the junior brothers, rode out with fifty horsemen, breaking through the Inca siege cordon at full gallop. While the actions of the Conquistadores were generally deplorable, one cannot but admire their raw courage at Sacsayhuamán. The ascent from the Plaza to the fortress is a stiff climb and the Spanish rode in what must have seemed a death ride, smashing every Inca barrier and obstacle in their way. Consider too the effects of the altitude and they must have been exhausted when they arrived up on the fortress plateau. One can imagine them forming up, catching their breath for a moment and looking in horror at the awesome citadel before them. The dismantled walls today remain an impressive obstacle; what must they have been like in May 1536 when they had their full complement of towers, turrets and bristling battlements; all fully manned by thousands of jeering natives, taunting the Spaniards to 'come and get it'.

Juan Pizarro formed his men and charged the mighty fortress. They succeeded in fighting their way through to the main gate, where they were driven back by a hail of stones, rocks and javelins hurled from the mighty machiolated walls. Juan Pizarro was killed, struck on the head by a rock hurled from the battlements above and the remnants of the assault retired to a small nearby hill where they spent a restless night, burying their leader lest the Incas gain heart from his demise. Over the night, the Incas received 5000 reinforcements; the Spanish were reinforced by twelve additional horsemen under Hernando Pizarro and spent the next day in their defensive position constructing scaling ladders.

That night they flung themselves against the walls. Individual Spaniards gained the battlements and once ensconced became killing machines. Iron and steel crushes flesh and wood every time and an estimated 1500 Incas were put to the sword in the fortress in the ensuing fight. The outcome of the battle was no longer in doubt. By the end of the following day the Spanish held Sacsayhuamán and their victory broke the spirit of the besieging forces, who now began to melt away. The Incas (basically a stone-age society) stood no chance against Spanish guns, germs and steel.

Inca stone-masonry is world-renowned but seeing it here up close, along the ruined battlements of Sacsayhuamán was astonishing. There is no attempt to create a uniform sized block and then lay this in some orderly fashion. No two stones are the same size or even shape and the stones are laid haphazardly and uncoursed. Yet there is a beautiful symmetry in this unevenness and the masonry obviously has inherent strength, as evidenced by the fact that it has withstood successive earthquakes, while colonial architecture has come crashing down.

From Sacsayhuamán we wandered along quiet roads to the ruined temple of Qenko with its carvings, altars and zigzag channels in the rocks said to have once funnelled sacrificial blood. At the end of the road lay the smaller fortress of Puca Pukara dominating yet another valley as it approaches Cusco. The views were splendid; as was the best stonework of the day at Tambomachay, a set of incredible Inca baths and water features, not to be confused with the Glaswegian hard-man of the same name.

At long last, our own Inca Trail started. The Inca Trail is part of the old network of roads by which couriers travelled to spread the will of the *Sapa Inca* (the emperor) and brought news back to the capital from the periphery of his empire. The forty kilometre hike is spread over four days, through the awesome Peruvian Highlands over passes reaching up to 4200 metres (13 500 feet), culminating with a visit to the famous ruins of Machu Picchu.

A bus picked us up at 7:30am on a sleepy Wednesday morning and we drove first to the busy Plaza San Francisco where we were immediately beset by a mob of Indians in a sea of upturned expectant faces: prospective porters looking for work. The cook, already on the bus, reached into the crowd and tapped heads of the lucky individuals who boarded, big smiley faces showing their delight at having gained employment for the next few days. It reminded me of stories my grandfather told me of the shipyard in Belfast where thousands would turn up at the gates each day and the gang foremen would come out to select who would work that day, a system open to corruption where many men paid the foreman a cut of their wages to guarantee a day's work. Thus was assembled our small party of eleven hikers, two guides, a chef and fourteen porters.

We climbed switchback roads out of the city, through somewhat run down suburbs and on into the mountains. We chatted with one our fellow hikers, Gerald, a 57-year-old gentle giant from Wisconsin on his first trip outside the US. He seemed a little concerned about what the next few days held in store, confessing to us that he had never hiked or spent a night in a tent in his life. Gerald had reached that point in life so beautifully portrayed by Jack Nicholson in the movie '*As Good as It Gets*', where the star poses the title of the film in a question, asking: did you ever wake up one day and ask yourself is this all there is to life? Is this all I will be? Is this as good as it gets? Gerald had asked this question and decided no, there had to be more. His wife didn't understand or wasn't interested so he found himself in a travel agent, booking a trip to 'somewhere exotic'. The young travel agent asked him where he wanted to go. He hadn't a clue and asked for suggestions. While pondering her recommendations he had noticed a poster on the wall, of an ancient city of jungly ruins with spectacular mountains all around. "Where's that?" he asked and that is how he came here to walk the Inca Trail.

The first day was a relatively easy four-hour walk to break us in to our new life on the trail. We followed a narrow winding path along the Urubamba river valley with a stop for a lunch of soup and pasta with a cheese sauce. The walking was easy, everyone stomping along at their own pace, and in the afternoon there was a brief ascent to an overview of the huge Inca terraces at Llaqtapata. Occupying a strategic crossroads in the river valley, the site is a nodal point on the old Inca trading routes leading on towards the Amazon and towards Machu Picchu. From our lofty perch we could make out the myriad of farm buildings in addition to houses and religious sites. As we were relishing the views in the afternoon sun, our porters had yomped on to set up camp for the evening in the 3000 metre high village of Wayllabamba. The cook further displayed his culinary skills in the evening with a stunning dinner of mussel soup, followed by trout with vegetables and rice, and ending with a delicious dessert of hot jelly tasting like spiced wine.

Day Two is notoriously the most difficult of the trek with a tiring slog of an ascent over the 4200 metre Warmiwanusca or 'Dead Woman's Pass'. The day started well with a 6am wake up in the tent by a porter bearing a cup of hot coca leaf tea. Breakfast consisted of fruit salad with yoghurt, porridge, pancakes, toasted rolls and tea, certainly one of the finest breakfasts we had in all our travels in South America. The ascent was surprisingly gentle, especially for me with my dodgy legs and podgy belly. I just took my time, aided by walking poles, to haul myself up the steep path and enjoyed a great morning's walk. The views from the top over the massed peaks of the Peruvian Highlands were simply fantastic. For me, the worst part of the day's hike was the descent down the other side of Warmiwanusca taking us down steep rocky paths with steps of up to eighteen inches in places. These descents jar and tear at knees and ankles and I was glad of the poles to take a little of my weight.

Today's trek ended around 2.30pm with a fabulous campsite perched on some terracing near the ruins of Runkuraqay. We lunched on soup followed by 'Chicken-a-la-King' with rice and then siesta'd under canvas, contentedly lying there with the tent flaps wide open. The terraces afforded breathtaking, uninterrupted views down the valley from the warmth and comfort of our sleeping bags. We lay there watching lost world clouds create a stunning array of vistas as they alternately covered, veiled and tantalisingly revealed the distant mountains. By 7:30pm it was pitch black and we stumbled over to the small tent where our party assembled for dinner. Tonight we dined on beefsteaks in gravy with roast potatoes and a hot chocolate dessert; loads of calories but hey, we needed them.

Day Three was an easier but longer walk and again started with the now yearned for coca leaf tea in the tent. One of the girls in our group was celebrating her birthday and the cook had made a chocolate covered sponge cake piped with cream for breakfast. How on earth he accomplished this using only a two-burner gas cooker is beyond our comprehension, but needless to say the cake was delicious and was eagerly woofed down by the group, along with all the other breakfast goodies.

We had a great morning visiting the ruins of the eagle's nest of a fort at Runkuraqay and then on to Sayamarca on another rocky outcrop overlooking a jungly valley. Our guides attempted some further explanations of the mysteries of the Inca world to us. The problem with interpreting the Inca ruins is that a lot of it is guesswork. The Inca civilisation left no written history and was systematically destroyed by the Spanish in their search for gold. All that remains today are the lifeless stone ruins. The purpose and function of the various forts, temples and dwellings along the trail can, for the most part, only be guessed at.

Lunch consisted of soup, chicken legs, various salads and spaghetti, taken in the dining tent, hastily erected when some low cloud rolled in. On emergence from the tent, the scenery had all but disappeared and we set off on the last leg to yet more precipitous ruins at Puyupatamarca, eerily spectacular in the murk. Today was a long haul and the paths took on a more jungly appearance as we entered the cloud forest nearing our goal: Machu Picchu. The descent from Puyupatamarca was another torturous Inca staircase, jarring on the knees with the added misery of stone steps rendered slippery by a light afternoon rain.

The third and final campground was at the hostel at Winaywayna. After a chicken dinner we met the cook and all his porters and presented them with a tip for their efforts. There was also beer to be had at the hostel and a party was in full swing when we got there but we were due for a 4am start on the last day and this put paid to any thought of an evening of excessive drinking. After one beer we turned in, dozing off to a gentle tree frog lullaby augmented by the light percussion from the patter of a light drizzle on the tent.

The pre-dawn wake up on the last day saw us off to reach Intipunku, the Sun Gate. This stone gateway, set across a saddle between two mountains, overlooks the ruins of Machu Picchu. This culmination of our four-day hike promised to be one of the highlights of the whole trip. The idea was to get there early and look on in stupefied amazement as the sun rose to illuminate the single most famous landmark in all of South America. The sun would shine like a beacon through Intipunku, slowly burning off the night time vestments of darkness and shadow, picking out first the highlights of the ruins and tantalisingly revealing, stone by stone, this wondrous Inca monument. By the dawn's early light we would 'ooh' and 'aah' in unison with our trekker mates, while worrying about the light settings on the camera, fretting lest it's too dark and we get shuddered, blurry recordings of the unveiling ceremony. As the ruins were fully exposed, we would probably indulge in a round of tearful hugs and back slapping in celebration of a glorious and successful hike. Then we'd all trot off down to explore the site in all its glory before the hordes of day-trippers arrived by train from Cusco. That was the theory anyway.

A groggy 4am breakfast of pancakes and coca leaf tea was scoffed followed by a two-hour hike in which we slithered along wet jungly paths, faintly illuminated by head-torch. The light bedtime drizzle had evolved into a penetrating and miserable mizzle and we were all thoroughly cold and dripping wet by the time some ghostly rocks poked out of the murk, announcing our arrival at the Sun Gate, a misnomer today if ever there was one.

It seemed like every trek party on the trail had gathered for the occasion with everyone shuffling and jostling for the best position to see the unveiling of our destination. As the sky slowly lightened to the east we all turned our heads west and stared into…well, into oblivion. The hollow in the mountains in which Machu Picchu is set, over which we had struggled to gain this point of supreme advantage, was completely socked in under a layer of dense jungle cloud. There was no Machu Picchu. It had been packed away neatly in cotton wool for the day. As the sun rose higher in the sky, it only confirmed that the ruin was gone, disappeared, completely buried in cloud, totally obscured, refusing to come and show itself.

After the sunrise fiasco we set off tired and frustrated into the cloud valley to the city itself. We walked as ghosts through quinoa-soup cloud-fog, our first exposure to the ruins by touch as we ran our hands over smooth Inca stone. Our guide tried his best to perform his tour… "If you look over here, on a clear day you would see…" But today it seemed we would see very little. We couldn't believe it. Machu Picchu, 'the Lost City of the Incas' and the highlight of all

South America was lost once more. It was like Iguazú Falls with the water turned off, or a melted Moreno Glacier. Threatening rain drove us indoors for a top-up breakfast and some coffee to take the edge off the damp chill. Condensation ran in little rivulets down the inside of the windows of the cafeteria making outside seem even murkier.

I pondered this landmark we had hiked for four days to see. The *Sapa Inca*, Pachacuti is thought to have built Machu Picchu in the mid 1400s, possibly as a family home or as a summer retreat. Others have postulated that it was a royal palace, a holy place, a temple or maybe even a place of learning, an Inca university. With no written history, its true purpose has not been handed down. Although it is only some fifty miles from Cusco, the Spanish never found Machu Picchu. It does not appear in any of their records and the city was abandoned at the demise of the Incas, remaining hidden from the outside world until 1912 when the American explorer Hiram Bingham rediscovered it.

By the end of our breakfast, revitalised by the caffeine intake, we emerged outside to find the sun high in the sky and the last wisps of the cloud-cover boiling off into the morning blue. We peeled off layers, waterproofs first, then thermals, and our jaws dropped as Machu Picchu was finally revealed at last. The most impressive feature is the overall location. The city was built on top of a mountain (Machu Picchu means 'old peak') surrounded by other, higher peaks, most notably the sugar loaf Huaynu Picchu (young peak) which dominates all the postcard photographs of the location. The lofty jungle covered mountains offer incredible views down to the snaking coils of the milk-coffee Urubamba river miles away in the valley below.

There are some 200 dwellings in the complex, ranging from small private dwellings up to larger temples or palace constructions.

The city was never finished and we visited on-site quarries where stones had been cut and polished. The masonry work is astonishing, considering that the hardest metal available to the Incas would have been copper. They cut stones by chiselling a series of holes across the cut (probably using obsidian or tools made from other harder rock). Wet wooden wedges were driven into the holes and heat applied, the thermal expansion of the wooden in-fills eventually pressuring a crack across the cut. A huge stone block, neatly prepared with a line of holes cut and ready for the firing process, lay on its side at the quarry as if abandoned only yesterday, begging the question: why did the work stop?

We meandered the streets and alleyways of the lost city and eventually made our way up to the Guardsman's Hut, the highest building in the complex and viewpoint for all classic panoramic photographs of the site. Surveying the complex, everything seemed incredibly neat and orderly. Freshly scrubbed stone buildings lined immaculately manicured emerald lawns and terraces, a far cry from the overgrown jungly mess that Bingham found. The site reminded me of Edinburgh Castle with the roof missing; indeed I fancied that if you roofed the dwellings and installed the doors and windows it would be ready to move back in.

I think it was the absence of any colourful history or background that disappointed most. There are no details of who built it, how or why this remote location was chosen, what purpose it served or anything of the individuals who lived and died here. The place lacked any real context and today all we can say of it is that it is here because it is here. Would that some Pizarro had descended on it with his plague of metal monsters from the Sun Gate, catching its sleeping denizens unaware in the morning gloom, putting the place to the sword before despoiling the city of its treasure hordes.

Or that it was the place from where the *Sapa Inca* finally fought back, the mountain fortress where the conquistadores were turned, finally defeated in battle by mighty Inca legions spewing forth from the mountains to drive them into the ocean. See here the very plaza where the captured Pizarro converted to Inti sun worship before he was sacrificed to the Sun God in thanks for deliverance from the Spanish devils…

We descended from Machu Picchu in the afternoon to the tourist railhead at Aguas Calientes. Here we said our farewells to the members of our little hiking group as we disbanded and took the train back to Cusco. We left Gerald contemplating another visit to the travel agent to look at other posters. Maybe Egypt or India next time? The spirit-lifting hike through the Peruvian mountains in such fine company will remain with us for the rest of our days and Machu Picchu, for all its attempts at hiding from us, and even its lack of history, turned out to be beautiful. It is a dream location, one of those top-ten-places-in-the-world everyone would love to see and a place that gives you the itch to travel. We had now scratched that particular itch and as we arrived back in Cusco another itch had taken its place: the desire to return to the road on two wheels and travel further in this South American wonderland.

Chapter 16: North Thru' Peru

On the map, the 350 miles down to the coast through Abancay to Nazca looked like nothing special, an easy day's ride. It proved to be one of the truly great motorcycling roads on this planet. The road had recently been completely tarmac'd and consisted of lashings of curvaceous hardtop, delicately ladled through some of the finest mountain scenery imaginable. Slalom plunges off the altiplano, chasing chasms cut in the Cordillera by turbulent rios as they rushed deep into the ruddy crust of the Earth. A switchback, hairpin Nirvana where we seldom had the bikes upright, bends so tight you felt you were in danger of being overtaken by your own rear wheel.

The rear brake saw constant use to bleed speed coming into the tight corners, grabbing that rear wheel halfway through the bend, making sure it stays planted at the back of the bike. Near Abancay I braked for the umpteen-thousandth corner that day when the pedal gave way and sank to the floor. Luckily I had no spectators to witness my botched recovery as I sat the bike up and teased the front brake to bring me to a halt. My rear brake had totally failed. The brake fluid had reached its boiling point through repeat usage, causing a vapour lock, rendering the brake useless. I let the brake cool for a few minutes until its performance was restored. I'll swear the saddle cover was pinched where my puckered ass had gripped it.

We found a grand old hotel in Abancay with some splendid Poinsettias on the front lawn, you know, those red leafed plants traditionally given to mums as gifts at Christmas? Here in Abancay they were fully grown trees, simply stunning in their scarlet foliage. Locals gathered to chat with us at the front of the hotel as we unloaded the bikes. We had come from Cusco, yes? We confirmed that we had indeed travelled from the city. On our new *camino*? It is such a wonderful road isn't it? It has brought such prosperity to Abancay. What did we think of it? The smiles on our faces spoke volumes of what we thought of their road and we were amazed that people would be so proud of a piece of hardtop.

Day two of the ride to the coast was, if such a thing were possible, even better than the first. It began by charging alongside the Apurimac River through a deep golden crevasse, criss-crossing occasionally over little Bailey bridges. We left the river and looked up at the mountains ahead to see a wicked zigzag scar slashed up and over their flank, the road ahead that hauled us over a 4200 metre pass and onto one of the most desolate sections of altiplano we would witness. Indians wrapped in blankets topped by bowlers waved as we sped straight across this barren moonscape, leaving us wondering how on earth they eked an existence up here on top of the world.

The only bad section of the whole ride was at a miserable little town called Puquio where, after refuelling at the outskirts, we were immediately dumped onto streets that looked like they were made from ploughed concrete. Fortunately the smooth *pavimiento* returned on the far side of town and we sped on towards another 4300-metre pass, green on one side, brown on the other, as we now rode the final leg to the coast. It was a case of 'best till last' as the road scratched through baked brown desert, the landscape softening as it rippled like coiled coffee cuir forever down to the sea. Switchbacks abounded again on our descent into furnace heat.

We could see the road for some distance way below us as it spiralled and tumbled crazily out of the mountains. We also spied what looked like a white motorcycle stopped by a small van. Shit! A bike cop... Hope he doesn't stop us for a bribe. As we drew nearer to the scene, a crazy woman ran out, waving her arms for us to stop. She was smiling and clearly elated at our arrival. So we met Miki, a young Japanese girl embarked on a round the world tour on her horribly overloaded Harley Davidson. She was riding out of the mountains enjoying the view, when she hit a pothole and the bike died, spluttering to a halt. The sun was setting and she was fearful of being stuck out here alone in the mountains in the dark. Some locals had stopped to help but there was little they could do; the bike was too big to fit in their van. A quick check revealed a total electrical failure and a search for the main fuse, the possible culprit, proved fruitless. In the end a bigger lorry half full of potatoes, with a human cargo on top, came to the rescue. The people on the back dismounted and once the problem was explained they simply man-handled the 600 pound motorcycle up off the ground and onto the lorry, where it lay nestled comfortably amongst the sacks of spuds. Miki rode up top on the lorry and we followed, crawling along in its diesel fumes at 20mph for the remaining few miles into Nazca.

With the bike unloaded and the three of us ensconced in a cheap but noisy hotel, we took Miki out for a pizza, small compensation for her misfortune on the road today. Over dinner we learned that she had travelled from Japan to Vladivostock then rode across Russia into Europe and now South America. She was tiny, not an inch over five feet tall and something of a techno gadget freak with a snazzy looking personal organiser that emerged from her bag of digital accoutrements to record our email address. Next morning she organised a pick-up truck to take her and the bike to Lima, where there was a Harley shop. We met her later in Ecuador, where she told us the failure was due to a fractured connector on the ground lead to the battery, killing all power to the bike.

We left Nazca to ride north along the coast to Lima. Big long roads, 'straighter than a preacher, longer than a memory' were the order of the day and we blasted along through mile after mile of sand and rock desert highway. By late afternoon we had reached the quaint seaside town of Paracas, site of a National Wildlife Reserve on the Pacific Coast. The town itself is quite small with a pleasant promenade lined with a handful of seafood restaurants and a few hotels. Travelling off-season we had the place to ourselves.

The friendly Hostal El Amigo offered clean rooms and the best pergola in Peru atop its flat roof. Swung from its beams and columns were a dangle of hammocks that quickly snared us in their nest of nets, forcing us to imbibe Pisco Sour from a frosted glass, while sinking back with a good book, interrupted only by the irritation of having to watch a hot red sun sink into a shot-peened sea. With the last 'oooh!' of the sunset and the last 'aaah!' of the Pisco Sour expired, we set out to explore Paracas in the dark, in search of eats. We limbered up with a post hammock stretch and yawn, before shuffling sleepily out of the hotel towards the seafront.

The soft lights from the array of eateries illuminated the inky dark night along the promenade, their pavement tables inviting us to come and dine on the best the Pacific has to offer. I was firing up my Pisco-pickled brain, running through its shaky Spanish vocabulary in the section labelled *'frutas del mare'*, when I first noticed the zombies. There hadn't been another living soul on the promenade and now it was come alive with slow ambling nightmares. Paracas: zombie capital, from young zombie girls in pretty dresses to older zombie blokes in beach shirts and slacks, all with that vacant dead-ahead stare, wide-open eyes betraying what they were, locked on us as they advanced at a slow hesitant shuffle. Each zombie bore a sheet of paper in both hands and as they approached they raised these votives towards us, a desperate yearning in their eyes. Why? What were they doing in the restaurants? Wake up you bastard! Too many Pisco Sours under the hot afternoon sun…you're still in that hammock, dreaming a nightmare. Snap out of it man.

The touch of Maggie's hand, as she gripped mine tightly in fear, snapped me from my somnolence to find the zombies still there. I wasn't still sleeping and this was real… As the first zombie made contact I realised the game. It was off-season; we were the only *Gringos* for miles. It had been a dead night and the restaurant staff had been quietly dozing in the absence of any custom. Then we appeared and they all came shuffling out, still half asleep, to stalk us. It was first night in Cusco all over again in slow motion and we were quickly surrounded by restaurant people clambering for ours, the only business on this night. Grabbing two of their flyers I rolled them up and held forth my hastily made crucifix, parting the way to a sanctuary recommended earlier by the owners of the hostel. We dined on fresh sole in a delicious tomato and onion salsa with a chilled bottle of Tacama Peruvian white, while outside the zombie restaurant touts returned to their graves.

The highlight of Paracas is the boat trip out to Las Islas Ballestas to see the seabird colonies. Our boat, a fast, open topped motor launch, zipped us through choppy seas, past limestone cliffs and over to the islands. The Islas are host to thousands upon thousands of sea birds, so many in fact that it is commercially viable to collect their waste. Saturated with rich nitrates and phosphates and harvested from the seabird nesting sites, *guano* (bird poo to you and me) is one of the best fertilisers known to man. By the 19th century, it was a major commodity and part of the dispute between Chile, Bolivia and Peru that led to the War of the Pacific.

The islands off the coast of Peru are acknowledged as producing the best bird poo in the world. This is not a flippant, light-hearted statement; I'm talking serious shit here. The islands sit in the Humboldt Current, the predominant climatic determinator in this part of the world. The Humboldt draws cold water from Antarctica up along the hot Peruvian coast towards the equator, resulting in a peculiar weather system where the clash of cold water and warm air minimises the fall of rain. The current also brings a rich seafood soup full of plankton, fish and other yummy aquatic nutrients, attracting the seabirds that come to feed and breed here on these remote islands, free from predators, in their millions. Their main diet is oily fish and when they poo, the sun bakes the nitrates into the droppings with minimal loss from evaporation. With no rain, the *guano* never washes away and is easy to collect.

Now for the really serious shit… By the mid 1800s, these *guano* reserves were up to 150 feet deep in some places and it has been estimated that a colony of one million birds will produce in excess of 11 000 tons of *guano* a year. In the years between 1840 and 1880, it is estimated that the Peruvians excavated over twenty million tons of bird shit for export, a business worth some $2 billion in profits. Most of this was controlled by British traders, who exported the poo back to Europe. By 1910 *guano* reserves were severely depleted, yielding a comparatively paltry 48 000 tons per year, leading the Peruvian government to establish a Guano Administration Office to better manage their reserves by preserving the birds and their environment. As the 19th century came to an end, cheap artificial fertilizers appeared on the market and with *guano* no longer the prize commodity, the industry went into decline.

As the islands drew near, growing specks in the sky heralded the first sight of our avian hosts. Nearing the rocky outcrops, the skies burst forth in a profusion of birds by the flock, flight, formation and flush. Our approach was paralleled by a wave-skimming squadron of cormorants, seven of them, all in line astern as they followed the leader back to roost, overtaking and hauling away from our speedy launch. They looked like a gaggle of torpedo bombers, coming in low at wave top height, under the radar, guano bombs primed and ready to launch. A series of dramatic shell splash columns off to port announced the next attack: this time a sortie of gannets bombing a large shoal of fish from the air. Their method of attack was spectacular. The large white birds circled overhead, heads lowered as they sought out individual targets.

Gannets and their smaller relatives, the booby, have fantastic binocular eyes set in the front of the skull to bore-sight down a long slender harpoon of a beak. With target lock achieved, they fold their slender wings tight in by their side and plunge from the sky, their body now a deadly air to sub-surface missile, diving from as high as thirty metres at speeds up to 100 kph. They have no external nostrils and the front of their skull contains air pockets that cushion the birds from their dive impact with the sea. Surfacing from a successful attack the bird then takes off, gaining the altitude necessary for the next strike. They have voracious appetites too, giving us the bye-phrase for gluttony 'to eat like a gannet', an undeserving sobriquet as the birds are, quite simply, ruthlessly efficient hunting machines. We scanned a strafe of graceful chalk-white boobies flying in perfect line astern, changing formation to line abreast as they turned towards us as if making a torpedo run on our boat. Further on, a circuit of graceful shark-grey terns with vivid scarlet beaks, feet and legs, winged over to dive bomb another shoal of fish, the sea a frothing white fury of foam in testament to the ferocity of their hunt.

We could smell and hear the islands long before we were close enough to see any individual birds; the heady fish-oil aroma of anchovy-laced poo alighting on the nostrils around the same time as the cacophony of hoots, screeches and wails made itself audible over the putt-putt of our motor launch. The islands themselves are a honeycomb of rock formed by the action of wind and water into fantastic escarpments, bridges, overhangs and caverns. Their flanks ran streaky white with bird poo, like badly done emulsion. In places the rocks shone bright white, tawny grey or charcoal black and as the boat drew nearer, these clumps of colour transmuted into individual bird colonies, huge roosts with thousands of birds occupying every last square inch of available real estate. All-black cormorants contrasted sharply with their white-chested cousins; their location of choice along sheer and towering cliff edges.

We passed whole shantytowns of boobies and gannets, with their long grey faces and spotless white plumage, and circled a smaller rock with its colony of little grey Inca Terns regurgitating fish for their impossibly large offspring. Here and there we spied the odd nun-in-a-wetsuit that is the Humboldt Penguin looking lost in the crowds. They were obviously not too fussy about where they nested and seemed as content to roost with strangers as with their own. On the lower levels seals basked, squinty eyed in the glorious sunshine, flopped lazily on the sun-bleached rocks, totally oblivious to the commotion and racket above. A crazy pier with a few sad, sagging derricks marked the landing to the poo collectors' station. I tried not to think too hard on the processes involved but I guess it must be a job largely performed by hand. The rocks are too irregular for the employment of any sort of scraping machine and care must obviously be taken not to harm the birds in any way, so I guess it must all be down to men with shovels and buckets. A shit job really!

Our northern progress continued on to the capital, Lima. We rode through Pisco, which seemed cluttered and indeed sour, and found little to detain us in Lima itself. The roads were marred by a horrible weather condition known as '*Garua*', a by-product of the Humboldt Current that causes cold water to condense in the hot air. This dense fog drifts inland for miles, totally obliterating the coastal scenery. It was a weird contrast to be riding through desert sand dunes cloaked in thick chill fog that had us donning extra thermal layers and all of this within ten degrees latitude of the Equator. The Garua also slowed us down, in places crawling along at 20mph on good paved roads that in normal circumstances would have seen us cruising at 60 to 70mph. The visibility was so poor, the fog so dense, that to ride any faster would have been suicidal.

North of Lima we faced another 'expected' hazard. This stretch of road is notorious for corrupt police operating a 'stop, your documents are confiscated unless you pay the fine' system. Later in Nicaragua we met an English motorcyclist who had been a victim. The first checkpoint fined him $100 for 'speeding'. Fifty miles later he was stopped a second time netting the police $30, all he had left on him. Fifty miles on, he simply refused to pull over when a third police car tried to stop him, by now realising that they probably heard over the radio that easy *Gringo* dollars were headed their way.

Having already been bitten by bent cops in Argentina, we took no chances and had our pre-rehearsed plan all ready. Sure enough, fifty miles north of the capital, we were pulled over at a checkpoint on a remote stretch of highway into the midst of a collection of sorry looking Mitsubishi Patrol SUVs, all with baldy tyres. These were leftovers from Peru's famous Japanese president, Fujimori, who apparently made many lucrative deals with Japanese businesses during his tenure. The police took delivery of a fleet of these 'Patrols', expensive vehicles with high maintenance, that are now slowly deteriorating due to unaffordable service costs.

We were immediately interrogated by the chief of this outfit, a big, heavyset man wearing a Castro Kepi and a green quilt padded jacket over green army denims tucked into high laced jump-boots. The first thing we noticed on handing over our dodgy documents was his broad smile and that he had soft brown cow-eyes that didn't exactly sit right with the uniform. He asked what we were doing out here on this desolate coastal road. We explained about our journey to ride from Chile to Alaska for Cancer Research. He handed us back our documents and sent us off with a handshake and his blessing for a safe road ahead. We rode off, exhaling and elated that it was not our turn today.

The road continued north slowly through lowlands greyed out by Garua with ascents up out of the murk to crest the odd headland and plateau. By late afternoon we reached the appalling city of Chimbote, the largest fishing port in Peru. To say the place stank is a severe understatement, like saying Hitler was not a very nice man. A light whiff of marine odour singed our sensitive nostrils a few kilometres south of the town, prompting an initial 'what's that funny smell?' This subtle aroma of foulish, fetid, pissy fish built in intensity as the city approached. Behind the docks lie a number of fish processing plants and their chimney effluvia blows straight inland to blanket the city in plumes of rancid smoke, drenching it in stench. We desperately tried to pull scarves up over our noses, at times positively retching at the malodorous smell, now the strongest *'eau de poisson'* on the planet. Fortunately the ring road was relatively fast enabling us to circumvent the reek at a rapid rate of knots.

We spent a day in Trujillo, our last major stop in Peru, where we visited the vast ruins of the Chima civilisation at Chan Chan. Built entirely of mud, these pre-Inca ruins stretch along the road for five kilometres and resemble a sprawling, lunatic sandcastle, testament to the arid conditions of coastal Peru. Anywhere else in the world and they would have been washed away. The main Tschudi temple complex is undergoing restoration, with incredible detail reproduced in the patterned borders and friezes around the various dwellings and courtyards. Looking back at photographs we took at Chan Chan it looks like a depressing place, its drab mud constructions blending drearily into a dull grey palette of the ever-present Garua. This dreary greyness followed us back into town, where it dampened down even the bright pastel coloured buildings around the Plaza des Armes, spurring our exit on towards Ecuador.

The ride north through Sullanca finally said farewell to the desert. Our sensory deprivations were at an end as our retinas exploded in a rush of lush green fields and palms with the odd banana plantation thrown in. We rode north to Tumbes and the border at Aguas Verdes. We were sad to leave Peru. From our troubled arrival it had developed into a land rich in experience, history and encounter. Like Argentina we felt we could get comfortably bogged down here, lost like a couple of latter day Paddington Bears on bikes. Ecuador waited and beyond the gnawing problem of how we would circumvent that Darien Gap.

Chapter 17: Ecuador

The customs post at Aguas Verdes was one of the biggest shambles of the whole trip, a sprawling shantytown-cum-*mercado*-cum-slum. The streets thronged with people and were lined with a ramshackle collection of shacks and market stalls selling everything from washing machines to dodgy DVDs. We arrived early in the afternoon to embark on the most hassled border crossing of the trip.

First we arrived in Ecuador without formally exiting Peru. There were so many hustlers, hawkers and hangers-on, all vying for our attention, that we sped up a little to avoid their attentions, riding on past the plain clothes Peruvian customs officers, who looked like just another bunch of dollar changers on the street. An Ecuadorian policeman corrected us and we went back, this time spotting the customs shack amongst the rabble. Exiting was straightforward: fill in a few forms, collect a few stamps and *'adios amigo'*, thanks for your lovely country. Another fifteen minutes should deal with the Ecuadorian side and we would be through and away from this mayhem.

Back in Ecuador they did indeed quickly stamp our passports for entry but we were then asked for *'Carnets de Passage'* for the bikes. The *carnet* is basically a customs declaration that you will not sell your vehicle in the country by guaranteeing a bond with a bank that can be cashed in by customs in the event you renege on this procedure. In researching the trip it seemed that none of the countries on our route required a carnet; a temporary *import permiso* was all that was required for each bike and that could be arranged at the border. With no *carnets*, we were sent to see a more senior officer in town to resolve the issue. Riding through dense, choked, dusty streets to the *Aduanas* HQ, smells of savoury market food assailed our nostrils amidst an aural assault of treble mutilated Latin dance music played through distorted ghetto blasters. At the *Aduanas*, I left Maggie with the bikes while I pushed my way to the door through a throng of hawkers selling pirate DVDs and CDs for a dollar, testament to the effectiveness of the FACT campaign in these parts.

Outside, Maggie found some shelter out of the sun, where she sat waiting patiently for the verdict. I was gone around half an hour and she began to get a tad nervous. Maybe something was wrong? After an hour something was definitely wrong. There had been a fight and I had been arrested. The doors to the *Aduanas* would burst open at any second and a storm of heavy duty officers would drag her kicking and screaming to join me in my cell. The market crowd would descend on the laden bikes and tomorrow morning all our worldly possessions would be for sale on a stall and never seen again. What was going on?

Inside I was ushered into an office and seated across a desk from the senior *hombre*, a fat, bald chap in a swivel chair. His desk placard announced he was a lieutenant in the *Aduanas*. He listened as the guy from the checkpoint explained our predicament, then sat back and sucked his teeth before delivering his judgement.

"It is quite simple," he explained. "You can enter Ecuador of course, but your bikes, no." My heart sank. What did he mean 'your bikes, no'? He said it was impossible to import the bikes without a carnet; they would have to go back to Peru; that's what he meant by 'your bikes, no'. I sat and calmly explained that we had ridden our bikes for over 9000 miles through South America to get here. We had survived accidents, strikes and lynch-mobs; not to mention ripio roads, dusty arid deserts and grotty garua to reach Ecuador, surely the jewel of all of South America, only to be told 'you may enter paradise but your bikes, no'. I showed him a calling card with our website and the Cancer Charity and the man softened. Well, there was a Brazilian passed a few days ago on a bike; same thing, no carnet. He would speak to the base *Commandante* and maybe they could organise something 'special'.

I was obviously being set up for a take. There would be a 'special circumstance', a dispensation that would allow our bikes entry, with a fee payable in dollars. As I sat there fuming and waiting, I pondered my options and determined to pay no bribe. I was totally disarmed by what happened next.

The lieutenant returned with a tall handsome man with slicked back hair and a thin pencil moustache. He was dressed head to toe in immaculate, sharp pressed navy whites adorned with his badges of rank and arm of service. He marched confidently into the office and the other *Aduanas* officers present immediately bucked up in the presence of the *Commandante*. My eye was drawn first to a pair of little brass dolphins on his shirt collar and then to a brass submarine badge over his right breast pocket. Struggling to get my mind round the fact that this customs post, miles from the sea, was run by a submariner, I was further disarmed by the man's charm and grace.

He asked for a summary of the predicament and the lieutenant explained our case with sympathy and some concern. Maybe I had misjudged these guys. The *Commandante* listened, stroked his chin while he deliberated for a minute or two and slowly paced the office. There was silence for about thirty seconds; then he began to speak, dispensing his verdict on the issue. We must understand that yes, in normal circumstances, a *carnet* was required; but this was surely a special case and he and his officers would do everything possible to help. What was needed was a letter waiving the carnet requirement, granting us 25 days in Ecuador, after which we must leave the country with the bikes. He would sign it personally. Suddenly everyone was smiling, the mood lightened by this declaration. Having shaken my hand and wished us good luck, the *Commandante* left. My new buddy, the lieutenant, was all happy and sat down to type up the letter immediately, a task he accomplished with some tentative mono-digit touch-typing and the tip of his little pink tongue poking out the side of his mouth. It was taken to the *Commandante,* who signed it immediately and we were clear to go.

The downside was that these proceedings had taken all afternoon and the sun was getting low in the sky when we at long last left town around 6:30pm. Our heart-stopping encounter with the *Aduanas* and the prospect of spending one second longer than absolutely necessary in the town now enticed us to break one of our cardinal rules of the road when travelling in Latin America: never, ever, ride at night. This was an oft repeated piece of advice we had picked up from experienced overlanders and every book and website. Road markings are almost non-existent. Cat's eyes? Only if the cat happened to get run over and expired in the middle of the road with its eyes wide open, looking in your direction. Oh, and all those animals you saw in the fields today? Turned out to graze the quiet, lush, roadside verges in the dark. Cars driving in the dark with their headlights deliberately switched off? Saves the car battery, of course!

We set off towards Santa Rosa hoping to find a tranquil one-nighter along the way. The first ten miles or so were fine but revealed no hint of accommodation in the rolling farmland. Then the lights went out. There is little in the way of sunset here; one minute all is sunshine and illumination, the next total darkness. The road effectively disappeared. At home even the smallest back roads are graced with a central marker and solid white lines at the edges offering some reference for guidance in the dark. Here there was nothing and we were riding on the lighter 'dark grey bit' under our front wheel illuminated by our headlights, taking care when darkness started to encroach from the side. Beyond this small cone of light lay a dark world of total blindness and invisibility. It was a terrifying ride and our speed dropped to a crawl as we picked our way through the night.

Strike one: an ancient pick-up truck, no headlights, drunk driving up the middle of the road. He appeared like a jack-in-the-box out of the gloom and we only saw him at the last minute, swerving hard into a ditch to avoid collision. He sped off into the black, his only illumination a single red taillight winking at us like a nocturnal Cyclops. We pulled into a small country gas station at closing time. The lady must have thought we were armed robbers, lunatics out on the road at this time of night. We asked tentatively if there was a small hotel nearby. Her reply, after double-locking the glass door to the office, a muted *'no hay hotels aqui'*. As we rode off, Maggie noticed a part of the darkness shifting to one side and took hasty evasive action. I saw her taillight jinking and then a pair of huge eyes caught in my high beam revealed the cause of the problem: a humungous black cow turned loose and wandering along the road.

An hour later, we crawled into Santa Rosa to find nothing saint-like and little to be rosy about in this cheerless concrete slum. We cruised the area around the plaza and found a seedy hotel where $16 bought us garaged parking, no breakfast and a shared room with two resident lizards and a large spider in the bathroom (cold douche of course). Dinner looked likely to be equally disappointing. A short stroll for a few blocks around the plaza confirmed a dearth of eateries. There were a few places selling burgers of dubious quality and origin, cooked on barbeque grills out on the street, but just as we were about to give up the aroma of fresh roast *pollo* led us to a little café doing rotisserie chickens and beer, Santa Rosa's saving grace.

We plonked our tired butts down on the cheap white injection-moulded picnic furniture out on the street and proceeded to demolish a whole fowl between us, shredded and eaten with our fingers to the sound of heavy rap belting out from a ghetto blaster in the back of the café. Sodium streetlights reflected in the grease of the red and white chequered plastic tablecloth, catching the circles of wet condensation left by our beer bottles. We supped suds and took in the street life of Rosa, mostly kids whizzing past our street corner on decrepit mopeds and bicycles, trying to look cool in front of a gang of young girls hanging round another little café down the street. Welcome to Ecuador.

In the morning we fled. Not even breakfast could entice us to spend a moment longer in this dreary town. We took the high road up into the mountains on approaches lined with mile after mile of banana plantations, their fruit clusters protected by unsightly blue plastic bags to keep the pests off. A pot-holed highland road swept us through verdurous valleys of lush green forest. It was an easy ride to our early afternoon halt in the old city of Cuenca, exchanging last night's cold concrete and gloom for colonial cobbles and quaint. At 2500 metres the city was cool, the first hint that our stay in these equatorial lands might not be quite the furious furnace we had anticipated at home before the trip. We took a beautiful apartment overlooking the white water of the Rio Tomebamba, within easy walking distance of downtown and settled in for a few days to kick off our bike gear, see the city and enjoy having our own little home after a few weeks on the trot of living in hotels.

On our first saunter through town it was immediately obvious that we had departed the lands of the tiny Bowler (doomed forever to remain none the wiser as to the means of their affixation) into the land of the Panama hat. Panamas originate in Ecuador but take their popular name from the construction of the canal, when thousands of workers wore them as sunshades. The people of Cuenca were friendly and hospitable, an easy-going crowd, content to take you or leave you in a way that suited us fine after the hustle and bustle of Peru.

Maggie selected some avocados in the market, opting for fruit that was all of uniform size, firm and green, a choice conditioned by supermarket standards in the UK. The fruit lady set her selection to one side and replaced it with some fruit that was knobbly, soft and, to be honest, a bit manky looking. When Maggie protested she smilingly explained that we had chosen unripe fruit and that if we wanted to eat the avocados today, we should take the manky fruit. We grudgingly took her advice, a little uncomfortable that maybe we were being duped but content on this occasion to bow to her experience.

Back at our apartment we had just converted the avocados into guacamole for dinner with a veggie chilli (the avocados were delicious, the best we ever had) when reception called to say that there was someone asking for us. A tall chap with thinning swept-back hair was checking out our bikes. A firm handshake and a broad friendly grin was our introduction to Eduardo, a local motorcyclist. He had been driving by with his wife Peggy when they saw the bikes. We passed a pleasant half hour or so chatting amiably in the afternoon sun, talking bike talk as they listened to our tales from the saddle, and we learned a little of life in Cuenca. Eduardo was a member of the local bike club and by the end of the conversation the couple offered their services to be our guides to Cuenca and its environs. This kindness of locals to strange visitors is always a little windfall on the road, leading to experiences and introductions that would otherwise likely be missed.

The following day we took a short excursion with Eduardo and Peggy to the nearby El Cajas National Park, a wetland wonderland with over 250 small lakes set in a world of broken craggy mountains. An emerald landscape bejewelled by water, this 'Killarney with condors' was yet another Andean landscape reminiscent of home. After a few short strolls in the park we lunched on *humitas* (corn and cheese mashed and rolled in corn leaf) with a nip of the local hot fruit and herb punch (very alcoholic) to keep the chill air at bay. In the late afternoon we returned for spectacular views over the city from the Mirador de Turi and ended the day with a gut-busting dinner of pork and beef at a local Asado.

In the morning one of our worst nightmares with the bikes was realised. At an elevation of over 2500 metres, we were back in that region where our high altitude starting problem was likely to manifest. To compound the issue the sky was overcast with a threat of rain so we had no sun to warm the engines up. Sure enough, both bikes suffered SADS and refused to start. Eduardo turned up with half the bike club, including a couple of mechanics, and eventually got the bikes running. Big hugs all around as we finally left Cuenca and our biker family there.

It was a murky wet day through mountains in rising temperatures and humidity, our first ride in persistent rain in nearly six months on the road. Heavy showers had us stopping to don wetsuits, riding on encapsulated in our very own personal saunas. A few miles up the road, with the rain off, we would stop to strip off again only to have to pull over to repeat the entire process for the next big shower. Thus we progressed at a snail's pace along badly holed roads that lead us ever on into these vast mountains shrouded in ominous cloud.

By early afternoon the rain abated and the cloud broke to reveal stunning vistas of snow-capped mountains and volcanoes up ahead. Our destination for the day was the little mountain town of Baños, sited at the foot of the mighty 5000-metre highly active Volcan Tungurahua. The views of the volcano were spectacular as we rode into town and we had planned to go on a night walk to see the lava fields of Tungurahua lit up in the dark. Sadly foul weather scuppered this idea and we set off instead for a soggy day's hiking along jungly paths that we abandoned in the face of increasingly heavy downpours.

Our hostel in Baños had heated indoor parking, so both bikes started fine, allowing us to depart for Quito, our last major stop in South America and a jump off for a side trip to visit the Galapagos Islands. Quito sits at 2800 metres and is the world's second highest capital city (after La Paz). We were soon on a good four-lane highway, zooming along with ever-more-staggering snow-coned volcanoes on the horizon; this city of just over two million souls is sited within striking range of over half a dozen of the country's nineteen active volcanoes.

For accommodation, we had selected a few likely hostels in downtown Quito from our *Lonely Planet* guide. At the end of the highway, we pulled over on the hard shoulder to change the road map in my tank bag to a street map of Quito when an extraordinary vehicle pulled up. It was a white Mazda pick-up truck bearing Queensland plates, with a flat deck out back and a huge orange and brown aboriginal spotted-snake motif scrolled across the bonnet. The driver got out and walked towards us. He was a giant of a man with a shock of short-cropped ginger-blonde hair and matching goatee. Sharp bright eyes and a neat smile flashed friendly intentions.

"G'Day mate. Where y'frum? What're the bikes? Looks like they've seen a few miles. Any problems? Chile t'Alaska? Peru? Argentina? Bolivia?" he said, reading off our pannier stickers. "What're you's doin' here? What brings ya ta Quito? Wher're y'staying?" The staccato of questions, one on top of the other, continued; he was obviously very curious and excited to meet us. His accent was weird, definitely Aussie, but with a twang of something strange thrown in, something I felt we ought to recognise. He was what would be known affectionately at home as 'a strapping big lad'. Tall and broad-chested, he stood there smiling in his grey T-shirt, his pinky white legs dangling from a pair of trendy shorts that gave him the look of a fifty year old naughty schoolboy.

"We're from Belfast, Northern Ireland, and we're on a charity ride from Chile to Alaska for Cancer Research," we explained, trying at a stroke to answer as many of his queries as possible.

"Fek me!" he exclaimed, "Sure amn't I from Carrickfergus just down the road." A big hand shot out and grabbed my paw and nearly shook me to death. Such was our introduction and acquaintance with Chris Halliday, a big man from back home, at the side of a road in Quito.

He gave us a quick run through his life, starting with his family's move to Australia when he was very young. His father worked for Harland and Wolff, the Belfast shipbuilder and worked all over the world for the Onassis family and their shipping interests. Chris grew up in Australia and had a keen interest in over-landing, having completed a number of journeys in both cars and bikes. He had been happily married until his wife left him for another man. There was a moment of real sadness in his voice as he told us this part. He had been involved in an international bike event in Australia and kindly offered to provide accommodation at his home for one of the competitors, an English policeman. The guy hit it off with his wife and that was the end of his marriage. Devastated, he had moved off to start a completely new life here in Ecuador where he was now running a hostel.

"Now tell me again, wher're y'staying?" he asked with a big smile.

We followed Chris to 'The Andes Range' near the airport; first night free and we could take it or leave it after that. Like Rio Mayo and Cusco, the 'Andes Range' was another nodal point of our trip, a location where we would make many new and lasting friendships. It felt like staying with a mate, as Chris showed us to our room and gave us the run of the house. Even better, he let the pair of us loose in the kitchen and the dinners that followed at his table were boozy, candlelit affairs lasting long into the evening, the food accompanied by good music and conversation with the kindred spirits who haunted the 'Range'. Chief amongst these was a sparkly American lass, one of Chris's most frequent houseguests, Colleen Pawling. She had abandoned a career as a lawyer in New York State to come and run a bear sanctuary here in Ecuador. We parted company with an invite to call and see her project at work.

The bikes saw little action during our stay in Quito. The weather was cloudy in the mornings with hot sunny afternoons, conditions that did not bode well for the bikes. True to form, they refused early morning ignition, only starting later in the day when it was warmer.

250

Fortunately Quito is blessed with a BMW dealer and we arranged for them to take the sick bikes for servicing and examination while we went off to see the marvels of nature that are the Galapagos Islands.

Chapter 18: Animal Crackers

A Galapagos cruise was the perfect punctuation to end our South American trails. A two-hour flight took us to Balta Island where we were united with the other twelve guests and our guide for the eight day tour, a little chap called Juan. Our boat, the 100-foot motor vessel *Beluga* was an elegant craft with pleasant quarters and a grand crew. The idea was to sail from island to island at night, while we were all asleep, minimising the likelihood of seasickness. Chilling out on a boat, in slightly more sumptuous surroundings than usual, offered a complete change from our normal mode of travel on the bikes. We arrived at each destination majestically transported there, courtesy of our valiant crew. Each dawn brought a new location with our man Juan on hand to reveal the mysteries and delights of the islands.

The stars of the show at Galapagos were always going to be the animals. For eons the wildlife here has been free from predators and consequently the animals display little fear or shyness when approached by humans. Previous wildlife encounters on our travels were distant affairs with us posed as remote, passive observers, ogling animals doing their stuff. Galapagos was different due to the intimate nature of the contact. At Islas Ballestas we had marvelled at seabirds on the wing or in their roosts as viewed through a pair of binoculars. Here we had to take care not to tread on the birds as we traipsed through their nesting sites.

We were captivated by the blue-footed boobies, their eggs and young scattered everywhere across *guano*-splattered terrain. We were close enough to view the birds eye to eye, held fascinated by their intricate plumage, that dazzling white down speckled immaculately with little brown-grey speed-flecks emanating from the face, spreading around the neck and down the back of the large head. Softly smoked velvety-brown wings folded back as if held by clasped hands, an appearance enhanced when they waddled up and down like a worried bet at a racecourse. The elegance and grace of this fine plumage is of course lost when you look down at the bird's feet. They look like they originally belonged to another bird, like the booby lost that bet and ended up with a forfeit pair of oversize, web-spanned paddles, dipped in the brightest blue paint in the universe, straight from a rainbow. I found a small rock and sat alone, staring at a mature female on her nest, a student's flour bomb splatted on the ground. This shell crater of *guano* had the earth scratched out from its centre to form a little depression in which the bird rested, seemingly content and oblivious to the bunch of giant, drab-footed tourists around.

Under her left breast I spied an egg, round and smooth like a worn ivory billiard ball, nestled deftly in soft feather down. At the right breast a baby grey pterodactyl stared out with beady black eyes. Like all chicks it bore absolutely no resemblance to its parent and sat there contentedly waiting for the next meal to arrive. I took some photographs of the nesting booby, no zoom required, just close as you like to get the shot, taking care not to stress the bird in the process. As I changed position for a slightly different angle, those striking eyes caught my full attention. Bore-sighted down that long broad pointed beak, their effect was somewhat cross eyed, yet I remembered watching these birds in action at Ballestas and appreciated what an efficient hunting machine the booby is for all its funny name.

No longer distant voyeurs, we relish these close-up animal encounters. A few days later and we are snorkelling off the Panga, our inflatable motorboat used for ferrying us on forays out from the *Beluga*. I have just left Maggie swimming with a giant turtle. I spot something small, sleek and silver darting through the aquamarine, leaving a telltale trail of pewter bubbles and I am soon on the tail of a flightless cormorant. The lack of predators has cost him his ability to fly, his wings reduced to stubby little paddles for swimming only. The volcanic seafloor is a perfect hiding place for small fish and crustaceans and my cormorant is oblivious to the ungainly little white whale with the funny plastic thing on its face, tailing him as he hunts. He holds me totally enthralled for a full twenty minutes as he roots out prey from nooks and crannies. Time stands still and the world disappears, the universe reduced to just me, the lucky observer, watching this little bird performing his magical underwater routine.

Another day, another duet; Maggie, this time, still in the water above a reef littered with a shattered spectra of tropical fish. She came up for air when Pete, one of our shipmates, called out for her to turn round and look behind. Turning slowly she found herself face-to-face, nose-to-nose, with a young sea lion. They looked like a pair of odd bookends, this snorkel-head at one end matched by the seal-head at the other. Maggie performed a slow pirouette; the young mammal mirrored her movement and the ballet began. She followed this with a contra-rotation and again, the sea lion did the same. She ducked her head under the water to find him staring at her. The sea lion swam slowly around her, twisting and turning. Maggie attempted to do the same, swimming back at the seal, copying his movements as best she could. He recognised the game and joined in, performing ever more complex rotations as she struggled to keep up. Finally, having totally wrong footed his dance-partner, he took off like a silky torpedo, leaving Maggie jilted but elated on the watery dance floor.

Giant Galapagos tortoises, land and marine iguanas, boobies, frigate birds, mockingbirds, sea lions and pelicans, we saw them all but the most thrilling encounter involved a pod of bottle-nosed dolphins. Breakfast was almost over on our third day on the *Beluga* when a shower of dolphins was spotted out beyond a sunken volcano crater known as the Devil's Crown. The breakfast table was hastily abandoned as we rushed to grab swimwear and snorkels before boarding the two Pangas and charging to head off the pod. 'Pod' is such an inapt collective to describe the furious pandemonium of mammals headed our way. It suggests three or four cutesy, smiley dolphins, a little family maybe, dossing around in a river estuary to the 'oohs' and 'ahhs' of spotters in a passing boat and is a totally inadequate description for the churning, boiling dolphin soup ahead.

The freezing cold water momentarily quenched our enthusiasm as we plunged into the path of the horde. Gathering my wits and orientation, I had just figured the direction of approach and turned in the water to meet the dolphins when I was greeted with a trio of ghostly grey-blue apparitions headed straight for me at a most rapid rate of knots. Certain collision was avoided when, with split second timing, the first dolphin broke left, the second right and the third dived straight down under me. I was mildly terrified to say the least, trying to scream 'fek!' with a mouth full of rubbery snorkel tube and salt water. They left me twisting and spinning, totally out of my element, trying to catch a last glimpse as they disappeared off into the murk.

Calm now; after this first contact a still quietness descended on the proceedings interrupted only by the clicks and whirrs of the dolphins communicating our transgression into their world. Looking through the water in every direction, it was choked full of dolphins. Not just on the surface: the maelstrom we had spied initially was but the upper layer and I was treading water over a huge layer cake of dolphins. They extended deep down as far as the light could penetrate to allow my feeble eyes to see, all swimming purposefully in one direction. Later on the *Beluga*, Juan estimated we were in the presence of over 500 animals, a rare occurrence that he had previously observed only once before in his sixteen years as a guide in the Galapagos.

This up close and personal interaction with the animals permits an almost unique access to nature at work. Small wonder that Charles Darwin, who spent just under four weeks at the islands, was so captivated by the variations in the animal species that live here. Initially the different islands seem to contain various combinations of the same animals, sea-birds, iguanas and so on, but closer study reveals how each species has evolved to adapt to the peculiar conditions on each island. In particular Darwin noticed how the beaks on the little finches on the isles have developed depending on their diet, ranging from broad, stubby little nutcracker beaks on the seed and nut feeders to the tweezer-mandibles of the insect eating varieties.

Today we pay lots of money to visit the isles and can only do so as part of an officially sanctioned tour group. Juan and the tour guides ensure that visitors do not interfere with the wildlife or the islands, asking us to 'leave only footprints in the sands and take only photographs and memories.' It was not quite the case in Darwin's day, when the islands held renown as a source of slow moving meat fests for passing ships. Darwin records in his '*Voyage of the Beagle*' how sailors performed their own experiments, tying heavy weights to sea iguanas to see if they could be drowned (amazingly they found one specimen was still alive after an hour under water).

Fascinating as this fauna may be, the islands are largely inhospitable to human habitation. They are remote from the mainland and have a dry, windy climate with poor soil and little rain, yet this has not deterred some from trying to settle here. In 1924 the scientific researcher William Bebe published a book called *'Galapagos: World's End'*, depicting the islands as a remote Utopia, a haven in the tropics far away from a post-World War world. Who amongst us has not indulged themselves with a daydreamed escape to such a paradise? To exchange that deskbound nine to five tedium in a dreary, wet grey climate for a timeless life in a hammock, supping everlasting rum from a chilled coconut, rocking gently to sleep serenaded by waves lapping softly on white coral sand as the soft scent of hibiscus wafts in the gentle breeze. A sun-tanned, semi-naked existence with a healthy diet of tropical fruits straight off the tree before popping back to the beach to net some tasty fish for dinner cooked in exotic leaves over an open fire. The reality of course is never quite like that.

The Galapagos Islands themselves are mostly big clumps of ugly, relatively newly formed lava-rock straddling the Equator some 600 miles out into the Pacific Ocean off the coast of Ecuador. Some of the islands, such as Isabella, are fairly new with fresh lava fields less than two hundred years old. One of the first things we learned to distinguish were the two main types of lava we would be walking on, identified by their Hawaiian names. First there is the quite smooth, if a little uneven 'Pahoehoe' lava, 'lava you can walk on barefoot'. This lava has oozed slowly from a molten fissure in the earth and coiled up in ropey folds. 'Pahoehoe' fields look like the surface of a dried up, crazy artist's palette, where coils of oils have been squished wastefully to cover the palette in a messy grey-black goo. The second type, known as 'Aa' (ah-ah), was formed from a more violent eruption, with the superheated lava full of gas when it flowed. This onomatopoeic name means 'lava you cannot walk on barefoot'. The set lava contains many bubbles and air pockets, forming a crumbly honeycomb with very sharp edges. We quickly dubbed it 'Ah-Fek' lava, from the profanity uttered when you realise that you have to traverse another large patch of it.

But, I digress; back to paradise… Floreana sounded like such a paradise. This island, one of the most southerly in the group, has a smattering of arable soil and a fresh water supply, making it a slightly better prospect for settlement. German dentist Friedrich Ritter thought so when he came here in 1929. Having studied philosophy and fancying himself as something of a Nietzsche, Ritter sold his practice and left his wife to set out for 400 square miles of island paradise with his girlfriend, Dore Strauch Koerwin, who abandoned her husband to join him. Their objective was to set up a self-sufficient home where they would live a simple, nudist, vegetarian existence living off the land.

Prior to leaving Germany, Ritter considered potential medical emergencies. He felt confident in his ability to cope with most minor ailments, with the exception of toothache. While he could treat Dore, he was obviously limited in what he could do in the way of self-treatment, so he decided to remove his own teeth. He had some dentures made and, as appearances in paradise would be of slight concern, they were made from stainless steel. Makes sense really: easy to clean, strong and durable, with two sets in case one gets lost. The couple lived in a self-built tin roofed shack where they came face to face with the realities of this 'good–life'. They kept chickens (for their eggs) and they harvested some of the island's fruits and edible plants. They also cultivated a small garden and then had to defend it constantly from the ravages of the wild hogs, cattle and asses that abounded on the island.

Ritter seems to have been a somewhat fickle and cantankerous man, full of contradictions. He came halfway around the world to settle his dream paradise only to write about it for the newspapers. He wanted to escape from the world, to be self sufficient, yet he rapidly took to scrounging whatever he could from every passing ship. The stories he wrote made sensational reading and attracted other wannabe Crusoes, a rag-tag assortment of adventure travellers who wanted a share of this desert island life.

These short-term visitors, to the annoyance of Ritter, lived in the old caves, alleged haunts of pirates who had used the islands as a safe-haven in preceding centuries. One day he was visited by one of these temporary residents, who brought the gift of some beef from an animal he had killed and butchered. Dore set to frying the meat for their visitor, to the admonishment of the crazy dentist, who ranted on about the evils of the carnivore. However the smell of sizzling, frying steak soon had his gastric juices flowing and temptation proved too much. Ritter decided it would be a far worse sin to waste good food and so, popping in his stainless steel gnashers, he did his Christian duty and tore into the meat platter before him. His vegetarian backsliding would ultimately lead to his undoing.

In August 1932 more permanent settlers arrived: another German family, Herr and Frau Wittmers, with their thirteen-year-old son. Emboldened by Bebe, they came to Floreana and established a small settlement. They became uneasy neighbours with Ritter, who was initially suspicious and mistrusted them, as he had all the other island arrivals. The Wittmers had chosen to settle higher up in the island, requiring a backbreaking journey to ferry all of their possessions to their new home. Ritter had a donkey and loaned it to help one day, only to refuse the next. Later on he refused to attend the delivery of their new baby, saying, "Come and get me when the crisis is really there. I don't want to have to sit around your house all day." Given that his dwelling was quite a hike away it was clearly impractical to leave the expectant mother for any length of time when birth was imminent.

These petty squabbles pale into insignificance compared with the events that unfolded following the arrival of the next permanent settlers. In October 1932, the grandly titled Baroness Eloise Wagner Bousquet set foot on Floreana with her two lovers, a Berliner named Philippson, and another German called Lorenz, with an Ecuadorian called Valdivieso in tow. They had travelled from Paris and now planned to build a luxury hotel on Floreana. Where Ritter and the Wittmers had merely exchanged the odd cross word, the Baroness was proving to be a neighbour from hell. Visitors were run off from the 'hotel site' at gunpoint, things went missing, crops were raided and the Wittmers' collapsible boat was stolen. Wittmer accidentally shot Ritter's prize donkey one night, when he mistook it for a wild ass raiding his garden. He later found that someone had deliberately led the poor beast there, knowing the probable outcome and hoping to fuel a dispute. He quickly buried the beast before Ritter found out what had happened.

Stories abounded in the press about the Baroness, now dubbed the 'Empress of Floreana', and how she wandered the island clad only in a bra and shorts with a pearl-handled pistol slung round her curvaceous waist, issuing orders to her slave lovers. Valdivieso soon fled, overworked and abused, leaving Philippson and Lorenz to serve the queen. It was rumoured that each day they had to fight for her favours, the smaller Lorenz coming off worse every time. Most of these stories are probably nonsense or rabble-rousing rubbish put about by either Ritter or the Baroness herself, both of whom were writing for American newspapers, but the thieving was present and Lorenz was bullied by Philippson to the point where, after being knocked unconscious, he fled and took up residence with the Wittmers.

What happened next is shrouded in mystery. Initially the Baroness tried to smooth things over, according to the diaries of the Wittmers, the only record of those days. They had quite taken to Lorenz, finding him a useful help around their settlement. On 27th March 1934, the Baroness came to visit with Frau Wittmers, announcing that some friends had dropped by in a boat and that she planned to leave with them, along with Philippson, for Tahiti. She asked that Lorenz look after the 'hotel', a ramshackle structure of wood, tin and canvas, until she sent word of her new location. The Baroness and Philippson were never seen nor heard of again.

There were no boats in or around Floreana at this time and no record of any boat sailing from anywhere in the Galapagos to Tahiti. What is clear is that Lorenz and Ritter soon settled down to disposing of the 'Hotel' contents, Lorenz passing most of his share on to the Wittmers or Ritter when he too announced his intention to depart the islands. He left in June on a reputedly unreliable motor vessel owned by a Norwegian from Santa Cruz, another Island of the Galapagos. Lorenz intended to travel back to Germany, having had quite enough of this island life. He never got there. The boat was reported missing and several months later the desiccated bodies of Lorenz and the Norwegian were found shipwrecked on the waterless desert island of Marchena, an out of the way island seldom visited by passing ships.

Rumours circulated that Lorenz had murdered the Baroness, his ex-lover, and her boyfriend, disposing of their bodies in the shark infested waters off the island and concocting the story of their departure for Tahiti. There was a government investigation into the matter, possibly inspired by Ritter, who had sent hints to the authorities that the Wittmers knew more about the disappearance of the Baroness than met the eye. But with no bodies, witnesses or hard evidence of foul play, there was little to be done. The death of Lorenz seemed like a nautical mishap with the enticement that justice had been served when the possible murderer foundered on the remote island while making his escape. All in all this was very convenient for Ritter and the Wittmers, who could now live once again in peace, but for Ritter this would be, literally, short lived.

He had taken to preserving meat by boiling it and storing it in jars. In November 1934 he opened one of these to entertain some visitors from a passing American ship and found the meat had spoiled and gone off. So he fed the spoiled meat to his chickens, most of which died after eating it. Never one to be wasteful, Ritter had these birds boiled and bottled. A few days later he ate some of this preserved chicken meat, fell ill from food poisoning and died. Dore Strauch Koerwin left the islands to return to Germany. Descendants of the Wittmers still live in the Galapagos today, having eventually abandoned Floreana and moved to one of the major islands.

Back in Quito, we collected the bikes from BMW. They had been serviced, cleaned and thoroughly checked out, with nothing obviously wrong with them, so we were still none the wiser about our starting problem. Big Chris had procured a can of 'easy-start', an ether aerosol used to start diesel engines, and we used this for the rest of our stay at high altitude. We had two last excursions in Ecuador: a trip to the mountains to visit Colleen at the Bear Tracking Station being one; but that would wait until we had our day out on a rose farm.

Carlos Cadena was one of our Galapagos shipmates, a tall, charming Ecuadorian with a broad smile and a warm handshake. Chatting to Carlos on board the *Beluga* we found that he makes his living exporting roses all over the world. Ecuador, we soon learned, has a huge flower industry and Carlos invited us to go visit 'Sisapamba Roses', one of the rose farms that he deals with. Ecuador's neighbour, Colombia, is actually one of the largest flower growing countries in the world with an industry ten times larger than that of Ecuador. Carlos explained that here in Ecuador, they go for the lower volume, higher quality end of the market. 'Sisapamba Roses' are a relatively small producer, concentrating on 34 varieties of roses in 23 different colours. Their seven-hectare plot contains some 450 000 individual rose bushes, mostly under glass. The plants are all hybrids and sadly grown only for their appearance, so that they are odourless; which was a pity as the heady scent of half a million rose bushes would have been a whiff to remember.

Production was running slowly when we were there, at around ten thousand stems a day; but this can ramp up to forty thousand stems per day during peak periods, such as St Valentine's Day and Mother's Day. The plants are meticulously inspected for any sign of pest or disease, with any infected deliveries immediately returned in their entirety, so tender loving care is the order of the day. The stems are cut, trimmed, packed and placed into cold storage ready for delivery anywhere in the world. Different markets have different requirements, some obvious others not so. Deep and seductive reds for those romantic Italians; while Russia, on the other hand, has taken a shining to a new green rose. In Armenia the preference is not for colour but stem length, anything up to eighty centimetres. We were staggered to learn that Armenians will pay \$40 for an individual long stemmed rose.

The trip to the Bear Tracking Station was our last ride in South America. We rode north to the market town of Otavalo north of the Equator. The line was marked by a little wayside globe marker with a plaque and some souvenir stalls and we stopped to take some photographs. As we mounted up to leave, we were amazed and baffled by the arrival of a small 50cc Yamaha scooter bearing Alaskan license plates. The tiny two-wheeler was horribly burdened with a bundle of bin bags containing the rider's earthly possessions. A tall, very amicable young English chap in sandals, who introduced himself to us as Rupert Wilson-Young, had ridden 'Britney' all the way here from Alaska. In an all too short exchange, we swapped stories and emails and after parting we tracked Rupert all the way to the bottom of South America on his incredible journey, but that is another story...

The tarmac ended just beyond Otavalo. We wound our way up into some fairly sumptuous scenery on the ride through the mountains to the little village of Apuela, where the tracking station was located. Well-surfaced dirt roads took us deep into lush jungle and canopied valleys with breathtaking views over the Northern Andes. We forded bubbling streams against backdrops of silver waterfalls before descending onto some fairly horrible broken rocky roads that led up a river valley to Apuela. Stopping in the Plaza, we asked directions for the *'Casa De Los Gringos'* or the *'Casa De Los Osos'* (house of the *Gringos* or bears). Sure enough, everyone pointed the way for us up an even rockier road that climbed high up and out of town and took us to the Bear Project, where we were warmly received by Colleen and her volunteers.

The station itself was a low block-built farmhouse with a shoddily tiled roof and a patchy grass and weed lawn out front. It was furnished with a variety of repaired and home-made chairs and plywood-box beds, on which we laid out our sleeping bags. We were warned not to leave anything edible lying around as the place was infested with rats. We went for a walk with Colleen to buy some provisions from the local store at the little village of Pucara. When we returned, much to our surprise, there were now four bikes sitting outside the station. The two new arrivals were another pair of F650s belonging to Rene Cormier, a Canadian, and Amy his American girlfriend, headed south having just arrived in South America. We pondered the chances of two couples, riding the same bikes, meeting in such a remote spot.... but such is life on the road. We sat down to a candlelit dinner of truly scrumptious vegetable soup, washed down with lashings of beer and dark rum. We also sampled Puro, the local hooch made from cane sugar, which we diluted with a lemon tea. This dulled our senses somewhat by bedtime, so we were not too disturbed by the rats squeaking in the rafters.

The Andean Bear Conservation Project is part of the *'Fundacion Espiritu del Bosque'* (Spirit of the Forest), an organisation with the objective of saving the Andean Bear from extinction through scientific study and rehabilitation of captive bears. The organisation depends on volunteers, mostly students or wildlife enthusiasts, who come from all over the world to give a little time to monitor the bears and help in the local communities. At the time of our visit they had seven bears in the area fitted with radio collars and the volunteers track their movements, generally early in the morning and again in the early evening when the bears are most active. The data is then collated in an attempt to learn more about the habits of these shy little creatures. The bears' only enemy is man and they are unwelcome visitors at local subsistence farms, where they raid the cornfields. The fact that they are an endangered species means little to an angry farmer confronted by broken fences and damaged crops and consequently bears are occasionally shot or trapped.

To begin with there was a big battle to win over the local communities, to raise awareness and make them appreciate the presence of an endangered species on their doorstep. It was a difficult task. Colleen spoke of being confronted by locals arguing "Hey, look here; you already killed all your animals and chopped down all your trees in Europe and North America, so what right do you have to march in here and tell us not to do the same thing? Sure, it's OK for you now; you have fine towns and cities, nice cars, schools and houses; well we want those things too and if we have to axe forest and kill animals to get them, then so be it". A hearts and minds approach was required and the people had to get something in return for not harming the bears.

Payback comes in the form of education. Many of these remote communities have no local school or if they do, have no teachers to work in them. Their children are keen to learn, so Colleen initiated a system whereby her volunteers live and teach in the communities. That way, they can track bears at dawn and dusk and spend daytime, when the bears are inactive, teaching the kids in the schools. It has been a successful approach that has really switched the communities on as to why the Andean Spectacled Bear is special and needs protection. In fact, there was news when we were there of one farmer deliberately planting a late cornfield to attract bears so that a volunteer teacher would have to be provided.

The return to Quito was via a different road from Apuela that had only recently re-opened after some horrendous landslides that left it blocked since February. The section as far as Otavalo (about 40km) was a gruesome experience, our first riding on mud. Heavy rain occasionally brings the whole mountainside down. When the resulting landslide blocks the road, earth moving dozers are required to shovel the dirt off the edge and cut further into the mountain to make a new road. We arrived in the middle of two of these operations and had to wait until they had shovelled a path through for us to continue slithering over the mud and earth of the new road.

In Quito we finally decided to bypass Colombia and it saddened us to miss what, by all accounts, is a beautiful country. Travelling north, we paid increasing attention to news on events in the area and what we heard was not good. FARC, the main rebel group, were celebrating their fortieth birthday with a series of major actions against government troops. Ambushes, bombs in crowded market squares, assassinations and kidnappings were daily occurrences. We had coped with strikes and civil disorder further south but the idea of straying into an area where helicopter gunships were seeing plenty of employment seemed a little too dangerous.

And so we set about exiting South America, organising our departure for Panama. A shipping agent arranged for the bikes to be flown to Panama City via Bogotá for $500 per bike. We would fly out the following day and the bikes would be there ready and waiting for collection. On our penultimate day in Quito, the bikes were loaded onto a huge aluminium pallet at the airport where we completed the shipping and packing processes, a simple and straightforward procedure, apart from the chaos of the ensuing drugs check.

The customs guy turned up, turned out in the finest in paramilitary paraphernalia. He looked a right little fascist in a neatly pressed grey, black and white street camouflage uniform, ready for all-out urban war. He sported a chunky black flak-jacket and was fully equipped and decked out with all manner of belts, pistols, ammo pouches, handcuffs, radios and so on. He was a mean, serious *hombre* with a dashing Zorro pencil moustache and a permanent frown. This look, obviously cultured and groomed over long hours in front of the mirror, was marred only by the fact that he stood in his jump boots around five foot two, even on his tippy-toes, and when he said something we both looked around everywhere to see who had spoken, before looking down to see it was him.

The function of this glum Ninja today was to check over our shipment to make sure we were not smuggling drugs, historical artefacts or up to any similar illegal shenanigans. He would perform this duty ably assisted by his sniffer dog. He asked us to remove our saddle packs and baggage from the bike and lay them out for the dog to sniff. If the dog found anything of interest he would ask us to open that particular bag; fair enough.

Now generally I love sniffer dogs. I get a kick out of seeing these highly trained animals in action, all bright eyed with their glistening coats, their little tails wagging manically as, senses honed, they sniff out the bad stuff, knowing there is a tasty treat if they find the goodies. Today I was in for a major disappointment when a scruff-bag, mangy looking, matt-coated Golden Labrador arrived, brought over in one of those plastic-box, doggy-cage things you see around airports.

We laid everything out as requested, but the poor dog had spent so long cooped up in his tiny kennel that all he was interested in was exploring his new found temporary freedom. He did so by dragging the Ninja on the other end of the leash over to an expensive looking BMW car in the parking lot, where he (the dog, that is) did an impressive piss over one of the wheels. Eventually the glum Ninja dragged the poor mutt back to work, puffing and swearing under his breath as he tried to maintain his composure. We looked on as the neatly arranged elements of his uniform were gradually misaligned; so that he arrived back at our gear with his kepi a kilter and his accoutrements all over the place.

In all this time we had been mildly amused and had to restrain our increasingly growing grins, but at the same time we were anxious to get the formalities over and done with. The dog walked around one or two of the bags but he clearly was not bothered by anything they might contain. We could have been smuggling kilos of coke and it would not have bothered him. No: he had found something far more interesting!

Prior to leaving Chris's place I had been petting Coco, the Siamese kitten, who snuggled up on my lap for a while. The dog must have picked up her scent because he now made a bee-line for my crotch. His nose seemed to go onto a sort of radar lock and I spent the next ten minutes trying to fight him off. We set off in a whirl around the loading bay, with me on one end of the dog, both hands round his snout as I tried to protect my vitals; the glum Ninja hanging on to the other end of the leash, trying to jerk him away. As the dog persisted I started to panic; what if Ninja decides I have something on my person and decides it's worth a closer look? Full body cavity search with the dopey dog delightedly looking on?

Maggie was by now doubled over in an apoplexy of hysterical laughter. What added to the mirth was the fact that the Ninja remained stoically glum throughout; his face never twitching or moving a muscle, the humour of the occasion totally escaping him. Eventually he prised the dog away and slapped it hard a few times, which killed our chuckles too. He grumpily dismissed us; search over and we were free to load the bikes for shipment. We started re-packing and the Ninja dragged the dog over to the next job: sniffing a consignment of cardboard boxes.

Still amused by the inspection, I was bent over checking some strapping and tie-downs when I felt a firm grasp on the back of my thigh, followed by a sharp series of tugs on my trouser leg. Turning round I looked down into the big brown eyes of the drugs dog, pink tongue lolloping out the side of his mouth, doing his doggie thing to my left leg. He had escaped his leash and made straight for paradise and boy was he locked on good. Maggie was floored, hooting and choking at this latest turn in the comedy of canine capers. The glum Ninja was now totally disgusted, his cool composure totally gone as he re-attached the lead and hauled the dog away for good.

Back at the hostel, Colleen turned up with news of two recently rescued Spectacled Bear cubs in a Quito animal clinic and offered to take us over to see them. Idiot villagers had stolen them from their mother when she went out from their den to look for food and were then spotted showing off their new found prizes by someone more sensible who appreciated that they are a protected species. The authorities were duly informed and the cubs rescued. It was impossible to return them to their mother as, even if the den could be located, she would likely reject them because they had been handled by humans. Now they would have to be hand reared on bottled milk at the clinic for the next few months.

We were reduced to a session of 'oohing' and 'aahing' as we watched them cavort and caper on the clinic floor, cute little sleepy balls of fluff just ready for mischief and aching to play. They quickly bowled over to see us and grabbed hold of my feet, lured by my dangling laces, and set about chewing at my boots, fitting just nice, like a pair of dodgy Christmas slippers. I felt more than a little sad when the nurse removed them, prizing their little paws from about my legs, ignoring their pleading whimpers. Eventually, once weaned onto solid foods, they would be moved to the Santa Marta Animal Rescue centre, the collection point for rescued animals. The inmates may have been shot by hunters or have histories similar to our little bears. The centre provides veterinary treatment and recuperation so that the animals can hopefully be released back into the wild.

First stop on our tour of the centre was a cage full of beautiful macaws and other protected parrots recovered from the illegal bird trade. Nearby were cages with squirrel, spider and capuchin monkeys and another cage held a ferocious jaguar that had recently been recovered from an illegal circus. Indoors we saw a tank with some fifty or sixty tarantulas, remnants of a consignment of 400 found in the post, on their way to an address in Switzerland by regular mail; most were dead on discovery but the survivors would eventually be sent back to the jungle and released to do their spidery things once more.

Santa Marta was also a haven for some beautiful ocelots and a hapless, lazy puma called Garfield. He had been kept as a pet, totally dependent on humans for so long that he can never be returned to his natural environment. When found, he had been overfed and deprived of exercise to the point that he suffered from obesity and has since resisted all attempts to activate him at the centre, preferring to lounge around all day in the sun. He had a fantastic big enclosure and they tried to get him to walk a little by placing his food at the other side of it. He simply refused to get up to fetch it, preferring to go hungry instead. His weight was originally estimated at around 80kg, heavy for a puma. But the tranquillised cat shocked everyone, weighing in at an actual 140kg. He is now on a controlled diet and reports are that he is losing weight, albeit very slowly.

Another in-house pet was a Galapagos tortoise, over a hundred years old, his carapace scarred with blast marks, where past owners took pot shots at him to impress visitors how tough his shell was. The whole visit to the Rescue Centre moved us. It was a unique opportunity to see first hand the good treatment the animals were receiving here and, for most of them, to witness their rehabilitation programmes in action. The work by the volunteers is marvellous and we really admired their determination to return these animals to the wild. Santa Marta is no zoo and we left content in the knowledge that at least some of the animals we saw would go on to fulfil a normal and natural life.

Then we left Quito, Ecuador and South America, with hugs and farewells to Colleen at the hostel and then a sad goodbye to big Chris too as he dropped us off at the airport. The past six months in South America had been something else. I read in Hugh Thomson's book 'The White Rock' about the impact of the discovery of the Americas on 16th century Europe. The problem was that the early Conquistadors were all lesser and bastard sons of the Spanish nobility, out to make their name and fortunes in these new lands. They returned to Spain and people asked 'what's it like?' They replied with wild-eyed stories of the biggest river in the world, snakes that can swallow whole donkeys, gigantic tortoises, snow-capped mountains even higher than the Pyrenees and fabulous treasure-laden cities, their streets lined with silver and gold.

Given the background of the narrators, these stories were treated with scepticism and disbelief and it took a full hundred years after Columbus' initial landing before the world accepted the facts and the truth about this new continent. By then more 'reliable' witnesses, scholars and clerics had made the journey and returned, confirming the wild and fabulous tales of the Conquistadors. I can totally sympathise with these impressions: South America is a fantastic, otherworldly place. It felt literally like we had travelled to another planet, a new world full of alien sights, sounds, smells and sensations.

South America had been a series of wonderlands, each populated by warm, hospitable people and amazing animals, with stunning flora and landscapes on an unimaginable scale. True, at times it had been a little raw, dangerous and hairy but these times were easily countered by the application of a little common sense and wit to steer us safely through and around the bad parts. Maggie's broken elbow on the Ruta 40, damaged motorcycles, run-ins with bent cops in Argentina, strikes in Bolivia, riding round the massacre in Peru; for some people these incidents reinforce popular prejudices against Latin America but we both shudder with horror at the thought that we could perhaps have chosen another path, one that on paper looked like it would lead to an easier life, but one that would have kept us at home and thereby missing all of this. Far more frightening, the misery of prolonging an already tired working career with escalating, never-ending stress and hassle does not bear thinking about. This journey invigorated and strengthened us in ways we could not previously have predicted.

The steady barrage of foreign tongues everyday and constantly meeting and dealing with new people kept us on our toes, exercising the old grey matter so that mentally we were alert, keen and ready for anything, more so than at any other time in our lives. Physically we were fit, well and healthy, in peak condition. I had lost nearly thirty pounds in weight (my beer belly had all but gone) simply through living a very active daily life that was a million miles away from sitting at a desk or lounging on a sofa. If truth be known, the worst day on the road had proven, by several orders of magnitude, to be better than the best day at the office. Sitting on the plane, ready to leave the runway in Quito, we both knew we'd just had some of the best days of our lives. But the end in South America is not the end of this journey. Before us, through the gathering clouds that buffet our Boeing, lies Panama and a whole new road ahead as we enter Central America and the next phase of our Pan-American Adventure.

www.panamericanadventure.com

"Adventures in Yellow" was originally documented, as it happened, on our website www.panamericanadventure.com. The website, in addition to the raw travel blogs, contains a full set of photograph galleries from the trip. It lists recommended references and provides a wealth of data on the bikes, the equipment and kit that we used and preparations for the journey itself.

The website also records a host of heartfelt 'thank you's to all the friends, colleagues and kind people who supported, encouraged and in some cases sponsored us; everyone who put us on the road and kept us going once underway.

Any errors and mistakes in the "Adventures in Yellow" and the website are mine, all mine!

Norman Magowan

Adventures in Yellow

concludes with

Part 2: Leprechauns to Alaska

Prelude: The Fire

That sunny Sunday afternoon marked our last full day riding the Alaskan Highway, 1422 miles (2288 km) of wilderness roads from Dawsons Creek that would end the following day at Delta Junction in Alaska. The weather had been kind: sun soaked days in the saddle, our two little yellow bikes gobbling up the miles at an easy pace. The monotony of the long road with its vanishing point always just over the horizon and endless tree lined vistas was broken by delightful encounters with wild bears, moose and bison. With such easy riding it was a great time for reflection on a journey almost done.

Our journey started eons ago in Valparaiso, Chile, from where we had ridden south through Argentina before turning north to chase the Pan-American Highway through Latin America and up into the US. I have to confess to feeling a little… what's the word? Smug. We deserved to be smug today. After all, tomorrow would be 'Mission Accomplished'. We would have done what it said on our pannier livery: completed the long ride 'from Chile to Alaska for Cancer Research UK'. But the problem I find with allowing oneself to be smug is that it is invariably followed by a swift kick in the bollocks.

We pulled in at the sleepy 'Mile 1002 Motel' in Beaver Creek, our last stop in Canada, deciding to halt the day's ride early and cross into Alaska fresh on the morrow. We unpacked the two yellow motorcycles. They were battered, worn and abused, signs of a hard 27000 miles on the road to date. Maggie's 'KG' with its Frankenstein scar in the tank, a hard gravel fall from Ruta 40 in Argentina that broke Maggie's elbow and almost terminated the trip in its infancy. I ran my hand affectionately over my own beloved 'KP' with her taped-on indicator and the big ding on the aluminium pannier courtesy of ignoramus cargo handlers in Panama.

There now followed the familiar routine of stripping the luggage off the bikes and lugging it into the motel room, trying not to mess up the place too much in the process. The room was basic but comfortable with curtains drawn to block out the afternoon sun. We would sleep well tonight. A cool shower and then a tramp along the boardwalk to the motel bar to sup some suds. The bar lady recommended 'Buckshot Betties' next door for dinner, everything fresh and home cooked. Sounded perfect to round off this most excellent day…

On the way to dinner I stopped to look back at the sight of the two bikes parked up outside the cosy motel. It was then that we saw the most spectacular apparition in the sky, something uniquely beautiful and at the same time very menacing. Way off to the north, stood a single, gigantic, white billowy cauliflower cloud. It soared thousands of feet up into the heavens like a tactical nuclear weapon of some destruction had just been unleashed. This enormous nebulous entity was skirted with a dirty grey apron and appeared as an aerial, diabolical, Portuguese-Man-of-War-monster-jellyfish made of many parts and tendrils, all floating, nay lurking, in the sky.

It seemed incredible that we had not observed this phenomenon on our way into town but it had indeed gone completely unnoticed by both of us until this very moment. Surely it could not just have arrived? We stood there gawping, baffled as to what it could be. A forest fire? But wouldn't that just fill the air with smoke? A single, massive, self-contained thunderstorm? But there wasn't another cloud in the rest of the sky, which extended blue and clear across the rest of the horizon. As I stood there jaw dropped, legs apart, I failed to appreciate that it could also be a sign that some God of Travel was lacing up a size 9 boot and I was ideally positioned for that swift kick. Puzzled, we wandered off for food.

Dinner was some of the best homemade pizza ever (a Kluane Special if I remember rightly), served by a friendly lass by the name of Carmen, who proved to be the waitress cum chef, owner cum manageress; in fact Buckshot Betty herself. We chatted after dinner with the restaurant's other guests, a Dutch couple cycling to San Francisco and a young German couple, who had started at Prudhoe Bay and were now cycling to Ushuaia. The usual joy of sharing our experiences from the road and learning a little in return of what to expect up ahead was heightened tonight by the fact that we were on the cusp of completing our mission. Tomorrow we would make it for sure.

The cyclists left and we sat on for another beer. Then the door opened and a squad of sooty, dishevelled fire-fighters came in, looking like they'd had a rough time. They plonked themselves down and ordered a round of soft drinks with some food to go. I chatted with a tall moustachioed crew chief, who hailed originally from Blackpool, and it was then that the God delivered that most awful kick...

They'd been out fighting a raging forest fire; maybe we saw it from the town earlier? The wildfire blaze had been burning for twelve days now and was rampaging beyond control. They had tried some controlled burnings to head it off, removing the fuel from its path, but a fickle wind blew the fire away from their clearances.

Part 2: Leprechauns to Alaska

The likely threat now was that the fire would swing round to cut the road to Alaska. If it did this overnight we would be stuck here, our journey ended, eighteen miles short of the border. We eagerly interrogated the crew chief. If the fire reached the road, how long would it take to clear? Days, maybe weeks, depends. If the road is burned up bad they'll have to rebuild it. Might take a lot of weeks, maybe months. Our hearts sank at this news. Our 'Mission Accomplished' was looking like 'Mission Denied'!